Communications in Computer and Information Science 2886

Series Editors

Rationale

The CCIS series is devoted to the publication of proceedings of computer science conferences. Its aim is to efficiently disseminate original research results in informatics in printed and electronic form. While the focus is on publication of peer-reviewed full papers presenting mature work, inclusion of reviewed short papers reporting on work in progress is welcome, too. Besides globally relevant meetings with internationally representative program committees guaranteeing a strict peer-reviewing and paper selection process, conferences run by societies or of high regional or national relevance are also considered for publication.

Topics

The topical scope of CCIS spans the entire spectrum of informatics ranging from foundational topics in the theory of computing to information and communications science and technology and a broad variety of interdisciplinary application fields.

Information for Volume Editors and Authors

Publication in CCIS is free of charge. No royalties are paid, however, we offer registered conference participants temporary free access to the online version of the conference proceedings on SpringerLink (http://link.springer.com) by means of an http referrer from the conference website and/or a number of complimentary printed copies, as specified in the official acceptance email of the event.

CCIS proceedings can be published in time for distribution at conferences or as post-proceedings, and delivered in the form of printed books and/or electronically as USBs and/or e-content licenses for accessing proceedings at SpringerLink. Furthermore, CCIS proceedings are included in the CCIS electronic book series hosted in the SpringerLink digital library at http://link.springer.com/bookseries/7899. Conferences publishing in CCIS are allowed to use our online conference service (Meteor) for managing the whole proceedings lifecycle (from submission and reviewing to preparing for publication) free of charge.

Publication process

The language of publication is exclusively English. Authors publishing in CCIS have to sign the Springer CCIS copyright transfer form, however, they are free to use their material published in CCIS for substantially changed, more elaborate subsequent publications elsewhere. For the preparation of the camera-ready papers/files, authors have to strictly adhere to the Springer CCIS Authors' Instructions and are strongly encouraged to use the CCIS LaTeX style files or templates.

Abstracting/Indexing

CCIS is abstracted/indexed in DBLP, Google Scholar, EI-Compendex, Mathematical Reviews, SCImago, Scopus. CCIS volumes are also submitted for the inclusion in ISI Proceedings.

How to start

To start the evaluation of your proposal for inclusion in the CCIS series, please send an e-mail to ccis@springer.com

Xiaobing Li · Kejun Zhang · Yun Wang ·
Yun Tie · Xinran Zhang · Qingwen Zhou
Editors

China Computational Art

First CCF Conference, CCAC 2025
Jinan, China, September 23–25, 2025
Proceedings

Editors
Xiaobing Li
Central Conservatory of Music
Beijing, China

Kejun Zhang
Zhejiang University
Hangzhou, China

Yun Wang
Beihang University
Beijing, China

Yun Tie
Zhengzhou University
Zhengzhou, China

Xinran Zhang
Central Conservatory of Music
Beijing, China

Qingwen Zhou
Central Conservatory of Music
Beijing, China

ISSN 1865-0929 ISSN 1865-0937 (electronic)
Communications in Computer and Information Science
ISBN 978-981-95-8255-6 ISBN 978-981-95-8256-3 (eBook)
https://doi.org/10.1007/978-981-95-8256-3

This Springer imprint is published by the registered company Springer Nature Singapore Pte Ltd.
The registered company address is: 152 Beach Road, #21-01/04 Gateway East, Singapore 189721, Singapore

Preface

Welcome to the Inaugural China Computer Federation (CCF) China Computational Art Conference (CCAC 2025). Organized by CCF and co-organized by CCF Computational Art Branch, the Central Conservatory of Music, Shandong University of Arts, the Shandong Association for Science and Technology, and additional partners, CCAC 2025 provided a key platform for leading experts and researchers from academia and industry to convene, present their latest work, and advance innovation in computational art and related technologies.

Nobel Laureate and renowned physicist Chen-Ning Yang extended his congratulations to the conference, remarking: "Science and art together can create a better future. I wish the China Computational Art Conference a great success!" As a landmark academic event in the field, CCAC 2025 brought together leading experts from across China to discuss the "AI+" paradigm and to advance the flourishing development of computational art.

CCAC 2025 opened with a formal ceremony featuring five distinguished keynote speakers: Xiaohong Guan (Academician, Chinese Academy of Sciences), Xiangrong Xiao (Vice President, Beijing Dance Academy), Wei Li (Vice President, Beijing Film Academy), Pinjing Lu (Vice President, Central Academy of Fine Arts), and Zhijie Qiu (President, Tianjin Academy of Fine Arts). In addition, Wen Ling (Academician, Chinese Academy of Engineering; President, Shandong Association for Science and Technology), Qingfeng Xu (President, Shandong University of Arts), and Xiaobing Li (Chair, CCF Computational Art Branch) delivered invited talks sharing the latest developments in the field.

The conference program included eight thematic forums and three paper sessions. The Electronic Music Marathon showcased 88 works spanning AI-generated music, live electronic performance, interactive and algorithmic music, audiovisual interaction, synthesizer performance, and multimedia music. A concurrent Computational Art Exhibition received nearly 200 submissions from China and abroad, covering mechanical and interactive installations, AI art, digital video, VR/AR/MR works, mathematical art, digital sculpture, interactive games, and new media art. Ultimately, 38 works were selected as Finalists, 57 as Screening works, and four were recognized with the Best Work Award. The exhibition at the Shandong Science and Technology Museum ran from September 23 to 25, while the exhibition at the Shandong University of Arts Art Museum continued through October, offering the public a close encounter with the creativity and vitality of computational art.

For the science and technology track of CCAC 2025, the conference welcomed submissions on topics including: theories and methodologies of computational art; datasets, models, tasks, and evaluation methods at the intersection of art and AI; generative AI and artistic creation; music and AI; visual arts and AI; performing arts and interactive technology; digital media art and design; digitalization and intelligent presentation of traditional art; applications of AI in art education; digital preservation of cultural heritage; ethical issues in art and technology; applications of VR/AR/MR in the arts; AI-based robotic performance systems; and research and application of art in the metaverse. A total of 19 valid submissions were received. Each was reviewed by at least three independent reviewers under a double-blind process. After rigorous evaluation, 8 papers were accepted (42.1% acceptance rate), all of which were presented orally at the conference. Parallel Chinese submissions in science and technology, art, and social sciences underwent a separate review process and are not included in these proceedings.

We express our sincere gratitude to all reviewers and organizers for their dedication to CCAC 2025. We especially thank the 25 reviewers for their time and thoughtful assessments, which ensured the high quality of this volume. We also thank all authors who submitted their work—your contributions were essential to the success of the conference. It was a pleasure to welcome you to Shandong for CCAC 2025.

September 2025

Xiaobing Li
Kejun Zhang
Yun Wang
Yun Tie
Xinran Zhang
Qingwen Zhou

Organization

Honorary Chairs

Yu Feng	Central Conservatory of Music, China
Qingfeng Xu	Shandong University of Arts, China
Qionghai Dai	Tsinghua University, China
Xiaohong Guan	Xi'an Jiaotong University, China

Conference Chair

Xiaobing Li	Central Conservatory of Music, China

Conference Co-chairs

Zhijie Qiu	Tianjin Academy of Fine Arts, China
Maosong Sun	Tsinghua University, China

Steering Committee

Mei Xu	Shandong University of Arts, China
Xihong Wu	Peking University, China
Li Peng	Shandong University of Arts, China
Yang Yu	Shanghai Conservatory of Music, China
Zhiou Wang	BLACKBOW, China

Local Chair

Gequn Wang	Shandong University of Arts, China

Secretary-General

Jia Luan	Shandong Normal University, China

Program Committee

Weiming Dong	Institute of Automation, Chinese Academy of Sciences, China
Ruo Si	Tsinghua University, China
Xiaohua Sun	Southern University of Science and Technology, China
Xu Tan	Tencent Hunyuan Audio, China
Long Tang	Shandong University of Arts, China

Organizing Committee

Sen Zhou	Shandong University of Arts, China
Chunjing Hu	Shandong University of Arts, China
Haibo Yu	Central Conservatory of Music, China
Lin Shen	Shanghai Normal University, China
Yunpeng Li	Wuhan Conservatory of Music, China
Cong Jin	Communication University of China, China

Forum Committee

Qi Qian	Central Conservatory of Music, China
Kun Qian	Beijing Institute of Technology, China
Yichun Zhang	China Institute of Arts Science and Technology, China
Chunna Yu	Tianjin Academy of Fine Arts, China
Xiaohui Wang	University of Science and Technology Beijing, China

Paper Committee

Zongquan Huang	Central Conservatory of Music, China
Kejun Zhang	Zhejiang University, China
Yun Wang	Beihang University, China
Zeguang Lu	Zhongke Guoding Institute of Data Science, China
Yun Tie	Zhengzhou University, China
Xiaoying Zhang	China Rehabilitation Research Center, Music Therapy Center, China

Jian Yang	Shanghai Conservatory of Music, China
Xinran Zhang	Central Conservatory of Music, China
Qingwen Zhou	Central Conservatory of Music, China

Reviewers

Yihang Bo	Beijing Film Academy, China
Shichao Chen	Institute of Automation, Chinese Academy of Sciences, China
Weiming Dong	Institute of Automation, Chinese Academy of Sciences, China
Lei Gao	Ryerson University, China
Shiming Ge	Institute of Information Engineering, Chinese Academy of Sciences, China
Junjie Geng	Communication University of China, China
Cong Jin	Communication University of China, China
Mao Li	Sichuan University, China
Zijin Li	Central Conservatory of Music, China
Meiyu Lu	Beijing University of Posts and Telecommunications, China
Yanru Lu	Beijing Technology and Business University, China
Luntian Mou	Beijing University of Technology, China
Yancong Su	Xiamen University of Technology, China
Yun Tie	Zhengzhou University, China
Jing Wang	Beijing Institute of Technology, China
Xiaohui Wang	University of Science and Technology Beijing, China
Yun Wang	Beihang University, China
Zhenyu Wang	North China Electric Power University, China
Baixi Xing	Zhejiang Sci-Tech University, China
Xiaoli Yue	China National Ethnic Museum, China
Junping Zhang	Fudan University, China
Kejun Zhang	Zhejiang University, China
Xinran Zhang	Central Conservatory of Music, China
Yanxiang Zhang	University of Science and Technology of China, China
Chenyu Zheng	Fudan University, China

Exhibition Committee

Xiaomo Bai	Sichuan Conservatory of Music, China
Baoyang Chen	Central Academy of Fine Arts, China
Feng Gao	Peking University, China
Bing Wei	Central Conservatory of Music, China
Jun Zhao	Shandong University of Arts, China

Performance Committee

Yuming Sun	Central Conservatory of Music, China
Yixuan Zhao	Central Conservatory of Music, China
Changlei Zhu	Shandong University of Arts, China

Publicity Committee

Xiankun Kong	Shandong University of Arts, China
Zhen Fu	Shandong Yougu Youlu Digital Technology Co., Ltd., China
Yancong Su	Xiamen University of Technology, China
Xinyan Wang	Linyi University, China
Lu Lu	Shandong Radio and Television Station, China
Yuan Zhang	Central Conservatory of Music, China

Organizers

Organized by

China Computer Federation

Hosted by

CCF Computational Art Branch

Shandong University of Arts

In Cooperation with

Springer

Communications in Computer and Information Science

Contents

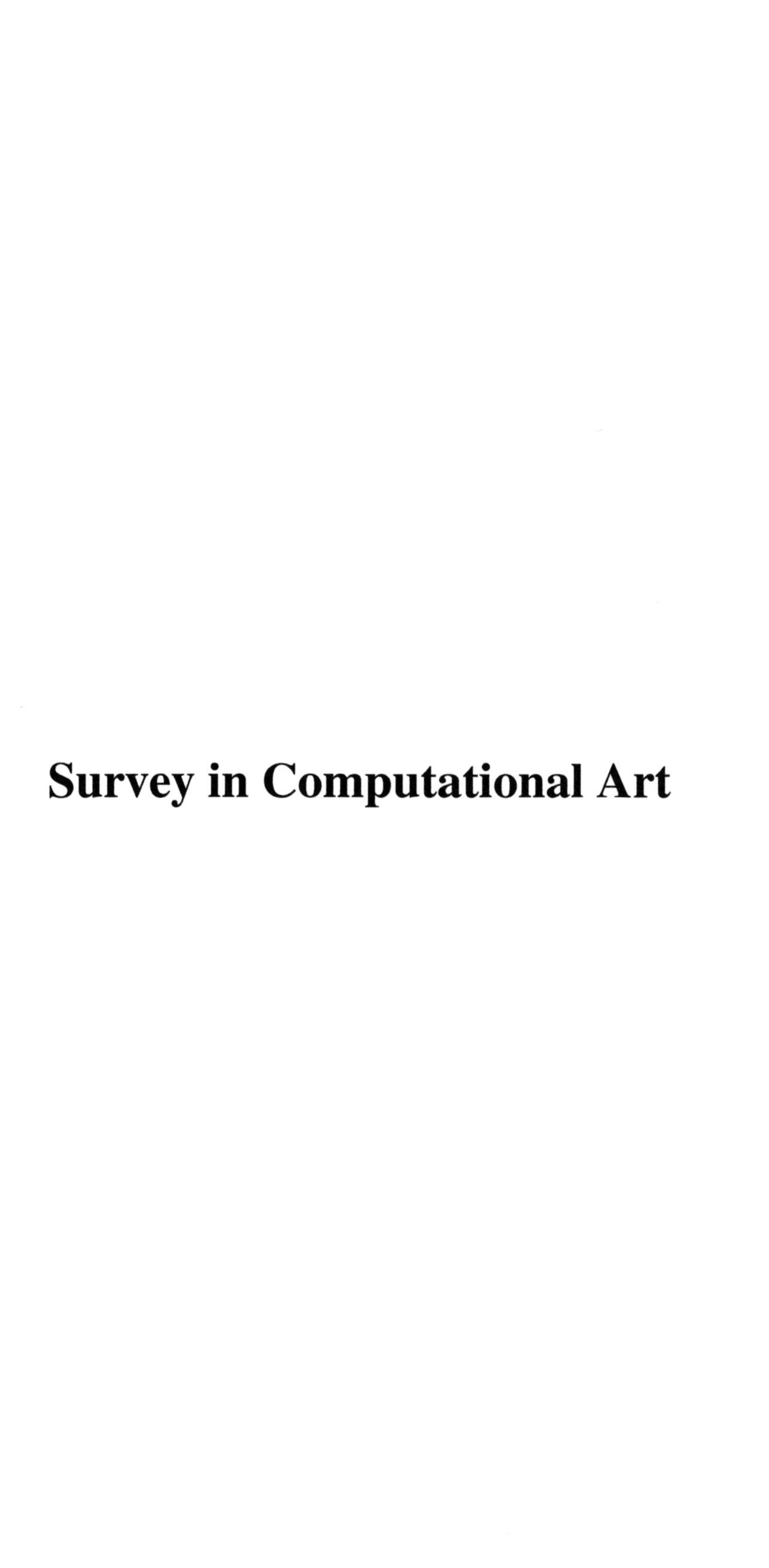

Survey in Computational Art

AI-Driven Intelligent Media: A Survey of Key Technologies in Symbolic Music Generation

Chenxiang Zhao and Cong Jin(✉)

Communication University of China, Beijing 100024, China
jincong0623@cuc.edu.cn

Abstract. With the rapid advancement of artificial intelligence, intelligent media has seen significant progress, particularly in the area of music generation. This paper presents a comprehensive survey of the core technologies in symbolic music generation, reviewing specific applications of autoregressive models, Variational Autoencoders (VAEs), Generative Adversarial Networks (GANs), and diffusion models. We analyze over a dozen representative papers published in top-tier conferences (e.g., ICML, AAAI, ISMIR, IEEE) over the past two years, summarizing and comparing them across five key aspects: model architecture, data representation, input/output formats, control mechanisms, and practical applications. Our analysis focuses on how multi-modal inputs, emotional and stylistic tag control, and structured representations are used to enhance the quality and controllability (e.g., over dimensions like emotion and style) of generated music. Furthermore, we provide insights into future research directions in symbolic music generation. This paper aims to provide a systematic and valuable technical survey for researchers working at the intersection of artificial intelligence and intelligent media.

Keywords: Artificial Intelligence · Intelligent Media · Symbolic Music Generation · Multi-modal Control · Emotion-based Generation · Diffusion Models

1 Introduction

With the rapid development of artificial intelligence, generative models have demonstrated unprecedented potential within the intelligent media landscape, achieving remarkable breakthroughs in music composition. This complex task integrates human emotion and structural logic. As a significant branch of AI-powered music generation, symbolic music generation focuses on creating multi-track music using MIDI or other structured formats. It addresses multiple dimensions, including melody, rhythm, and harmony. This not only pushes the boundaries of human-computer collaborative creation but also provides robust technical support for a variety of intelligent media scenarios, including virtual YouTubers, dynamic game audio, and content for short-form video platforms.

In recent years, deep learning architectures like Transformer, VAE, and diffusion models have continuously revolutionized the paradigms of symbolic music generation.

X. Li et al. (Eds.): CCAC 2025, CCIS 2886, pp. 3–18, 2026.
https://doi.org/10.1007/978-981-95-8256-3_1

The introduction of mechanisms such as emotional control, style transfer, and multi-modal prompting has made the generated content more refined and personalized [1]. For instance, the Text2MIDI model enables the direct generation of multi-track music from textual descriptions [2], while the XMusic framework pioneers new paths for multi-modal music generation by integrating various media inputs like images, videos, and humming [3]. These advancements have not only enriched the creative tools available but have also spurred deeper exploration into key challenges such as controllability, structural coherence, and real-time generation.

This paper focuses on representative symbolic music generation technologies from the past three years at the intersection of AI and intelligent media. We systematically review and compare these technologies from the perspectives of model architecture, representation methods, control mechanisms, and task-specific adaptations, aiming to provide a clear developmental roadmap and future direction for subsequent research. The remainder of this paper is organized as follows: Sect. 2 reviews the core technologies, Sect. 3 provides a comparative analysis, Sect. 4 presents case studies, and Sect. 5 discusses challenges and future directions.

2 A Technical Review: From Deep Generative Models to Multi-modal Music Construction

Symbolic music generation, as a key application of generative AI in the media domain, has evolved from traditional rule-based systems and Markov chain models to a phase dominated by deep neural networks. Current mainstream technologies for symbolic music generation can be categorized as follows: sequential modeling, latent space generation, diffusion-based modeling, and multi-modal-driven generation.

2.1 Sequential Generation Models: The Evolution from RNN to Transformer

Symbolic music generation has a history that predates the deep learning era. Early approaches were often rooted in rule-based systems and statistical models. For instance, systems like David Cope's Experiments in Musical Intelligence (EMI) utilized grammatical rules and pattern matching to analyze and recreate the style of classical composers [4]. Concurrently, statistical methods like Markov chains and n-grams became popular for modeling the probabilistic transitions between musical events (e.g., notes or chords). These models could capture local dependencies effectively but were fundamentally limited in their ability to model long-range structure and hierarchical relationships, often resulting in music that lacked overarching coherence and long-term development. The advent of deep learning, particularly Recurrent Neural Networks, marked a paradigm shift by offering a way to learn these complex temporal dependencies directly from data.

Early symbolic music generation was primarily based on Recurrent Neural Networks (RNNs) or their variants (like LSTM and GRU), which captured temporal dependencies between notes to generate melodies. However, RNNs suffer from limitations in modeling long-range dependencies, often resulting in poor structural and hierarchical coherence [5].

This limitation stems from the vanishing and exploding gradient problems inherent in processing long sequences, where information from earlier time steps is progressively diluted. Despite this, models based on Long Short-Term Memory (LSTM) and Gated Recurrent Unit (GRU) cells offered significant improvements by using gating mechanisms to control the flow of information. Prominent examples from this period include Google Magenta's Melody RNN, which demonstrated the ability to generate compelling monophonic melodies with learned structure [6]. The DeepBach model, cited as [5], specifically applied LSTMs to generate four-part chorales in the style of J.S. Bach, showcasing how these networks could handle polyphonic and harmonic constraints. Nevertheless, the sequential nature of RNNs remained a bottleneck, as the computation for a given time step depends on the completion of the previous one, hindering parallelization and still struggling with dependencies over very long time scales (e.g., across entire musical sections).

Since 2019, the Transformer architecture has rapidly gained prominence due to its self-attention mechanism, which excels at modeling long sequences. MuseNet (OpenAI, 2019) was the first to apply Transformer to multi-track MIDI music generation, supporting a variety of styles and instrument combinations and demonstrating the architecture's strong generalization capabilities on musical sequence tasks.

The Transformer's superiority lies in its self-attention mechanism, which allows the model to weigh the importance of all other notes in a sequence when generating the next note, regardless of their distance. This non-sequential processing enables parallel computation and, more crucially, captures long-range dependencies directly. The Music Transformer [7] further refined this by introducing relative positional encoding, which is better suited for music's relational and motivic nature than the absolute positional encoding used in the original Transformer. This allowed it to generate music with more expressive timing and dynamics. Building on this, models like the Pop Music Transformer [7] focused on specific domains, using beat-based representations to better model the metrical structure common in pop music.

Subsequently, models like Music Transformer, PopMAG, and DeepJ have further improved upon positional encoding, structural modeling, and style control modules, making the generated music more coherent and artistic.

2.2 Latent Space Modeling: The Exploration of VAEs and GANs

To enhance the diversity and controllability of music generation, Variational Autoencoders (VAEs) and Generative Adversarial Networks (GANs) have been introduced to this field. VAEs employ an encoder-decoder architecture to learn a compressed, continuous latent representation (or latent space) of the input data. By sampling from this space and feeding the vectors to the decoder, new musical pieces can be generated. The continuous nature of this space is a key advantage, as it allows for meaningful operations like interpolation between two different musical pieces, effectively creating a smooth blend of their styles. Google's MusicVAE is a seminal work in this area, demonstrating the ability to reconstruct and generate melodies, as well as interpolate between them to create novel musical ideas that are stylistically coherent [8]. This makes VAEs particularly powerful for tasks requiring creative exploration and stylistic fusion. GANSynth, on the other hand, focuses on high-fidelity audio generation. However, its primary focus is not on the symbolic layer; it laid the groundwork for subsequent audio-symbol collaborative modeling.

In the symbolic domain, GANs have also been explored, though with different architectural considerations. A notable example is MuseGAN, which uses a GAN framework to generate multi-track polyphonic music [9]. Its architecture features multiple generators—one for controlling overarching compositional elements (e.g., chord progressions) and others for generating individual instrumental tracks conditioned on these elements. This approach attempts to impose a hierarchical structure on the generation process. However, GANs are notoriously difficult to train due to issues like mode collapse, where the generator produces only a limited variety of samples, and the challenge of balancing the generator and discriminator. In music generation, mode collapse can lead to repetitive and uninteresting outputs, while unstable training can prevent the model from learning complex harmonic and rhythmic patterns.

VAE-based models excel at stylistic adjustments and melodic variations by manipulating latent variables, making them ideal for personalized media content creation. However, these models often suffer from unstable training and can produce content that lacks clear structural coherence. In recent years, some works have attempted to alleviate these issues by introducing multi-view information and musical structure constraints. The Multi-view Midivae model proposed by Lin et al. is a case in point [10], with its core innovation being the parallel deconstruction and modeling of music from two orthogonal perspectives. The first is the Track-view, which uses intra- and inter-instrument Transformer encoders to capture instrumentation relationships and global harmonic structures. The second is the Bar-view, which also employs a Transformer architecture but models music at the bar level along the time axis to capture local details, rhythmic patterns, and temporal progressions. The latent vectors from these two views are then fused into a unified latent representation, z, via a Multi-view Information Fusion (MIF) module. During the generation phase, this fused latent vector guides the decoders of both views to work in concert, ultimately producing structurally consistent and expressive long-form multi-track music through an adaptive weighting scheme.

2.3 Diffusion Models and Structural Control: Enhancing Interpretability and Cohesion

Since 2022, Diffusion Models have become a research hotspot in music generation. Unlike models that generate sequences token-by-token, diffusion models operate through a process of gradual refinement, which makes them particularly effective at ensuring global structural coherence. Their methodology can be conceptualized in two distinct stages:

First, the forward diffusion process defines a procedure for systematically destroying structure in the data. Starting with a clean data sample, such as a MIDI piano roll representation x_0, a small amount of Gaussian noise is added at each step over a long sequence of T steps. This creates a chain of increasingly noisy samples $x_1, x_2, \ldots, xT$. The schedule of noise addition is carefully controlled so that by the final step T, the sample xT becomes indistinguishable from pure, unstructured noise. This forward process is fixed and does not involve any learning.

Second, the reverse denoising process is where the learning occurs. The goal is to train a neural network to reverse the noising process one step at a time. The model is given a noisy sample xt and the timestep t, and its task is to predict the slightly less noisy sample x(t-1). For generation, one starts with a sample of pure random noise (equivalent to xT) and iteratively applies this learned denoising function for T steps. Each application of the model subtly refines the noise, gradually introducing structure, until a clean, coherent data sample emerges. Represented by Google's MusicLM, which models long audio tracks using vocoders and a hierarchical structure, these models establish a connection between the symbolic and audio layers. Symbolic diffusion models like DiffRoll and SymbolicDiffusion directly construct this diffusion-denoising process on MIDI representations, not only improving generation quality but also enhancing the ability to model structural elements like musical phrases and rhythms. A key challenge is how to impose complex, non-differentiable music theory rules. The work by Huang et al. [11], for instance, addresses this challenge by designing a novel Stochastic Control Guidance (SCG) algorithm. Its core idea is not to compute gradients but to adopt a "generate-evaluate-select" strategy at each reverse-denoising step. The model prospectively generates multiple candidate samples, estimates their corresponding "clean" music using Tweedie's Formula, and then uses a non-differentiable rule function as a black-box evaluator to calculate a "cost." Finally, it selects the candidate with the lowest cost to proceed. This mechanism enables "plug-and-play" guidance for pre-trained models.

The work by Zhang et al. [12] explores another powerful control mechanism by integrating vector quantization (VQ) into the diffusion process, creating a VQ-Diffusion model. In this setup, a VAE is first trained to encode musical segments into a discrete codebook of latent vectors. The diffusion model then operates in this compressed, discrete latent space rather than the high-dimensional data space. This has two major benefits: first, it significantly improves computational efficiency; second, the discrete codes can capture high-level compositional styles, making it easier to guide the generation process by manipulating these codes. Another significant model in this domain is Symbolic Music-Diffusion, which adapts the diffusion framework to a specialized token-based representation of music, jointly modeling pitch, duration, and instrumentation, thereby enhancing the harmonic and rhythmic coherence of the generated multi-track pieces [13].

Meanwhile, other studies are exploring different control dimensions. For example, Zhang et al. introduced vector quantization (VQ) into the diffusion process to capture compositional styles [12], while Tian et al.'s XMusic framework is dedicated to building a scalable and universal generation architecture [3].

2.4 Multi-modal Prompt-Based Generation: The Cross-Disciplinary Fusion of Text, Images, and Humming

To meet the demand for multi-source inputs in intelligent media scenarios, a growing body of research is shifting towards multi-modal-driven music generation. Text-to-Music is currently the most prominent direction. The core technology of such models lies in achieving precise alignment between text semantics and musical features. The Text2Midi model proposed by Bhandari et al. is a representative end-to-end solution [2]. This framework utilizes a pre-trained large language model (FLAN-T5) to encode text prompts. It injects the resulting text semantic vectors into an autoregressive Transformer music decoder via a cross-attention mechanism. This architecture allows the decoder to dynamically "attend" to relevant parts of the text description when generating each MIDI token, thereby accurately mapping abstract concepts to musical elements.

The internal workflow of such a model involves a sophisticated interplay between two main components. First, a text encoder, typically a powerful pre-trained Large Language Model (LLM) like FLAN-T5, is responsible for interpreting the user's text prompt. It processes the text (e.g., "a relaxing piano melody with a slow tempo") and outputs a sequence of semantic vectors, known as text embeddings, which numerically represent the prompt's meaning.

Second, an autoregressive music decoder, usually a Transformer architecture, takes on the task of generating the musical sequence token by token. The crucial link between these two components is the cross-attention mechanism. At every step of the generation process, before producing the next musical token, the decoder's cross-attention layers consult the text embeddings produced by the encoder. This allows the decoder to dynamically weigh the importance of different parts of the text. For instance, when generating tokens related to rhythm, it might "attend" more strongly to the embeddings corresponding to "slow tempo," while for instrument selection, it would focus on the embeddings for "piano." This continuous, step-by-step alignment ensures that the final musical output remains faithful to the initial textual description.

To address data scarcity, the work also employs a semi-supervised pre-training strategy, significantly improving semantic consistency.

Building on text control, researchers are pursuing finer-grained structural and emotional modeling. For example, the MMT-BERT system by Zhu et al. introduces multi-track modeling and chord-aware mechanisms to handle more complex musical hierarchies [1]. The Muser framework by Ji and Yang focuses on emotion-driven generation, injecting affective dimensions into symbolic music by modeling melodic features and their emotional expressions [14].

Beyond text, other modalities have greatly enriched the interactive possibilities of music generation. For instance, the Image2Music framework enables "composing from a picture," while models like Sing2Music and Melody-to-MIDI allow users to drive arrangement by humming.

The technical challenge in these "humming-to-music" systems is multi-faceted. It involves not only accurate pitch transcription from a noisy vocal input but also the musically intelligent task of harmonization and arrangement. The system must infer an appropriate chord progression, instrumentation, and rhythmic accompaniment based solely on a monophonic melody. This often requires pre-trained models that have learned common musical patterns and stylistic conventions, effectively acting as a virtual composer that completes the user's initial idea [15].

Furthermore, exploring real-time interactivity has become a crucial direction. The AI improvisation system proposed by Wang demonstrates a model's potential for real-time generation and strong interactivity [16]. The work of Guo and Herremans systematically analyzes the interplay of various control mechanisms in symbolic music generation, offering new insights for building highly customizable music generation systems [17].

3 Analysis and Comparison of Representative Models: A Tale of Three Paradigms

To better understand the current landscape, this section provides a comparative analysis of the three dominant paradigms: Transformer-based sequential models, diffusion-based stepwise models, and multi-modal prompt-driven models. We will evaluate them across several critical dimensions: generation quality (fidelity and coherence), controllability (the ability to steer the output), computational efficiency (training and inference costs), and user accessibility (ease of use for non-experts). This analysis, summarized in Table 1, reveals a clear trade-off between these paradigms, suggesting that the future of music generation lies not in a single "best" model, but in their intelligent integration.

3.1 Transformer-Based Models: Excelling in Style and Local Coherence

Represented by foundational models like Music Transformer [7] and MuseNet, this paradigm leverages the self-attention mechanism to capture complex, long-range dependencies in musical sequences. Their strength lies in learning "musical grammar"—the intricate rules of rhythm, melody, and harmony at a local level. This allows them to excel at style imitation. When trained on a large corpus of a specific style (e.g., pop piano), models like the Pop Music Transformer [7] can generate compositions that are remarkably faithful to the source genre's conventions.

However, their autoregressive, token-by-token generation process presents two key limitations. First, they are prone to error accumulation; a poorly chosen note early in the sequence can derail the entire subsequent generation, leading to a loss of long-term structural coherence. While they can maintain consistency over a few bars, they often struggle to develop musical ideas across entire sections (e.g., maintaining a consistent verse-chorus structure). Second, their control mechanisms are often indirect, relying on priming with an initial sequence or fine-tuning on a specific dataset. This makes fine-grained control over the global structure challenging compared to other paradigms.

3.2 Diffusion Models: Mastering Structural Integrity at a Computational Cost

Diffusion models address the structural weaknesses of Transformers. Their iterative refinement process, which starts from a global structure (noise) and gradually adds detail, is inherently better suited for maintaining long-form coherence. Google's MusicLM, operating in the audio domain, and symbolic counterparts like SymbolicDiffusion [12], demonstrate this by generating music with greater structural and rhythmic integrity over longer durations. The ability to apply guidance during the reverse process also offers powerful and explicit control. For example, a composer can enforce a specific chord progression or rhythmic motif as a hard constraint, which is difficult to achieve in a standard Transformer.

This power comes at a significant price. The iterative denoising process requires hundreds or thousands of steps, making inference significantly slower than the single-pass generation of a Transformer. This latency currently limits their application in real-time or interactive scenarios. Furthermore, training these models is computationally expensive, requiring massive datasets and GPU resources. Their performance in terms of structural rigor is outstanding, making them ideal for applications with high demands for "long-form track continuity," such as narrative video scoring and procedural game soundtracks, but less suitable for rapid prototyping.

3.3 Multi-modal Prompt-Driven Models: Democratizing Creation via Semantic Control

This paradigm, building on the success of large models like GPT-4 and CLIP, reshapes the entry point for music creation. Models like Riffusion [18], MusicGen [19], and Mubert AI [20] prioritize user accessibility. By allowing users to generate music from natural language text, images, or even video tags, they lower the barrier to entry, empowering creators without formal music theory knowledge. The core technology, cross-attention, enables a powerful form of semantic control, translating abstract concepts like "a melancholic, rainy-day jazz piano track" into concrete musical output.

The primary challenge lies in the "semantic gap"—the inherent ambiguity in mapping subjective human descriptions to precise musical parameters. The quality and relevance of the generated music are heavily dependent on the capabilities of the underlying large language or vision models and the diversity of the text-music paired data used for training. Furthermore, these models often rely on other generative backbones (like Transformers or diffusion models) to perform the actual music synthesis, inheriting their respective strengths and weaknesses. Their main contribution is not necessarily in musical quality per se, but in creating a highly intuitive human-computer interface for music generation.

3.4 Trend of Technical Fusion and Practical Trade-Offs

As shown in Table 1, the current landscape of music generation models presents a "trilemma": Transformers excel in style, Diffusion models in structure, and Multi-modal models in usability. In practical applications, however, it is often necessary to combine the strengths of multiple models. For example, one might first use a text prompt to generate a basic melody (Text2Melody), then use a structural model to optimize phrasal logic (Diffusion), and finally use a Transformer to arrange multi-track details, achieving holistic control.

Therefore, in media scenarios, the ability to flexibly select and combine models based on application goals is a more practical challenge than the "model performance race."

Table 1. Comparison of Three Mainstream Paradigms in Symbolic Music Generation

Model Category	Core Mechanism	Music Representation	Advantages	Disadvantages	Typical Application Scenarios
Transformer	Self-Attention	Event sequence (REMI, etc.)	Strong long-range dependency High style imitation	Weak structural control Error accumulation Local incoherence	Style transfer Music continuation Song prototyping
Diffusion	Iterative Denoising	Embedding Sequence	High-fidelity generation Strong structural integrity	Slow inference High training cost Costly conditional guidance	Film/game scoring Narrative BGM High-fidelity tracks
Multi-modal	Conditional Generation (Cross-Attention)	Event Sequence, Embeddings	User-friendly (prompting) Multi-modal input	Relies on large pre-trained models Semantic alignment challenge	Short-video/ad music Real-time AIGC tools Personalized content

4 Case Studies: Practical Applications of Models in Media Content

Generative music models are no longer confined to the laboratory; they are rapidly permeating digital media content creation workflows as tools or platforms. Scenarios represented by virtual YouTubers, short-form video platforms, and digital marketing are becoming critical testing grounds for these models.

4.1 Music Content for Virtual YouTubers: From Anthropomorphism to Controllable Performance

Virtual YouTubers (VTubers), a widespread phenomenon in today's digital media, heavily rely on music content to sustain their "persona" and "emotional connection." VTuber groups like Japan's Kizuna AI and China's A-SOUL have made music a core part of their content strategy.

In these projects, AI music models typically undertake two types of tasks: 1) Custom background music generation, using models like MusicGen to create bespoke soundtracks based on the plot theme or live stream content to enhance immersion; 2) AI song prototyping, where melodic ideas are generated from text prompts and then "semi-automatically processed" by human composers to create original songs. This "human-computer collaboration" workflow significantly reduces the production cost of music content while maintaining personality.

For instance, NetEase's "AI Virtual Idol Project V" has a built-in generative melody engine that allows fans to input keywords to create "idol support songs," showcasing the potential for media innovation of music generation models in "fan co-creation" mechanisms.

Technically, these systems often employ a hybrid approach. A multi-modal model, such as a simplified text-to-melody generator, might be used to translate fan keywords into a basic melodic contour. This melody is then fed into a more sophisticated Transformer or diffusion-based model that handles harmonization and multi-instrument arrangement, ensuring the final output is musically plausible. The business model here is equally innovative, shifting from passive content consumption to active fan engagement. It not only strengthens the bond between the virtual idol and its community but also generates a vast pool of user-generated content, which can be used to further train and personalize the AI models, creating a virtuous cycle of engagement and content creation.

4.2 Automated Soundtracking for Short Videos and Ads: The Union of Content Algorithms and Emotional Drivers

On short-form video platforms like TikTok, Douyin, and Instagram, music is not just a background element but a key factor in evoking emotional resonance and driving content dissemination. Therefore, automatically generating suitable soundtracks for each video has become a key objective for platform algorithm optimization.

SAMI, a music tool under ByteDance, employs a hybrid music generation model. It automatically analyzes emotional tags from video content (e.g., "motivational," "healing," "high-energy") and then generates short music tracks that match the mood. This integration of algorithmic and emotion-driven approaches greatly enhances user creation efficiency and strengthens the platform's control over content style consistency.

Furthermore, the copyright advantages of generated music cannot be ignored. Compared to traditional music, AI-generated music can circumvent copyright disputes, making it more flexible for commercial monetization on these platforms.

Platforms like ByteDance's SAMI and other similar services from companies like Amper Music (now part of Shutterstock) or AIVA are becoming integral to the content creation infrastructure. These platforms often maintain vast libraries of pre-generated musical stems categorized by genre, mood, and energy level. When a user uploads a video, computer vision and natural language processing models first analyze the video's content to extract relevant tags (e.g., "travel," "food," "upbeat," "sentimental"). A recommendation engine then matches these tags to the music library. For more dynamic needs, generative models can create bespoke tracks on the fly, sometimes even allowing users to adjust parameters like tempo or instrumentation. This "soundtracking-as-a-service" model represents a significant market, as it solves a critical pain point for millions of creators who lack musical expertise and a budget for licensed music.

4.3 Digital Marketing Scenarios: Emotionally-Adapted Music to Drive Brand Expression

In brand communication and interactive advertising, the emotional adaptability of music determines the audience's emotional receptiveness. For example, luxury brands use "dream-like" ambient music generated by MusicLM in immersive ads to enhance a "premium" and "ethereal" mood. Gaming ads, on the other hand, use Stable Audio to generate fast-paced, drum-heavy tracks to quickly engage users emotionally.

Creative advertising agencies are widely adopting Meta's AudioCraft toolkit. It allows the generation of "personalized soundtracks" based on product positioning, user gender, and psychological profiles, thus transforming music from a "generic background" to a "precise communication medium."

This "music-as-a-tag" strategy has significantly increased brand content conversion rates and user recall in digital marketing, reflecting the leap of music generation models from "tools" to the "communication strategy" dimension.

This strategic shift is powered by the models' increasing ability to respond to fine-grained emotional and stylistic prompts. For instance, an ad agency can now generate dozens of variations of a jingle, each tailored to a specific demographic segment identified through user data. A version for a younger audience might be generated with prompts like "energetic, synth-pop, viral dance beat," while a version for an older audience might use "calm, orchestral, inspiring." This level of personalization was previously cost-prohibitive. Furthermore, models like Meta's AudioCraft are designed as open-source toolkits, accelerating the adoption of these techniques across the industry and empowering smaller agencies to compete with established players on creative execution.

4.4 Interactive Scoring for Gaming and Media

A rapidly growing application area is dynamic and interactive scoring for video games and other interactive media. Unlike linear media, games require music that can adapt in real-time to player actions, narrative progression, or environmental changes (e.g., shifting from exploration to combat). AI music generation models are uniquely suited for this task, enabling procedural music systems that generate endless, non-repetitive soundtracks that are emotionally coherent with the gameplay. Companies like AIVA and Melodrive have developed tools specifically for this purpose, showcasing the potential of AI to create deeply immersive and personalized auditory experiences.

4.5 Co-creation with Professionals

Beyond automated content generation, a significant application area is the integration of AI models into the workflows of professional musicians and composers. In this context, AI serves not as a replacement but as a powerful collaborator or "composer's assistant." Tools built on generative models can help break creative blocks by suggesting novel melodic fragments, harmonic progressions, or rhythmic patterns. For example, a film composer working on a tight deadline could use a model to generate multiple thematic variations based on an initial motif. Similarly, a pop producer could use a tool to instantly generate a bassline or drum pattern that fits a given chord progression. AI-powered tools like Orb Producer Suite offer plugins that integrate directly into Digital Audio Workstations (DAWs) like Ableton Live and Logic Pro, joining long-standing virtual arrangement software like Band-in-a-Box in this evolving creative ecosystem. These tools leverage models trained on specific musical theories and styles, providing controllable and musically coherent suggestions that professionals can then edit, arrange, and develop into a final piece. This human-in-the-loop approach preserves artistic agency while significantly accelerating the creative process.

4.6 Summary: The Emergence of "Generative Collaborative Systems" in Intelligent Media

These three case studies show that the application of music generation models in the intelligent media domain is not an isolated module. Instead, it is embedded within a collaborative system of content production, style control, emotion management, and communication strategy. It not only improves efficiency but also redefines the pathways of content expression. It is a direct manifestation of the transformation of "media logic" in the dimension of music.

5 Trends and Challenges: The Leap from Technical Tool to Cultural Mechanism

The role of music generation models in the intelligent media ecosystem is gradually shifting from a "technical tool" to a "cultural mechanism." Its influence is no longer limited to improving content production efficiency but extends to multiple layers, including media expression, creative concepts, and communication ethics. This shift heralds the entry of media logic into a new phase of "generative collaboration," which also brings challenges that warrant vigilance.

5.1 From Independent Creation to Human-Computer Collaboration: The Reconstruction of Authorship

Generative music models are rewriting the paradigms of traditional music creation. From composers to arrangers, from content creators to end-users, an increasing number of actors are being integrated into the collaborative chain of "prompt-model-feedback."

This process not only redefines the boundaries of musical "authorship" but also alters the narrative power dynamics of media. AI is no longer a passive "tool" but an active agent that can generate emotionally resonant content driven by prompts. Its output carries a certain "representational" quality, reflecting a form of cultural imagination understood through algorithms.

Take TikTok, for example. The platform encourages users to pair their content with AI-generated melodies, making "music style" a part of the viral tagging system. This means that music generation models, to some extent, control the "latent rules" of content style distribution—they are both a source of creation and a filter for aesthetics.

5.2 The Challenge of Aesthetic Homogenization and Creative Freedom

While models enhance the convenience of content creation, the risk of aesthetic homogenization they bring cannot be ignored. Current mainstream models are mostly trained on large datasets of Western pop music. This data bias can lead to a triple dilemma: First, creative convergence, where models tend to generate the most frequent and "safest" musical patterns, causing different users' creations to exhibit high similarity in rhythm, harmony, and melody, lacking personalization. Second, the convenience of generation might induce creative inertia, causing creators to shift from active ideation to passive selection, thus diminishing the depth and originality of their work. A deeper issue is cultural flattening, where the unique expressive power of specific cultural contexts (e.g., unique modes, rhythmic patterns) may be standardized and compressed by the "mainstream" paradigm of the model, eroding the local cultural vitality of music.

This phenomenon can be understood through the lens of "algorithmic culture," where the affordances of the platform and the biases of the model steer creation towards a globalized, commercially viable mean. The reliance on large, homogenous datasets like the Lakh MIDI Dataset, which is heavily skewed towards Western pop and rock, means that models may struggle to generate authentic-sounding music from genres with different scales, rhythmic structures, or harmonic languages (e.g., traditional Indian raga, Arabic maqam, or complex jazz). Addressing this requires a concerted effort in data curation, including the creation of more diverse, culturally representative datasets, and the development of models capable of few-shot or zero-shot style transfer to less-represented musical traditions.

Therefore, designing music models with cultural diversity and customizable spaces is a key challenge for the next phase of development.

5.3 Ethical and Copyright Challenges

The "authorship" and "copyright ownership" of generated music currently lack a unified global standard. Although most platforms state that generated music is free for commercial use, does it constitute "stylistic plagiarism" when a model's output highly imitates a deceased or living composer? When a user uploads a model-generated melody as their original work, does it infringe on the rights of the model's developers? These questions have repeatedly led to legal disputes.

For example, in 2023, the trial version of OpenAI's MusicLM was delayed due to copyright concerns, as its samples were potentially too close to the original training data. This case highlights that the "input legitimacy" and "output originality" of a generative model do not form a naturally established causal chain, but require joint construction by media platforms, model developers, and the legal community.

The legal landscape is further complicated by the distinction between the model itself, the training data, and the generated output. For instance, is the copyright of a generated piece held by the user who wrote the prompt, the company that trained the model, or does it fall into the public domain? In the United States, the Copyright Office has generally held that works created solely by AI without sufficient human authorship are not copyrightable. However, the threshold for "sufficient human authorship" in a prompt-model-feedback loop remains a gray area. This legal uncertainty creates risks for commercial users and could stifle innovation if not addressed through clear international standards and legislation.

5.4 The Interplay Between Platform Power and User Autonomy

It is crucial to recognize that generative models themselves have become a "latent medium" for regulating user behavior on platforms. Through default prompt templates, style restrictions, and other means, platforms can guide users to generate specific types of content, thereby achieving strategic goals of "emotional control," "aesthetic guidance," or even "public opinion shaping."

This makes generated music not just content itself, but a part of a digital governance and communication mechanism. If a music generation model is integrated into a recommendation algorithm, it could form a new cultural control chain—seemingly "everyone can create," but in reality, "styles are constrained."

5.5 The Challenge of Evaluation and Interpretability

A fundamental technical challenge that underpins many of the aforementioned issues is the difficulty in objectively evaluating the quality of generated music. Unlike in other domains with clear metrics (e.g., BLEU scores for machine translation), musical quality is inherently subjective and multi-faceted, encompassing aspects like creativity, emotional resonance, structural coherence, and stylistic appropriateness. Current evaluation methods often rely on a combination of human listening tests, which are expensive and difficult to scale, and proxy computational metrics that measure statistical similarity to a training set, which may inadvertently penalize novelty.

Closely related is the problem of interpretability. Most deep generative models operate as "black boxes," making it nearly impossible to understand why a model made a specific compositional choice. Why did it choose a minor chord here instead of a major one? What feature in the input text prompted this specific rhythmic figure? A lack of interpretability hinders our ability to debug models, control their output with precision, and trust them in high-stakes creative applications. Future research into explainable AI (XAI) for music generation will be crucial for building more transparent, controllable, and truly collaborative creative tools.

6 Conclusion

This paper has provided a comprehensive survey of key technologies in symbolic music generation, charting the evolution from sequential models like Transformers to the modern paradigms of diffusion and multi-modal, prompt-driven systems. We have systematically analyzed and compared these approaches, highlighting a fundamental trade-off between the stylistic proficiency of Transformers, the structural integrity of diffusion models, and the user accessibility of multi-modal interfaces. Our analysis reveals that these models are no longer isolated tools but are becoming integral components of a larger "generative collaborative system," profoundly reshaping creative workflows.

Through a series of case studies in virtual YouTubers, automated soundtracks, digital marketing, and professional music production, we have demonstrated how these advancements are being applied in the intelligent media landscape. These applications show a clear trend towards hierarchical and hybrid systems, where different models are leveraged at various stages of the creative process, from initial ideation to final arrangement.

Looking forward, the primary challenge lies in navigating the complex interplay between technological advancement and its socio-cultural implications. While AI offers unprecedented creative possibilities, critical issues such as aesthetic homogenization, copyright ambiguity, the concentration of platform power, and the technical hurdles of evaluation and interpretability demand careful consideration. Future work must therefore focus not only on improving model fidelity and control but also on developing culturally diverse, ethically aligned, and explainable music generation systems. Fostering interdisciplinary collaboration between AI researchers, media creators, musicologists, and ethicists will be crucial in shaping a responsible and innovative future for this dynamic field.

Acknowledgments. The authors would like to thank the anonymous reviewers for their valuable comments and suggestions that helped improve the quality of this paper.

Disclosure of Interests. The authors declare that they have no known competing financial interests or personal relationships that could have appeared to influence the work reported in this paper.

References

1. Zhu, J., Sakurai, K., Togo, R., Ogawa, T., Haseyama, M.: MMT-BERT: chord-aware symbolic music generation based on multitrack music transformer and MusicBERT. arXiv preprint arXiv:2409.00919 (2024)
2. Bhandari, K., Roy, A., Wang, K., Puri, G., Colton, S., Herremans, D.: Text2midi: generating symbolic music from captions. In: Proceedings of the AAAI Conference on Artificial Intelligence, vol. 39, no. 22, pp. 23478–23486 (2025)
3. Tian, S., Zhang, C., Yuan, W., Tan, W., Zhu, W.: XMusic: towards a generalized and controllable symbolic music generation framework. arXiv preprint arXiv:2501.08809 (2025)
4. Cope, D.: Experiments in musical intelligence. In: Proceedings of the International Computer Music Conference, pp. 163–170 (1987)
5. Hadjeres, G., Pachet, F., Nielsen, F.: DeepBach: a steerable model for Bach chorales generation. In: Proceedings of the 34th International Conference on Machine Learning (ICML), pp. 1362–1371 (2017)
6. Oore, S., Simon, I., Dieleman, S., Eck, D.: This time with feeling: Learning expressive musical performance. Neural Comput. Appl. **29**, 959–967 (2018)
7. Huang, Y.S., Yang, Y.H.: Pop music transformer: beat-based modeling and generation of expressive pop piano compositions. In: Proceedings of the 28th ACM International Conference on Multimedia, pp. 1180–1188 (2020)
8. Roberts, A., Engel, J., Raffel, C., Hawthorne, C., Eck, D.: A hierarchical latent vector model for learning long-term structure in music. In: Proceedings of the 35th International Conference on Machine Learning (ICML), pp. 4364–4373 (2018)

9. Dong, H.W., Hsiao, W.Y., Yang, L.C., Yang, Y.H.: MuseGAN: multi-track sequential generative adversarial networks for symbolic music generation and accompaniment. In: Proceedings of the AAAI Conference on Artificial Intelligence, vol. 32, no. 1 (2018)
10. Lin, Z., et al.: Multi-view Midivae: fusing track- and bar-view representations for long multi-track symbolic music generation. In: Proceedings of the 2024 IEEE International Conference on Acoustics, Speech and Signal Processing (ICASSP), pp. 941–945 (2024)
11. Huang, Y., et al.: Symbolic music generation with non-differentiable rule guided diffusion. arXiv preprint arXiv:2402.14285 (2024)
12. Zhang, J., Fazekas, G., Saitis, C.: Composer style-specific symbolic music generation using vector quantized discrete diffusion models. In: Proceedings of the 2024 IEEE 34th International Workshop on Machine Learning for Signal Processing (MLSP), pp. 1–6 (2024)
13. Guan, Z., et al.: Symbolic music-diffusion: a diffusion-based framework for symbolic music generation. In: Proceedings of the 31st ACM International Conference on Multimedia, pp. 141–151 (2023)
14. Ji, S., Yang, X.: Muser: musical element-based regularization for generating symbolic music with emotion. In: Proceedings of the AAAI Conference on Artificial Intelligence, vol. 38, no. 11, pp. 12821–12829 (2024)
15. Donahue, C., McAuley, J., Puckette, M.: Synthesizing audio with generative adversarial networks. In: Proceedings of the International Conference on Learning Representations (ICLR), pp. 1–13 (2019)
16. Wang, S.: Real-time symbolic music generation using deep learning methods—an interactive AI-based improvisation system for musicians. Unpublished Manuscript (2024)
17. Guo, R., Herremans, D.: An exploration of controllability in symbolic music infilling. IEEE Access **12**, 34887–34898 (2024)
18. Schneider, F., Kamal, O., Jin, Z., Schölkopf, B.: Moûsai: efficient text-to-music diffusion models. In: Proceedings of the 62nd Annual Meeting of the Association for Computational Linguistics, vol. 1, pp. 8050–8068 (2024)
19. Copet, J., et al.: Simple and controllable music generation. In: Advances in Neural Information Processing Systems, vol. 36, pp. 47704–47720 (2023)
20. Drott, E.: Copyright, compensation, and commons in the music AI industry. Creative Ind. J. **14**(2), 190–207 (2021)

Computational Interactive Visual Art

A Multimodal Interactive System for Autobiographical Memory: AI-Assisted Reflection and Expression

Chongjun Zhong, Jiaxing Yu, Wenqi Wu, Songruoyao Wu, Hanshu Shen, and Kejun Zhang(✉)

Zhejiang University, Hangzhou, Zhejiang, China
zhangkejun@zju.edu.cn

Abstract. Autobiographical memory is a narrative form grounded in personal experiences. By recalling and organizing past events, individuals can document significant moments, facilitating emotional regulation and stress relief. While extensive research has demonstrated its positive impact on well-being, tools designed to support autobiographical narration remain underdeveloped. Compared to single modality, multimodal forms have been shown to be superior in memory retrieval. However, these methods often struggle to realize self-expression due to the limitations of the user's creative abilities. To address this gap, we propose an innovative multimodal autobiographical narration system combining large language models (LLMs) and generative AI (GenAI). The system combines audio and visual formats by utilizing an LLM-based agent to guide users in recollection and a GenAI to tackle creative challenges. User studies show the system effectively supports high-quality autobiographical narratives and quickly generates multimodal works aligned with users' content, providing a powerful tool for self-reflection and creative memory expression.

Keywords: Autobiographical Memory · Reflection and Self-Expression · Multimodal Narration · Large Language Model (LLM) · Generative Artificial Intelligence (GenAI)

1 Introduction

Autobiographical memory, an important way for life-logging, has been trending among end-users to trace past events, express themselves, and further share the events with others [6]. Typically, these memories are recorded as descriptive narrative form. Rather than merely recalling memory events, reminding individuals of positive events - especially the event details - can trigger people's positive emotion [35]. Although numerous studies have highlighted the benefits of autobiographical memory in mental health [15], research on autobiographical narration tools remains unexplored, making it challenging for end-users to properly record their significant events. While some artists have attempted some

X. Li et al. (Eds.): CCAC 2025, CCIS 2886, pp. 21–46, 2026.
https://doi.org/10.1007/978-981-95-8256-3_2

creative autobiographical narration tools, like photography [1], painting [41], and music [36], these methods usually require specialized knowledge, making them less accessible to end-users (Fig. 1).

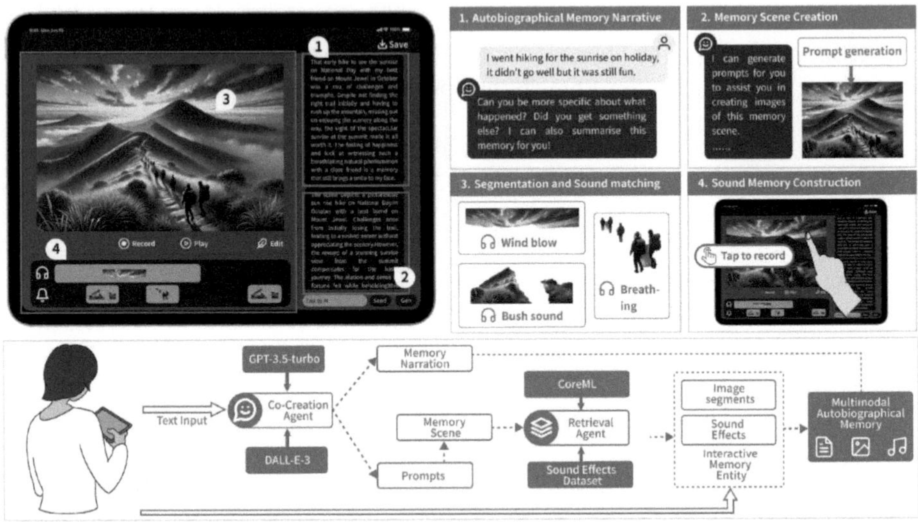

Fig. 1. Reverba, or "reverberate" in Latin, is a multimodal interactive system for autobiographical memory. The figure shows the functional demonstration of Reverba and its structure. (Top) System interface and the four main functions: (1) Autobiographical Memory Description. (2) Memory Scene Creation. (3) Segmentation and Sound Matching. (4) Sound Memory Construction. (Below) The functional structure of Reverba.

Traditional autobiographical memory research focuses mainly on simple self-reports [49,52]. These studies provided a theoretical foundation and research framework for autobiographical memory, but research methods remained limited to text-based and oral forms of reporting. With the development of research on cross-sensory channel, researchers began to explore the impact of different sensory modalities on autobiographical memory retrieval [61]. Compared to a single modal, multimodal cues can significantly enhance the retrieval of autobiographical memories [38] and stimulate more creative forms of memory expression [59]. However, there is still a lack of multimodal tools that allow users, without any specialized knowledge, to create reflective and creative autobiographical narrations.

In recent years, with the development of large language models (LLMs) and Generative Artificial Intelligence (GenAI), integrating multimodal creative formats into the design of tools for autobiographical narration has become possible. Users can use natural language to provide prompts to AI creation systems, which can intelligently generate corresponding creations [26]. This creative process significantly reduces the need for specialized knowledge, offering a more user-friendly interaction format. In some existing works, researchers have explored the intelligent use of LLMs for storytelling [65], proving LLMs' capabilities in narration and multimodal presentation. Therefore, we are motivated to use LLM-based agents to assist end-users in autobiographical narration and employ GenAI to help users create visual and auditory representations of their memories, achieving multimodal presentations of autobiographical memory.

We propose Reverba, a human-AI co-creation system based on LLM, which assists and guides users in narrating autobiographical memories by transforming those descriptions into audio-visual works. With Reverba, users interact with an LLM-powered agent that facilitates deep recollection and reflection through guided questioning, summarizing their autobiographical narrative. In the creative phase, the LLM-based agent generates prompts for image creation based on the user's memory descriptions, which users can refine iteratively with the agent to produce images that meet their needs. Afterward, users can enhance the images by adding sound effects that correspond to the content, thus creating a multimodal autobiographical memory. To reduce interaction complexity and improve creative detail, the system performs semantic recognition and segmentation on the generated images and automatically recommends sound effects based on these results. This allows users to add sound effects to specific parts of the image, constructing a vivid and immersive Reverba experience.

To evaluate the usability and effectiveness of Reverba in assisting users to create multimodal autobiographical memories and promoting self-reflection and self-expression, we conducted a laboratory study with 12 participants. Our findings indicate that Reverba effectively enhances memory recall and fosters self-reflection. Specifically, the system helped participants explore and reconstruct memories more deeply, enriching both emotional and sensory experiences. The multimodal co-creation process also sparked creativity and increased participants' willingness to share their memories. Additionally, interactive prompts allowed participants to reflect on their memories from a more positive perspective, facilitating emotional processing. These results highlight Reverba's potential to help users create meaningful and emotionally engaging autobiographical memories.

In summary, we highlight our contributions as follows:

(1) An end-to-end workflow that enables end-users to naturally narrate and creatively express their autobiographical memories. The system seamlessly transforms textual descriptions into multimodal works that enhance the emotional depth and vividness of the memory.
(2) A novel interaction method that allows end-users to effectively create multimodal memory in natural language, and intuitively add soundscapes to the memory through images, enabling creative expression of autobiographical memories.
(3) A comparative evaluation showing that Reverba outperforms traditional autobiographical memory methods in enhancing memory recall, enriching emotional and sensory experiences, increasing creativity, and fostering reflection.

2 Related Work

This work is motivated by previous researches on autobiographical memory, creative memory technologies and human-AI co-creation. In this chapter, we first introduce the background of autobiographical memory, with a focus on its methodological frameworks and research methods. We then briefly review previous research work on creative memory technologies and human-computer co-creation as a way to illustrate our design intent.

2.1 Construction of Autobiographical Memories

Autobiographical memory (AM) refers to the recollection of personal experiences and life events [6,31], and it plays a critical role in shaping one's identity and self-reflection [6,14,15,35]. In recent years, there has been a growing interest in tools and systems that assist individuals in recollecting, organizing, and expressing their autobiographical memories.

The development of tools for autobiographical memory has evolved alongside advancements in technology. Early efforts in AM tools primarily focused on writing and journaling, often facilitated by basic software or paper-based methods. In the late 19th century, Francis Galton pioneered the systematic study of autobiographical memory [28]. He triggered participants' recollections of past events by providing specific vocabulary and recorded the content and timing of their memories. In 1974, Crovitz and Schiffman improved upon Galton's method by developing the widely used cueing recall paradigm [17]. Participants were asked to recall related events based on provided cues and to record details such as the event's time, location, and emotional aspects. This method subsequently became a classic paradigm in autobiographical memory research. As digital tools progressed, applications such as personal diaries and digital scrapbooks gained popularity [8,18,32,55], allowing individuals to document and organize their memories through text [8,46], photos [55,58], and other media [32,37].

In research on autobiographical memory, researchers typically guide participants through reflection and recollection by asking questions [9,29,42,60]. These questions can be categorized into solution-focused questioning and problem-focused questioning [60]. Solution-focused questioning is a question style centered around finding solutions, aiming to help individuals shift their focus away from the problem itself and towards potential solutions and positive changes for the future, rather than overemphasizing the causes or negative impacts of the issue [30]. This approach is effective in enhancing positive emotions, boosting self-efficacy, and encouraging specific actions [19,29]. On the other hand, problem-focused questioning is a question style centered around the problem, aimed at exploring the causes, manifestations, and impacts of the issue in depth. Unlike solution-focused questioning, problem-focused questioning focuses more on the present and past states of the problem rather than future solutions [60]. This type of questioning is commonly used for diagnosing, analyzing, and understanding the root causes of problems, but it can also reinforce an individual's fixation on the problem, potentially leading to increased negative emotions [29,30].

Reverba draws inspiration from the cueing recall paradigm. During the autobiographical memory narration phase, it interacts with users around the time, location, and emotional details of their memory events. The system combines both solution-focused and problem-focused questioning approaches to balance the analysis of the problem with the exploration of potential solutions. This approach deepens users' reflection on past experiences while preventing the increase of negative emotions, thus providing more comprehensive support for individual growth and development.

2.2 Creative Personal Memory Technologies

Recording traces of our lives is a fundamental way to reflect on our experiences and share our life stories with others [16]. With the advancement of technology, digital personal memory technologies have introduced new possibilities for this process [33], significantly influencing how we capture and articulate these stories, shaping not only how we recall the past but also how we share memories with others and interpret our identities. Understanding the value of lifelogging in the personal domain can provide valuable insights for designers and researchers working on the development, implementation and evaluation of these technologies. The study by Petrelli et al. [48] revealed that people are not particularly interested in detailed digital documentation of their lives; instead, they prefer to sift through and reconstruct past life clues. Similarly, researchers argue that by supporting and fostering users' personal creative processes [7], creative expression can be transformed into emotional compensation, contributing positively to individuals' emotional well-being [40,47]. Therefore, future research on personal memory technologies should shift its focus from mere recording and retrieval of life data to empowering users with self-determined selection, self-driven creation, and meaningful construction of their experiences.

Currently, researchers in human-computer interaction have begun exploring creative approaches to personal record-keeping [2,53,57]. For instance, bullet journaling, a paper-based method for personal information tracking and planning, has been demonstrated as a creative self-tracking and reflective practice [2,53]. Unlike traditional written diaries, bullet journaling emphasizes the user's ability to filter, review, and reflect on life events, as well as to creatively express these insights. Additionally, Qian Wan et al. [57] proposed a system for the creative recording and reflection of dreams, allowing users to recall and reconstruct their dreams with the assistance of LLMs and GenAI.

Artificial intelligence technologies, particularly LLMs [43] and GenAI [44], have advanced significantly in recent years, offering powerful capabilities in language understanding and generation. These technologies can generate personalized and emotionally resonant content based on user input, significantly enhancing the efficiency and creativity of user-driven creation. Despite these advancements, no existing research has yet utilized AI technologies to assist users in the autonomous creation and creative expression of personal memory data. Inspired by these possibilities, we propose integrating LLM-based AI and generative AI into the system design of Reverba. By leveraging the understanding and generation capabilities of AI, our system enables users to intuitively and efficiently review, organize, and customize their life records, imbuing personal memory data with emotional resonance and profound meaning.

2.3 Multimodal Human-AI Co-creation Based on LLMs

Large Language Models (LLMs), with their powerful text comprehension and generation capabilities, have transformed the paradigm of human-AI interaction. Represented by products like ChatGPT [43], LLMs not only highlight the potential of generative AI in producing personalized textual content but also underscore the critical role of interfaces and interactions in facilitating communication with AI. Ding and Chan classified Human-AI text co-creation tasks based on the level of human intervention required, ranging from minimal to extensive [22]. It can be observed that iterative human-AI interaction plays a crucial role in complex and interconnected creative tasks, as these tasks require deep human collaboration and are likely to become a focal point of future research. Furthermore, with the ongoing advancements in LLM research, many LLM platforms have expanded beyond text-based interaction to support multimodal input and output formats such as images and speech [10,26,51]. This development directly addresses our challenge, prompting us to integrate multimodal LLMs into the creation and customization of personal memories, allowing end-users to co-create with LLM-based AI through iterative interaction.

Research on human-AI co-creation has been actively explored and applied across various fields [20,21,24,51,63,64]. Zhang et al. [64] proposed an iterative and interactive approach to human-AI co-creation in music, enabling users and AI agents to alternate in composing and modifying musical pieces. Yuan et al. [63] introduced an LLM-based interactive story-writing system, facilitating collaborative text creation between users and AI. The Drawing Apprentice [20,21] was developed as a real-time improvisational co-creative sketching agent. Similarly, Singh et al. [51] designed a multimodal writing support interface that provides users with suggestions through text, visuals, and audio. These studies primarily focus on the applications and contributions of AI in human-AI co-creation, emphasizing iterative interaction and multimodal integration in creative tasks.

LLM technology provides an effective solution for supporting self-reflection and self-expression through iterative human-AI co-creation. Reverba addresses this need by integrating multimodal creation and utilizing LLM-based iterative co-creation to help users express personal memories.

3 System Design and Implementation

Reverba, or "reverberate" in Latin, is an LLM-based multimodal autobiographical memory system with an innovative interface. It assists the end-user in the narration of autobiographical memories, and provides them with intelligent multimodal memory creation capabilities. Reverba provides three key functionalities: autobiographical memory description, memory scene creation and sound memory construction.

3.1 Autobiographical Memory Description

End-users can interact with the system co-creation agent (short for CCA) in natural language to describe their memories. As shown in the figure below, after the user initially describes their memory, the CCA will guide the user to further recall memory details through a questioning process based on the cue recall paradigm. During the process of deepening the recall, the CCA will also guide the user to reflect on the experience in order to gain deeper insights. When the user feels that the recall is complete, they can send a summary command to the CCA, which will organize the previous communication content and generate a complete autobiographical memory description. This memory description process can be iterated repeatedly until the user is satisfied (Fig. 2).

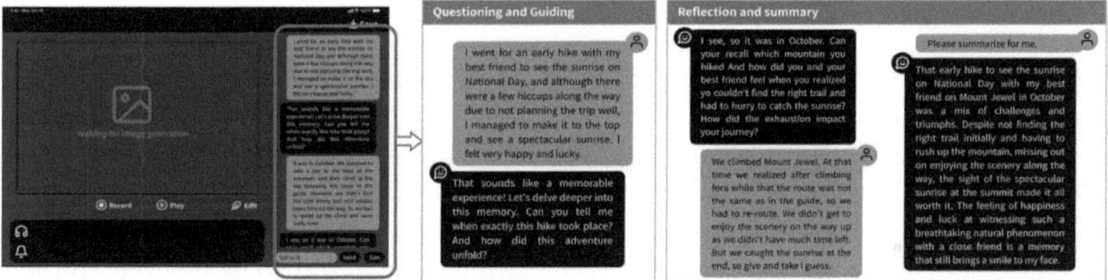

Fig. 2. The process of autobiographical memory recall and description generation through a conversational interaction between a user and the co-creation agent (CCA) by questioning, guiding, reflection, and summary.

3.2 Memory Scene Creation

Users also complete the creation of memory scenes through interaction with the co-creation agent (CCA). As shown in the figure, when the user clicks the generate button (displayed as "Gen" in the system interface), the CCA will automatically generate prompts for image generation based on the complete autobiographical memory description. Using these prompts, the CCA will generate a memory scene image for the user. The user can communicate with the CCA to modify the prompts, allowing for iterative image generation until the user feels that the image adequately represents their memory scene (Fig. 3).

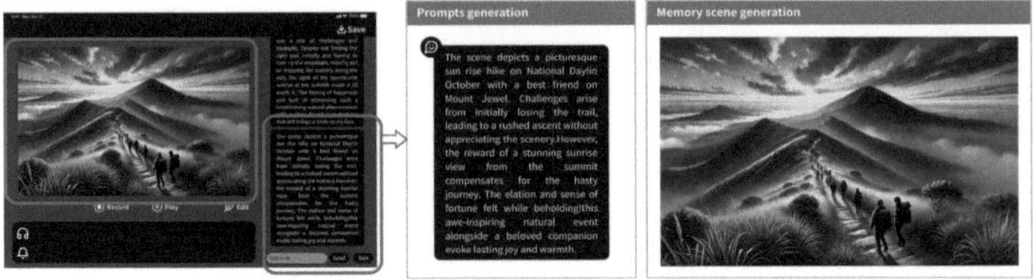

Fig. 3. The process of memory scene creation which includes memory scene prompts generation and image generation.

3.3 Sound Memory Construction

After completing the memory scene creation, users can add corresponding sound elements to the memory scene based on the visual imagery in the image. The system automatically performs semantic segmentation on the image and recommends sound effects based on the segmentation results. Specifically, sound memory construction consists of two functional modes, editing and creation.

Editing Mode. In the editing mode, users can select or replace appropriate sounds for the visual imagery in the memory scene. Specifically, users can tap on an image to select a visually segmented element, which will be highlighted. Subsequently, the system's built-in retrieval agent will search the sound library and recommend relevant sounds for the user to choose from. If the recommended sounds do not meet the user's needs, they can also search for the desired sounds. Each sound will have two playback modes: one for a one-time sound effect and the other for a looped ambient sound, which the user can set according to their preference (Fig. 4).

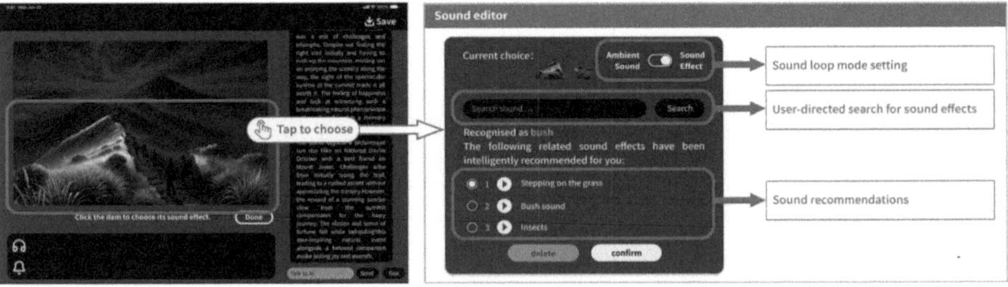

Fig. 4. The editing mode of sound memory construction which allows users to select or replace appropriate sounds for the visual imagery.

Creation Mode. After configuring the sound elements, the parts of the memory scene where sound effects have been applied will be highlighted. Once the user clicks the button to enter the recording mode, they can control the playback of each sound element by clicking the highlighted areas. All sound effects and ambient sounds will be recorded in the order of the timestamps when clicked, and displayed on two separate tracks for the user to review and modify. The recording process can be repeated as needed. After completing the recording, the user can replay the multimodal memory and save it (Fig. 5).

Fig. 5. The creation mode of sound memory construction which enables users to create multimodal memory.

3.4 Implementation

Reverba is developed for the iOS platform based on SwiftUI, which allows for the rapid construction of user interfaces using declarative syntax and enhances the performance and interactive experience through deep integration with system features. It consists of two primary components: the co-creation agent and the retrieval agent. These two agents collaborate seamlessly, enabling the system to efficiently generate multimodal memory outputs (Figs. 6 and 7).

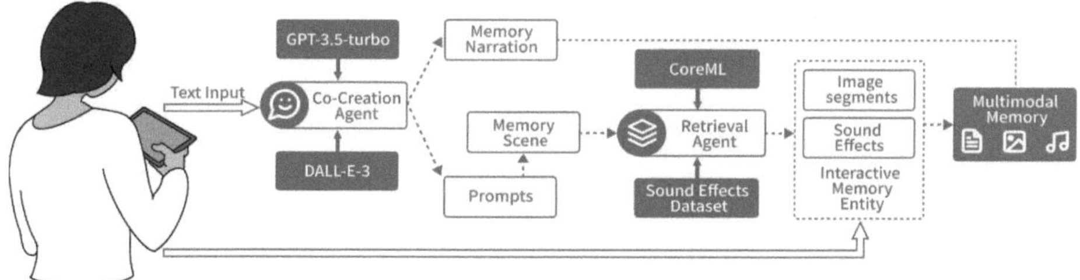

Fig. 6. An overview of Reverba. It includes two primary components: the co-creation agent and the retrieval agent.

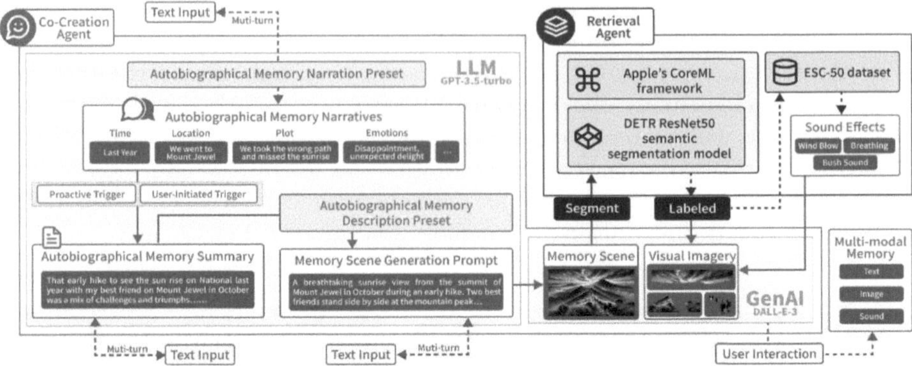

Fig. 7. Detailed workflow of the components of Reverba: co-creation agent and retrieval agent. The co-creation agent helps the users describe their memories and turn the memories into the image. The retrieval agent segments the imagery and retrieves sound effects.

Co-creation Agent The Co-creation Agent is a conversational system that incorporates GPT-3.5-turbo[1] as a large language model and DALL-E-3[2] as a text-to-image generation model. Through tailored presets, the agent enables autobiographical memory recall and description generation, as well as memory scene creation. Specifically, the agent first operates under the "autobiographical memory narration" preset, leveraging the GPT-3.5-turbo API to engage users in multi-turn dialogues and guide them in articulating their memories. Once sufficient information is gathered, users can manually initiate the trigger, or the agent can automatically generate a summarized description of the autobiographical memory. If the user is satisfied with the generated description, the agent switches to the "image description generation" preset, creating a visual description of the memory. This description is then passed to DALL-E-3 API to generate a corresponding memory scene.

Retrieval Agent The Retrieval Agent serves as a foundational component supporting the sound memory construction. After a memory scene is generated, the agent leverages Apple's CoreML framework[3] and the DETR ResNet50 semantic segmentation model[4] to intelligently segment and identify objects within the scene, extracting detailed image segments that represent semantically meaningful entities. For each segment, the agent assigns an object category label derived from the segmentation results. To retrieve a corresponding sound, the label is compared against the audio sample labels available in the

[1] https://platform.openai.com/docs/models#gpt-3-5-turbo.
[2] https://platform.openai.com/docs/models#dall-e.
[3] https://developer.apple.com/documentation/coreml.
[4] https://developer.apple.com/machine-learning/models.

ESC-50 dataset[5]. Specifically, the system employs Levenshtein Distance to compute string-level similarity between the segmented object label and candidate audio labels, thereby quantifying their lexical proximity. The retrieval module then selects the sound effect with the highest similarity score, ensuring accurate audio representation. Together, these elements form an interactive memory entity, enabling users to reconstruct sound memories with greater immersion and precision.

4 Study Design

To assess the usability of Reverba and the effectiveness of presenting multimodal autobiographical memories, and to explore its role in facilitating users' self-reflection and self-expression, we conducted a laboratory study with 12 participants. In the experiment, we introduced the system to the participants, then asked them to create autobiographical memory narratives both with and without the assistance of the system, using the GenAI model to create memory scenes. Specifically, we aimed to answer the following research questions:

- RQ1: Is Reverba easy to use, and can it assist users in efficiently creating vivid multimodal autobiographical memories?
- RQ2: Does the process of creating memories with Reverba help users achieve self-reflection and self-expression?

To answer RQ1, we conducted surveys after each of the two creative tasks to gather participants' evaluations of the creation process and outcomes using both methods. Additionally, we included an evaluation of the system's usability. To answer RQ2, we asked participants to think aloud during the creative process, expressing their thoughts and feelings, and conducted semi-structured interviews about their overall experience after the creative tasks. Subsequently, the researchers performed thematic analysis on the qualitative data.

4.1 Participants

We promoted the user study through social media and recruited participants from within the university. Ultimately, 12 students, aged 20âĂŞ29 (9 male, 3 female), volunteered for the study. Among the 12 participants, almost all had used large language model tools and were proficient in their usage. Only two participants had some experience with AI-based image generation tools, though they had used them infrequently. All participants were Chinese, and the study was conducted in Mandarin. After the experiment, each participant was paid 100 RMB (approximately 13.60 USD) as compensation for their participation.

[5] https://github.com/karolpiczak/ESC-50.

4.2 Study Process

Before the study, we obtained participants' consent via message and then invited them to our lab. The experimental research took place in a closed room with only one researcher and one participant. Two creative tasks were set up during the experiment.

For Task 1, participants were asked to recall an autobiographical memory based on a given theme without any system assistance, then use the DALL·E 3 model to create an AI-generated image based on their memory description. No prompts or assistance were provided during the creation process. After obtaining a satisfactory image, participants completed a survey evaluating the creation process and outcome of their memory scene.

For Task 2, participants were required to recall autobiographical memories and create corresponding multimodal memory scenes based on the given theme, using our system. Before starting Task 2, the researcher demonstrated the system's features. After completing Task 2, participants filled out the same survey as for Task 1, plus an additional usability evaluation of our system.

To avoid carryover effects, a fully balanced Latin square design was used in the experiment [56]. Two different memory themes were set: (a) an experience that made you feel very proud or successful, and (b) an experience that made you feel disappointed or failed. These two themes were evenly distributed across the two tasks. Additionally, the order of the tasks was randomly assigned, with a 5-minute break between the tasks for the participants. Therefore, there were 4 condition combinations, with 3 participants assigned to each group.

All participants were instructed to think aloud during the creative process and express their thoughts, feelings, and opinions about using the system at any time. When non-verbal responses (e.g., pauses, hesitation, laughter) were observed, participants were asked to clarify their thoughts at those moments. After the creation process, the participants' memory stories were shown, and they were asked about their feelings and evaluations.

Once all creative tasks were completed, semi-structured interviews were conducted to gain deeper insights into participants' feelings, emotional experiences, reflections (e.g., how communication with the agent influenced their recollection of past experiences), and self-expression (e.g., why they presented the memory in this way during creation). The entire process lasted about one hour, and we recorded, videotaped, screen-captured, and transcribed all sessions for further analysis.

4.3 Data Analysis

The quantitative research data comprised three parts. First, we conducted expert scoring on the autobiographical memory descriptions provided by participants in two creative tasks, evaluating them across three dimensions: completeness, emotional depth, and reflectiveness. We invited two psychology graduate students to participate in the scoring process. Prior to scoring, we provided training on the scoring guidelines to ensure a consistent understanding of the evaluation criteria.

After the scoring was completed, we assessed the consistency of their ratings. According to the weighted Kappa analysis, the inter-rater reliability between the two experts was 0.65, indicating a good level of agreement in their evaluations. For the evaluation of the memory scene creation process and outcomes, we referenced studies on LLM evaluation methods [13], taking into account our research questions, and set four dimensions: relevance, generative quality, time efficiency, and overall satisfaction. Participants provided subjective assessments on these dimensions for both creative tasks. Third, we used the System Usability Scale (SUS) [12] to evaluate the usability of our system. All three parts of the quantitative research used a 5-point Likert scale. Paired-sample t-tests were used to analyze the data from the first two sections. The SUS data were interpreted based on the scoring criteria proposed by Bangor, Kortum, and Miller [3] and Sauro [50].

For qualitative data analysis, we used thematic analysis [11]. The primary researchers transcribed the participants' thoughts and interviews, then analyzed the video recordings and transcriptions, generating initial codes with timestamps and potential themes. The researchers shared the preliminary findings with the research team to facilitate collective discussion and analysis. During this collaborative process, when questions or disagreements arose regarding coding and themes, the team reviewed short audio excerpts corresponding to timestamps and discussed the issues to refine the coding dimensions for better alignment with the research questions. This iterative process continued until consensus was reached among all team members.

5 Findings

We analyzed both the quantitative and qualitative data from the experiment. By summarizing user feedback on interaction and creation results, we provided preliminary answers to the two research questions.

5.1 System Function Evaluation: Effective and Vivid

Through the analysis of two sets of participant self-assessments' quantitative data, we addressed RQ1 from the perspectives of creation effectiveness and experience, as well as system usability. The image displays the statistical results of participant ratings on Reverba's usability. To facilitate comparison, the negative scores in the SUS were reversed. In this experiment, the SUS score of our system was 75.4. According to the scoring criteria proposed by Bangor et al. [3] and Sauro [50], our system demonstrates good usability. As shown in the figure, participants generally found Reverba easy to use. It is worth noting that P3 faced some issues with creation due to network connection problems. After adjustments and resets by the researchers, P3 was able to continue and complete their creation, so the evaluation was influenced to some extent (Fig. 8).

In the image generation phase of autobiographical memory, Reverba also received positive feedback from participants. Table 1 shows the results of a

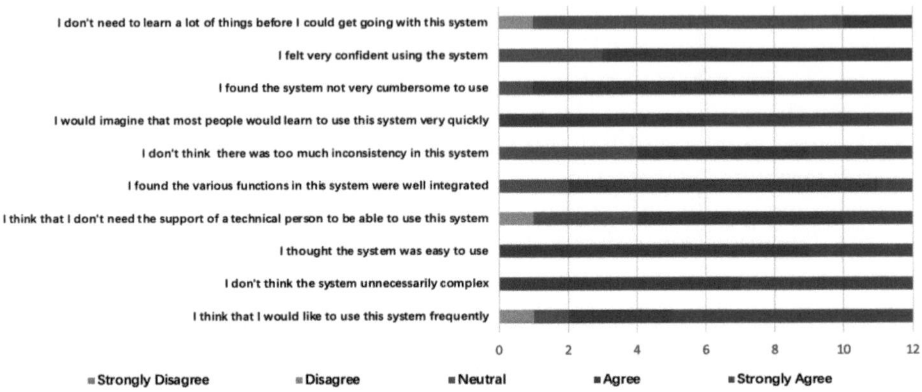

Fig. 8. SUS score statistics of Reverba.

paired-sample t-test on participants' ratings of the creation effectiveness and experience for two tasks. In terms of accuracy, relevance, generation quality, and overall satisfaction, Reverba demonstrated significant superiority. This indicates that the co-creation agent in Reverba effectively assisted users in creating autobiographical memories. Based on participant feedback, they found that the prompts generated by the CCA (Co-creation Agent) based on the recollection description provided a quick and relatively accurate basis for image generation (P1, P2, P5, P8). Therefore, for participants who were not familiar with text-to-image AI tools, this effectively lowered the threshold for prompt engineering. Several participants expressed appreciation for the system's initially generated images (P4, P6, P8), noting that the images created from the system-generated prompts accurately depicted the memory scenes they had in mind. However, in the dimension of time efficiency, our system did not show statistically significant superiority. Upon observing the creation process, we found that different users had varying demands for image details. Additionally, due to model limitations, the final image generation results may not always meet participants' requirements. For example, P11 needed to create a scene of a surgical operation in an operating room, but the generated images often failed to accurately display details of human organs. As a result, P11 felt that the created image was somewhat distorted and had to repeatedly modify the prompts to avoid displaying organ details in the image, which extended the creation process.

All participants agreed that the multimodal presentation of autobiographical recollections enhanced the vividness of the work. Most participants found the addition of sound effects to the images innovative, significantly enhancing the expressiveness of the memory scenes. The inclusion of sound heightened the atmosphere of the work and quickly transported the viewer into the memory.

Table 1. Paired t-test analysis results of the creation effectiveness and experience for two tasks.

Name	Pair (Mean ± SD)		Difference	t-value	p-value
	Task1	Task2	(Task1 - Task2)		
Accuracy	3.50 ± 0.80	4.17 ± 0.58	−0.67	−2.966	0.013*
Relevance	3.92 ± 0.51	4.67 ± 0.49	−0.75	−3.447	0.005**
Generation Effect	3.58 ± 0.79	4.25 ± 0.62	−0.67	−2.966	0.013*
Time Efficiency	3.42 ± 1.00	3.75 ± 0.87	−0.33	−1.301	0.22
Overall Satisfaction	3.58 ± 0.67	4.25 ± 0.45	−0.67	−3.546	0.005**

* p<0.05, ** p<0.01

5.2 In-Depth Autobiographical Recollection in Interactive Creation

During their interaction with our system for creative production, participants continually advanced their recollection and depiction of memory details. This process deepened the users' autobiographical recollections, making their memories clearer and more vivid through interactive creation.

Text Interaction Facilitates Deep Recollection. Initially, most participants provided relatively brief descriptions of their experiences, typically including an overview of the event and their general emotional response. However, as they engaged more deeply with the CCA, they began to recall the finer details of their experiences, such as the background of the event, the environment at the time, and the emotional journey they went through. In this process, researchers observed a significant amount of thinking and recollecting from the participants. Through their verbal reflections, it became clear that participants recalled details they had long forgotten. For example, P8 reflected on a badminton competition experience. During their interaction with the CCA, they recalled a small incident on the court they had not previously noticed: "When the match reached halftime, my opponent requested a change of shuttlecock. At the time, I didn't pay much attention to it, but looking back now, I think it could have been a strategic move on their part. It unconsciously affected my game performance". Most participants (P1-4, P6-12) expressed that the system greatly enhanced the completeness of their autobiographical recollections and enriched the details of their memories. However, P5 had a slightly different perspective. They felt that the CCA's questions and prompts "sometimes led my thoughts astray" and "posed questions that seemed irrelevant".

P1 stated that the interaction with the CCA allowed her to more systematically organize her memories. She explained,

> *"Without the systematic guidance, my memories would come to me in fragmented pieces. But with this (CCA), the questions helped me recall things along a logical chain, and in the end, it integrated these fragments into a*

whole, like piecing together a puzzle. I was able to review the experience in a more holistic way".

Finally, we conducted a quantitative analysis, where expert evaluations of participants' autobiographical recollection descriptions were performed. We applied a paired-sample t-test to the expert evaluation scores for the two creative tasks, and Table 2 presents the analysis results. The findings indicate that our system significantly enhanced the completeness, emotional depth, and reflectiveness of participants' autobiographical recollections.

Table 2. Paired t-test analysis results of the expert evaluation scores for two tasks.

Name	Pair (Mean ± SD)		Difference	t-value	p-value
	Task1	Task2	(Task1 - Task2)		
Completeness	4.17 ± 0.58	4.63 ± 0.48	−0.46	−2.421	0.034*
Emotional Depth	3.63 ± 0.48	4.29 ± 0.58	−0.67	−3.084	0.010*
Reflectiveness	3.21 ± 0.62	4.00 ± 0.77	−0.79	−3.383	0.006**

* $p<0.05$, ** $p<0.01$

Image Creation Facilitates Recall of Visual Details. We found that when participants engaged in text-based communication with the CCA to refine their autobiographical recollections, they tended to focus more on the development of the events and their internal emotional experiences. However, when they transitioned into image creation, they paid more attention to concrete, visual memory details. For instance, when P4 attempted to create an image of a scene where he went hiking with classmates to watch the sunrise, he noted that he recalled many details of the landscape, such as the types of plants along the way, and even the colors of the leaves. In a subsequent interview, he mentioned,

"I wouldn't necessarily recall these visual details when describing the memory in words. The image creation process subconsciously made me revisit the details of the scene, even if I might not end up depicting all of them in the image. Still, it allowed me to recall more things".

Sound Effects Enhance the Recollection of Multisensory Memories. The majority of participants (P2, P8-12) expressed appreciation for the sound effect addition feature. Typically, 2–3 sound effects were added, usually including one ambient sound (looped) and 2 other sounds (single-play). Similar to the impact of image creation, participants also searched for auditory details of their memories during the sound effect addition phase. Interestingly, more than one participant (P4, P6, P10) mentioned that the sound effects provided a more dimensional experience. For example, P4 added footstep sounds, breathing sounds, and bird calls to his work.

> *"Together, these sounds really recreated the atmosphere of my hike. The mountain was very quiet in the early morning, so the bird calls sounded crisp. Our group's footsteps and breathing were also very clear, and I could almost recall the damp, slightly cool air from that time".*

P6 recreated a scene of him attending a concert with his girlfriend. During that concert, a cup of milk tea spilled from above, which became a memorable incident. After adding the"pouring water" sound effect to the work, he said it felt as though he was reliving the "wet and sticky sensation" he had when the milk tea spilled on him. He then added a "splashing" sound effect because he felt it perfectly represented that tactile feeling.

P1 was the only participant who did not feel that sound effects were essential. She acknowledged that sound effects made her autobiographical recollection presentation more expressive, "but it was just an enhancement. Without the sound effects, the final presentation didn't seem to be affected".

5.3 Self-expression in Multimodal Creation

Building a Sense of Story All participants agreed that compared to single-modal text narratives, the multimodal presentation in our system significantly enhanced the sense of story. P2, while creating an image, paid close attention to the overall tone of the image. She believed that the color tone effectively set the atmosphere and emotional tone of the memory, something that is difficult to convey through text alone. She added that she particularly liked how the CCA used sunlight breaking through dark clouds to symbolize her shift in mindset. "The overall gloomy tone conveyed the sense of loss and suppression I felt at that time. But the sunlight breaking through the clouds contrasted strongly with that tone, and this contrast gave the scene a strong sense of story". P8 used sound effects to create a metaphor for his emotions. He added "drizzling rain" and "howling wind" sounds to represent his frustration after losing the competition and the low-pressure atmosphere of the competition venue. "A lot of emotional content, I don't like to express with words—it feels awkward. But images and sounds can convey these emotions in a subtle and effective way".

In addition, P3 used sound effects to add a sense of time flow to the static image, helping to construct the storyline. He depicted an experience of experimental results acceptance. "It's hard to show the passage of time in an image because it's just a snapshot of a moment. So, I added footstep sounds, keyboard sounds, and discussion sounds to reflect the development of the entire process".

Creativity and Willingness to Share. Regarding the perception of creativity, different participants held opposing views. We found that, although image generation provided greater creative space and creative support for most participants, its unpredictability was greater compared to adding sound effects. As a result, some participants (P3, P11) felt a stronger sense of control and self-efficacy during the sound effect addition phase, which made them feel more creative.

This form of creative self-expression also made autobiographical memories more intuitive compared to text-based narratives, leading to a higher willingness to share. P5 mentioned in the interview,

> *"I don't have to tell my friends a long story to share my experience; instead, I can just show them the audio-visual work I created and add some verbal description, which is much more effective. Moreover, this creative method is so novel that it makes me more willing to share this memory with others".*

5.4 Emotional Experience in Reflection

When asked about their experiences during the process of autobiographical reflection, many participants (P5-7, P11-12) mentioned a shift in perspective. Autobiographical recollection allowed them to revisit their past selves and gain new insights. P11 noted,

> *"The entire autobiographical recollection and creation process allowed me to step outside the subject of the memory and view the experience from an objective third-person perspective. This experience was fascinating, and I hadn't noticed it before".*

It is this sense of objectivity that led participants to focus less on the negative emotions of past experiences. While they still revisited their emotional experiences during the reflection process, the negative feelings were much diminished. Meanwhile, the positive emotions from past memories continued to provide them with a sense of healing.

Additionally, the CCA made an effort to avoid triggering negative emotions during its communication with participants. P5 remarked that the CCA offered *"lots of encouragement and praise"* during their conversations, which made him more inclined to reflect on what was previously an unpleasant experience from a more optimistic perspective. P1 also discovered that the CCA, when summarizing her autobiographical recollections, subtly modified the more negative aspects of her narrative, presenting it in a *"warmer"* light, which she appreciated.

5.5 Summary

Our research findings indicate that Reverba effectively supports autobiographical memory recall and self-reflection, and provides end-users with a tool for self-expression through creative multimodal co-creation. The main findings are as follows:

(1) **Enhancing Memory Recall.** The system encourages participants to delve deeper into their memories, helping them reconstruct and personalize their recollections in a more meaningful way.

(2) **Enriching Emotional and Sensory Experience.** By integrating image and sound creation, the system enhances the sensory experience of memories, making them more vivid and emotionally engaging.
(3) **Increasing Creativity and Willingness to Share.** Multimodal co-creation made the presentation of memories more vivid and expressive, sparking participants' creativity and increasing their willingness to share their memories.
(4) **Therapeutic Reflection.** Through the system's interactive prompts, participants were able to revisit past memories from a more objective and positive perspective, reducing negative emotions.

6 Discussion

In this study, we present a multimodal interaction system, Reverba, designed to assist users in reflecting on and creatively expressing autobiographical memories. This system combines large language models and generative AI to help users refine their autobiographical narratives, allowing them to create images for memory scenes and enhance the presentation of these scenes with sound effects. The results from our user study indicate that the multimodal creative features of Reverba significantly enhance memory recall and enrich users' emotional and sensory experiences. Compared to traditional methods, participants reported more vivid and emotionally profound autobiographical memories while using the system, leading to deeper self-reflection and introspection.

In this section, we will introduce our key research findings and further discuss the relevance and scalability of Reverba in relation to existing research, placing it within the broader context of human-computer interaction studies.

6.1 Multimodal Developments in Autobiographical Memory Research

Research on autobiographical memory typically relies on textual descriptions or verbal narration [49,52], which, while providing surface-level recollections, still fall short in conveying emotional depth and multi-sensory expression [45]. Existing tools and methods are mainly focused on recording and reviewing memories, often failing to fully stimulate users' emotional expression and engagement [27].

To address this, the Reverba system introduces a multimodal interaction approach that integrates visual and auditory elements, offering a more vivid and profound representation of autobiographical memory. By combining large language models (LLMs) and generative AI (GenAI), users can not only describe their memories through language but also transform them into images and sounds, enriching their emotional experiences and enhancing creative expression. With the addition of image generation and contextual sound effects, users can make each memory more nuanced and layered. This multimodal interaction provides more possibilities for memory expression and enables users to freely explore and create emotionally, facilitating the emotional representation of memories and offering individuals greater space for emotional regulation and self-exploration.

Most importantly, Reverba drives a shift in autobiographical memory research from single-dimensional recollections to multi-dimensional, multi-sensory experiences, providing researchers with a new methodology for enhancing the presentation and emotional depth of memories by integrating multi-sensory information. This shift challenges traditional methods in the field of autobiographical memory and offers new perspectives and tools for future research. As technology progresses, future researchers can further explore how to use multi-modal techniques to enhance the therapeutic, creative, and emotional value of autobiographical memory, thus opening up new applications in fields such as psychology and art therapy.

6.2 Innovative Pathways for Emotional Expression and Self-regulation

In psychological research and emotional therapy, emotional expression and self-reflection are crucial for achieving mental health and emotional regulation [5,34,39]. Traditional therapeutic methods often focus on cognitive restructuring and verbal expression [4,23,54], but many patients, when facing negative emotions, often find it difficult to accurately convey the complex feelings and painful experiences within them through language and text [23,25]. Therefore, helping individuals release emotions and self-regulate through innovative approaches has become an important research direction in emotional therapy.

Reverba employs a multimodal interaction approach, integrating visual and auditory elements, to effectively facilitate emotional expression and regulation. The system guides users through an intelligent creative process to recall and express personal experiences, not only through verbal descriptions but also by visually and sonically representing the emotions and details of memories. This artistic form of creation allows users to express their emotions more freely, thus enhancing the depth of self-reflection. Especially when dealing with negative emotions, visual and auditory elements can more concretely present the emotional hues of memories, overcoming the limitations of verbal expression and providing individuals with a richer sensory experience, helping them release emotions and regulate their feelings. Through this innovative approach, Reverba offers a new supportive tool for emotional therapy, enabling better regulation of negative emotions and promoting mental health.

Additionally, the application of Reverba in multimodal creation has advanced the development of "creative co-creation" in human-computer interaction research. Traditional human-computer interaction is often limited to functionality and task-oriented objectives, whereas Reverba integrates AI with users' creative expression, offering a more free and personalized creative experience. This "co-creation" model breaks the traditional one-way interaction in human-computer communication, enhancing the interaction and collaboration between users and AI, leading to the co-creation of content that is both creative and emotionally profound. Future research could further optimize AI interaction to increase freedom and personalization in the creative process, positioning AI not merely as a tool but as an effective collaborator in users' creative and self-expressive endeavors.

7 Limitations and Future Work

Although we have previously outlined how Reverba has gained participants' approval in user experiments and validated its usability and effectiveness, there are still certain limitations in the development and evaluation of our system.

7.1 Uncontrollability Due to the Technological Black Box

Despite the pre-setting of the co-creation agent (CCA), we observed considerable variation in conversation styles among participants during the experiment. Some participants found the way CCA posed questions during autobiographical recall to be rather rigid and mechanical. Specifically, CCA would often present a series of questions in a numbered list format, prompting participants to provide additional details of their memories. On one hand, this conversational style differs significantly from everyday communication habits, making participants feel uncomfortable and perceive the system as "lacking warmth". On the other hand, receiving multiple questions at once left some participants feeling overwhelmed, and they expressed a preference for a more gradual, guiding interaction from CCA. However, it is worth noting that this issue did not arise for all participants during the creative process. Given that the recall guidance stage does not require CCA to provide excessive creativity, we plan to fine-tune the model's presets in the future to ensure that interactions between users and CCA are more natural and conversational.

In the memory scene creation (image generation) phase, there remains significant uncertainty. Each time the image is regenerated, unexpected results may occur. Sometimes, the newly generated image perfectly meets the participant's needs or inspires new ideas; however, there are many occasions when the generated image shows unforeseen deviations or errors, requiring participants to revise the prompt and once again wait for an unknown outcome. This unpredictability can sometimes be frustrating. It is worth noting that the latest DALL-E model integrated into ChatGPT allows for the regeneration of specific regions of an image while keeping the rest of the image intact, which significantly reduces the trial-and-error cost of image generation. In the future, we will take into account both system functionality design and user interaction logic to update the image generation feature, aiming for a more controllable and refined creative process.

The black-box nature of AI models inevitably introduces randomness [62], which acts as a double-edged sword in the creative process. Excessive constraints on the model to reduce uncontrollability may lead to content homogenization, thereby stifling the creativity in human-AI co-creation. Therefore, we believe that when designing and developing interaction systems driven by AI models, it is crucial to balance functional objectives, interaction methods, and model capabilities to strike an optimal balance between controllability and innovation.

7.2 Individual and Group Differences in Study Design

Qualitative research data is one of the main sources of our experimental conclusions, and the collection of linguistic materials heavily relies on the participants' ability to express themselves. This presents a significant challenge for autobiographical recall experiments, as some participants may struggle to effectively describe past experiences and personal feelings, even with guidance. As a result, the collected data may exhibit considerable individual differences, and some data may fail to fully capture the depth of participants' experiences and emotions.

Moreover, individual differences in the experiment are also reflected in the participants' selection of recalled events. Compared to pleasant, leisure-type memories, participants' experiences of setbacks often provoke deeper reflection. While we reduced the influence of different types of recalled events to some extent by employing a fully balanced Latin square design, it is undeniable that we could not completely control all potential variables that might affect the data.

Finally, there may be group differences in the selection of participants for the experimental design. The subjects of this user study were all Chinese youths with strong educational backgrounds. However, younger generations' habits when using mobile devices may differ from those of other groups. Additionally, regional culture may influence creative habits, which means that the findings of this study could be biased and may not be applicable to other groups. Future work could expand the study to include populations outside of Chinese youth to further validate these findings.

8 Conclusion

In this study, we introduced Reverba, an innovative multimodal autobiographical memory narration system powered by large language models (LLMs) and generative AI (GenAI). The system is designed to assist users in reflecting on and creatively expressing their autobiographical memories by guiding narrative reflection and generating images and sounds. With Reverba, users interact with an LLM-powered agent that guides deep recollection through questioning and summarizes their autobiographical narrative. In the creative phase, the agent generates image prompts based on the user's memory descriptions, which can be refined iteratively. Users then enhance the images by adding sound effects, creating a multimodal autobiographical memory. The results of a user study involving 12 participants demonstrate that Reverba plays a crucial role in enhancing memory recall and fostering self-reflection. The system enables participants to explore and personalize their memories more deeply. By integrating image and sound, it enriches the sensory experience, making memories more vivid and emotionally engaging. The multimodal co-creation process sparks creativity and encourages memory sharing. Interactive prompts guide participants to revisit memories from a positive perspective, reducing negative emotions. Overall, these findings highlight the potential of Reverba to support the creation of meaningful autobiographical memories, offering a novel approach to self-exploration and emotional expression.

References

1. Abdul Rahman, A., Azmi, N.N.: Exploration of fine art photography as a medium for self-expression. Int. J. Art Des. (IJAD) **8**(1 SI 2), 96–106 (2024)
2. Ayobi, A., Sonne, T., Marshall, P., Cox, A.L.: Flexible and mindful self-tracking: design implications from paper bullet journals. In: Proceedings of the 2018 CHI Conference on Human Factors in Computing Systems, pp. 1–14 (2018)
3. Bangor, A., Kortum, P.T., Miller, J.T.: An empirical evaluation of the system usability scale. Int. J. Hum.-Comput. Interact. **24**(6), 574–594 (2008)
4. Beck, J.S.: Cognitive Behavior Therapy: Basics and Beyond. Guilford Publications (2020)
5. Bennett-Levy, J., Thwaites, R.: Self and self-reflection in the therapeutic relationship: a conceptual map and practical strategies for the training, supervision and self-supervision of interpersonal skills. In: The Therapeutic Relationship in the Cognitive Behavioral Psychotherapies, pp. 255–282. Routledge (2007)
6. Bluck, S.: Autobiographical memory: exploring its functions in everyday life. Memory **11**(2), 113–123 (2003)
7. Boals, A.: The use of meaning making in expressive writing: when meaning is beneficial. J. Soc. Clin. Psychol. **31**(4), 393–409 (2012)
8. Bolger, N., Davis, A., Rafaeli, E.: Diary methods: capturing life as it is lived. Annu. Rev. Psychol. **54**(1), 579–616 (2003)
9. Bradburn, N.M., Rips, L.J., Shevell, S.K.: Answering autobiographical questions: the impact of memory and inference on surveys. Science **236**(4798), 157–161 (1987)
10. Brade, S., Wang, B., Sousa, M., Oore, S., Grossman, T.: Promptify: text-to-image generation through interactive prompt exploration with large language models. In: Proceedings of the 36th Annual ACM Symposium on User Interface Software and Technology, pp. 1–14 (2023)
11. Braun, V., Clarke, V.: One size fits all? What counts as quality practice in (reflexive) thematic analysis? Qual. Res. Psychol. **18**(3), 328–352 (2021)
12. Brooke, J., et al.: Sus-a quick and dirty usability scale. Usability Eval. Ind. **189**(194), 4–7 (1996)
13. Chang, Y., et al.: A survey on evaluation of large language models. ACM Transa. Intell. Syst. Technol. **15**(3), 1–45 (2024)
14. Conway, M.A.: Autobiographical memory. In: Memory, pp. 165–194. Elsevier (1996)
15. Conway, M.A., Rubin, D.C.: The structure of autobiographical memory. In: Theories of Memory, pp. 103–137. Psychology Press (2019)
16. Crete-Nishihata, M., et al.: Reconstructing the past: personal memory technologies are not just personal and not just for memory. Hum.-Comput. Interact. **27**(1–2), 92–123 (2012)
17. Crovitz, H.F., Schiffman, H.: Frequency of episodic memories as a function of their age. Bull. Psychon. Soc. **4**(5), 517–518 (1974). https://doi.org/10.3758/BF03334277
18. Dale, O., Hagen, K.B.: Despite technical problems personal digital assistants outperform pen and paper when collecting patient diary data. J. Clin. Epidemiol. **60**(1), 8–17 (2007)
19. Dameron, M.L.: Person-centered counseling and solution-focused brief therapy: an integrative model for school counselors. J. Sch. Counseling **14**(10), n10 (2016)
20. Davis, N., Hsiao, C.P., Singh, K.Y., Magerko, B.: Co-creative drawing agent with object recognition. In: Proceedings of the AAAI Conference on Artificial Intelligence and Interactive Digital Entertainment, vol. 12, pp. 9–15 (2016)

21. Davis, N., Hsiao, C.P., Yashraj Singh, K., Li, L., Magerko, B.: Empirically studying participatory sense-making in abstract drawing with a co-creative cognitive agent. In: Proceedings of the 21st International Conference on Intelligent User Interfaces, pp. 196–207 (2016)
22. Ding, Z., Chan, J.: Mapping the design space of interactions in human-ai text co-creation tasks. arXiv preprint arXiv:2303.06430 (2023)
23. Dirkse, D., Hadjistavropoulos, H.D., Hesser, H., Barak, A.: Linguistic analysis of communication in therapist-assisted internet-delivered cognitive behavior therapy for generalized anxiety disorder. Cogn. Behav. Ther. **44**(1), 21–32 (2015)
24. Du, X., An, P., Leung, J., Li, A., Chapman, L.E., Zhao, J.: Deepthink: designing and probing human-ai co-creation in digital art therapy. Int. J. Hum Comput Stud. **181**, 103139 (2024)
25. Erkic, M., et al.: Impaired emotion processing and a reduction in trust in patients with somatic symptom disorder. Clin. Psychol. Psychotherapy **25**(1), 163–172 (2018)
26. Feng, Y., et al.: Promptmagician: interactive prompt engineering for text-to-image creation. IEEE Trans. Visualization Comput. Graph. (2023)
27. Fioretti, C., Smorti, A.: How emotional content of memories changes in narrating. Narrat. Inq. **25**(1), 37–56 (2015)
28. Galton, F.: Psychometric experiments. Brain **2**(2), 149–162 (1879)
29. Grant, A.M.: Making positive change: a randomized study comparing solution-focused vs. problem-focused coaching questions. J. Systemic Therapies **31**(2), 21–35 (2012)
30. Grant, A.M., O'Connor, S.A.: The differential effects of solution-focused and problem-focused coaching questions: a pilot study with implications for practice. Ind. Commer. Train. **42**(2), 102–111 (2010)
31. Greenberg, D.L., Rubin, D.C.: The neuropsychology of autobiographical memory. Cortex **39**(4–5), 687–728 (2003)
32. Hammerl, S., Hermann, T., Ritter, H.: Towards a semi-automatic personal digital diary: detecting daily activities from smartphone sensors. In: Proceedings of the 5th International Conference on PErvasive Technologies Related to Assistive Environments, pp. 1–8 (2012)
33. Harper, R., Randall, D., Smyth, N., Evans, C., Heledd, L., Moore, R.: The past is a different place: they do things differently there. In: Proceedings of the 7th ACM conference on Designing interactive systems, pp. 271–280 (2008)
34. Herwig, U., Kaffenberger, T., Jäncke, L., Brühl, A.B.: Self-related awareness and emotion regulation. Neuroimage **50**(2), 734–741 (2010)
35. Holland, A.C., Kensinger, E.A.: Emotion and autobiographical memory. Phys. Life Rev. **7**(1), 88–131 (2010)
36. Istvandity, L.: The lifetime soundtrack: music as an archive for autobiographical memory. Popular Music Hist. **9**(2) (2014)
37. Jin, Y., Cai, W., Chen, L., Zhang, Y., Doherty, G., Jiang, T.: Exploring the design of generative AI in supporting music-based reminiscence for older adults. In: Proceedings of the CHI Conference on Human Factors in Computing Systems, pp. 1–17 (2024)
38. Knez, I., Ljunglöf, L., Arshamian, A., Willander, J.: Self-grounding visual, auditory and olfactory autobiographical memories. Conscious. Cogn. **52**, 1–8 (2017)
39. Laireiter, A.R., Willutzki, U.: Self-reflection and self-practice in training of cognitive behaviour therapy: an overview. Clin. Psychol. Psychotherapy: Int. J. Theory Pract. **10**(1), 19–30 (2003)

40. Malchiodi, C.A.: Expressive Therapies. Guilford Publications (2013)
41. Maré, E.A.: "I paint, therefore I am": self-portraiture in the era of the self-aware and self-reflexive artist. South African J. Art Hist. **29**(3), 156–178 (2014)
42. Neipp, M.C., Beyebach, M., Nuñez, R.M., Martínez-González, M.C.: The effect of solution-focused versus problem-focused questions: a replication. J. Marital Fam. Ther. **42**(3), 525–535 (2016)
43. OpenAI: ChatGPT (2025). https://openai.com/index/chatgpt/. Accessed 21 Jan 2025
44. OpenAI: Dall·e 3 (2025). https://openai.com/index/dall-e-3/. Accessed 21 Jan 2025
45. Pascuzzi, D., Smorti, A.: Emotion regulation, autobiographical memories and life narratives. New Ideas Psychol. **45**, 28–37 (2017)
46. Pasupathi, M., Mansour, E., Brubaker, J.R.: Developing a life story: constructing relations between self and experience in autobiographical narratives. Hum. Dev. **50**(2–3), 85–110 (2007)
47. Pearson, M.R., Wilson, H.: Using expressive counselling tools to enhance emotional literacy, emotional wellbeing and resilience: improving therapeutic outcomes with expressive therapies. Counselling Psychotherapy Health **4**(1), 1–19 (2008)
48. Petrelli, D., Van den Hoven, E., Whittaker, S.: Making history: intentional capture of future memories. In: Proceedings of the SIGCHI Conference on Human Factors in Computing Systems, pp. 1723–1732 (2009)
49. Rubin, D.C.: Remembering Our Past: Studies in Autobiographical Memory. Cambridge University Press (1999)
50. Sauro, J.: A practical guide to the system usability scale: background, benchmarks & best practices. Measuring Usability LLC (2011)
51. Singh, N., Bernal, G., Savchenko, D., Glassman, E.L.: Where to hide a stolen elephant: leaps in creative writing with multimodal machine intelligence. ACM Trans. Comput.-Hum. Interact. **30**(5), 1–57 (2023)
52. Sotgiu, I., Sotgiu, I.: A "brief" history of the psychology of autobiographical memory. The Psychology of Autobiographical Memory: History, Theory, Research, pp. 17–92 (2021)
53. Tholander, J., Normark, M.: Crafting personal information-resistance, imperfection, and self-creation in bullet journaling. In: Proceedings of the 2020 CHI Conference on Human Factors in Computing Systems, pp. 1–13 (2020)
54. Thoma, N., Pilecki, B., McKay, D.: Contemporary cognitive behavior therapy: a review of theory, history, and evidence. Psychodynamic Psychiatry **43**(3), 423–461 (2015)
55. Volpe, C.R.: Digital diaries: new uses of photovoice in participatory research with young people. Children's Geographies **17**(3), 361–370 (2019)
56. Wagenaar, W.A.: Note on the construction of digram-balanced Latin squares. Psychol. Bull. **72**(6), 384 (1969)
57. Wan, Q., Feng, X., Bei, Y., Gao, Z., Lu, Z.: Metamorpheus: interactive, affective, and creative dream narration through metaphorical visual storytelling. In: Proceedings of the CHI Conference on Human Factors in Computing Systems, pp. 1–16 (2024)
58. Wang, X., et al.: Promoting personalized reminiscence among cognitively intact older adults through an ai-driven interactive multimodal photo album: development and usability study. JMIR Aging **7**(1), e49415 (2024)
59. Wardell, V., Palombo, D.J.: Stability and malleability of emotional autobiographical memories. Nat. Rev. Psychol. 1–14 (2024)

60. Whitmore, J.: Coaching for performance. N. Brealey Pub. (1996)
61. Willander, J., Sikström, S., Karlsson, K.: Multimodal retrieval of autobiographical memories: sensory information contributes differently to the recollection of events. Front. Psychol. **6**, 1681 (2015)
62. Yu, J., Wu, S., Lu, G., Li, Z., Zhou, L., Zhang, K.: Suno: potential, prospects, and trends. Front. Inf. Technol. Electron. Eng. 1–6 (2024)
63. Yuan, A., Coenen, A., Reif, E., Ippolito, D.: Wordcraft: story writing with large language models. In: Proceedings of the 27th International Conference on Intelligent User Interfaces, pp. 841–852 (2022)
64. Zhang, K., et al.: Wuyun: exploring hierarchical skeleton-guided melody generation using knowledge-enhanced deep learning. arXiv preprint arXiv:2301.04488 (2023)
65. Zhang, R., et al.: Let storytelling tell vivid stories: a multi-modal-agent-based unified storytelling framework. Neurocomputing 129316 (2025)

Fine-Grained Egyptian Coffin Line Drawings: Data Augmentation for Cultural Heritage Line Drawing Generation

Jiacheng Li[1], Letao Wang[2], Qingyang Wu[3], and Binbin Zhang[1](✉)

[1] World Arthistory Institute, Shanghai International Studies University, Shanghai 201620, China
zhangbinbin@gmail.com

[2] Shanghai Key Laboratory of Brain-Machine Intelligence for Information Behavior, School of Business and Management, Shanghai International Studies University, Shanghai 201620, China
0221147016@shisu.edu.cn

[3] Institute of Language Sciences, Shanghai International Studies University, Shanghai 201620, China

Abstract. Generating high-fidelity line drawings from cultural heritage artifacts is essential for archaeological and art historical documentation and analysis. This task is particularly challenging for ancient Egyptian artifacts due to limited training data and substantial stylistic diversity, ranging from densely patterned motifs to sparse hieroglyphs. We present Line-Density Aware Augmentation (LDAA), a novel data augmentation strategy that mitigates these challenges by analyzing the line density of ground-truth drawings and probabilistically synthesizing diverse, challenging training samples through the strategic recombination of high- and low-density regions from different images. Integrated with established generative frameworks like Pix2Pix and CycleGAN, LDAA enables models to effectively adapt to varying artistic styles and smooth transitions between them. Extensive qualitative and quantitative evaluations show that our approach significantly outperforms traditional methods, such as Canny edge detection, and baseline deep learning models, producing line drawings with higher structural accuracy and perceptual quality—even on severely eroded surfaces. Beyond providing a robust tool for cultural heritage preservation, LDAA offers a transferable augmentation paradigm applicable to other data-scarce computer vision domains.

Keywords: line drawing generation · data augmentation · egyptian coffin · digital preservation of cultural heritage

1 Introduction

Line drawing plays a crucial role in archaeology and cultural heritage preservation, offering a distilled yet precise representation of artifacts. For ancient

X. Li et al. (Eds.): CCAC 2025, CCIS 2886, pp. 47–67, 2026.
https://doi.org/10.1007/978-981-95-8256-3_3

Egypt—whose murals, reliefs, and inscriptions are often faded, eroded, or structurally fragile—line drawings preserve essential contours, proportions, and symbolic motifs. Grounded in this context, an ongoing Sino-Egyptian joint archaeological project is currently focused on the digitization of painted wooden mummy coffins unearthed from the Saqqara necropolis. These drawings function simultaneously as research tools for scholars to study craftsmanship and stylistic evolution, and as lasting visual records that safeguard the aesthetic and historical value of ancient works for broader audiences (Fig. 1).

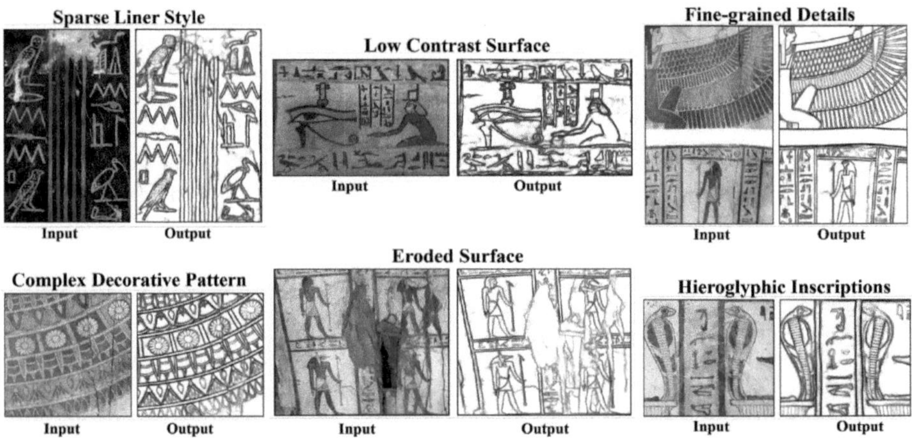

Fig. 1. Illustration of key challenges in automated line drawing generation for cultural heritage, such as substantial variation in artistic styles (e.g., intricate patterns versus sparse hieroglyphs) and surface abrasion. To address these challenges, we propose an image augmentation technique—Line-Density Aware Augmentation (LDAA)—designed to improve the robustness of generative models under diverse conditions. As shown in the examples above, LDAA enables models to effectively process a wide range of challenging inputs, from stylistically varied artworks to low-contrast, heavily eroded artifacts, thereby demonstrating its practical effectiveness and strong generalization capability.

Traditionally, such drawings were created by hand: artists placed tracing paper over photographs, illuminated them with light boxes, and carefully replicated the lines. In recent years, digital tools and graphics tablets have replaced tracing paper, yet the process remains labor-intensive and time-consuming. More critically, hand-drawn results inevitably reflect the subjective interpretation of the artist—selecting which lines to include, how to simplify forms, and how to interpret ambiguous or weathered details. These factors limit the scalability and consistency of line drawing production, especially in large archaeological projects (Fig. 2).

Automated line drawing generation offers a promising solution, combining efficiency with reproducible accuracy. However, conventional edge detection algorithms such as Canny [2] struggle with the complexities of aged artifacts, often

Fig. 2. The left image depicts the original cultural heritage artwork, while the right image shows its corresponding hand-drawn line illustration. [1]

producing fragmented or noisy outlines that fail to capture subtle but crucial features. Generative models, such as Pix2Pix [3] in the Generative Adversarial Network (GAN) [4] family, have shown the capacity to transform raw images into high-fidelity line drawings by learning style patterns from paired datasets. Yet, in the context of Egyptian cultural heritage, their performance is hampered by the scarcity of high-quality, domain-specific training data capable of representing the unique textures, curvatures, and line densities of coffin paintings and reliefs (Fig. 3).

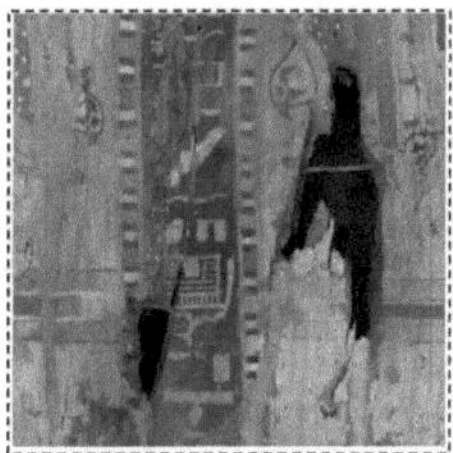

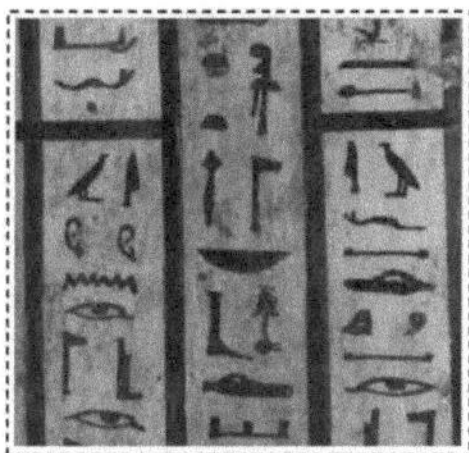

Fig. 3. Representative challenges in generating line drawings from Egyptian artifacts. (a) Eroded surfaces—pigment loss and surface damage obscure underlying details, hindering the inference of continuous lines. (b) Hieroglyphic inscriptions—demand high precision to preserve legibility and scholarly integrity. (c) Dense coffin linework—requires resolving fine, closely spaced details without unintended merging or oversimplification.

This study addresses the challenge by integrating data augmentation techniques with the Pix2Pix and CycleGAN framework to enhance the automatic generation of line drawings from Egyptian artifact images. We combine multiple datasets—BSDS500 [5], BIPED [6], and our own curated Egyptian line art corpus—and introduce a novel line-density blending strategy to overcome data scarcity. This approach improves the model's capacity to render fine details and adapt to the heterogeneity of ancient Egyptian imagery. As shown in our evaluation (Sect. 4), our method achieves state-of-the-art results with a PSNR of 24.78, SSIM of 0.93, and LPIPS of 0.132, outperforming all baseline methods.

The contributions of this work are twofold. First, it delivers a precise visual tool for archaeological research, enabling systematic analysis of craftsmanship, decorative logic, and stylistic evolution. Second, it extends beyond academia by translating the aesthetic DNA of Egyptian art—its rhythmic human gestures, symbolic arrangements, and balanced compositions—into visually intuitive forms. In doing so, it fosters wider cultural engagement and helps ensure that the visual and humanistic values of ancient heritage are sustainably preserved.

2 Related Work

2.1 Digital Line Drawing and Its Use in Arts

The evolution of digital line drawing has progressed from manual drafting, which was accurate yet labor-intensive and subjective, to automated approaches that initially relied on classical edge detection techniques such as Canny [2] and Sobel [7]. These early methods, however, struggled with noise, lighting variations, and complex textures, often resulting in the loss of critical details. A major shift occurred with deep learning, especially Generative Adversarial Networks (GANs) [4], which enabled robust image-to-image translation through models like Pix2Pix [3] and CycleGAN [4], while Pix2PixHD [8] further improved realism with multi-scale discriminators. Nevertheless, GANs faced challenges such as instability and mode collapse, leading to the rise of Denoising Diffusion Probabilistic Models (DDPMs) [9], which achieved higher fidelity and diversity by simulating noise reduction. ControlNet [10] built on these advances by introducing structural guidance for precise outputs, and together these methods have been widely adopted in cultural heritage projects.

In particular, the digitization of Dunhuang murals has benefitted significantly: ControlNet has supported tasks such as damage repair, color restoration, and line drawing extraction [11], while specialized frameworks such as DunhuangGAN [12], convolutional–self-attention contour networks [13], and Diffu-Mural [14], which combines multi-scale diffusion models with ControlNet [10], have further advanced high-fidelity line art and restoration.

Despite these successes, current research still faces key limitations. First, most work has concentrated on Dunhuang murals, leaving other cultural traditions—such as ancient Egyptian heritage—largely unexamined. Second, many heritage contexts lack high-quality paired data that aligns original painted surfaces with expert line drawings, restricting the adaptability of existing deep learning methods. To address these challenges, we propose the LDAA (Line Drawing for Ancient Artifacts) algorithm, which we integrate into the Pix2Pix [3] and CycleGAN [4] frameworks. This approach is designed for data-scarce scenarios and enhances both efficiency and accuracy in generating line drawings from Egyptian cultural artifacts, representing a crucial step toward extending digital preservation methods beyond their current regional and data-rich confines.

2.2 Image Data Augmentation and Image Mix Methods

Image data augmentation has become an essential technique for improving the generalization of deep learning models, and several systematic reviews have provided comprehensive overviews. For example, Shorten and Khoshgoftaar [15] categorized augmentation methods into three major categories and fifteen subcategories, including basic manipulations such as kernel filters and image mixing. Similarly, Yang et al. [16]divided augmentation into basic approaches—such as image manipulation, erasing, and mixing—and advanced approaches—such as auto augment, feature augmentation, and generative models. Unlike other strategies such as Dropout [17], Batch Normalization [18], or Transfer Learning [19], augmentation directly operated at the data level, addressing overfitting, data scarcity, and class imbalance.

The present study places particular emphasis on Image Mix methods, which generated novel training examples by combining two or more images either entirely or in selected subregions, thereby expanding diversity. Mixup [20]created convex combinations of images and labels, encouraging linear behavior between samples, while subsequent methods such as CutMix [21], Fmix [22], Augmix [23], and SaliencyMix [24] refined this principle using patches, random masks, or saliency guidance. However, these approaches were not specifically designed for line drawing tasks, and their effectiveness in this context has not been systematically explored. To fill this gap, we propose LDAA (Line-Density–Aware Augmentation), a method tailored to line drawing generation. LDAA improves structural fidelity and perceptual clarity, while also providing a generalizable augmentation paradigm for fine-grained image-to-image translation tasks in cultural heritage preservation and beyond.

3 Line-Density Aware Augmentation (LDAA)

This section presents our method for generating high-fidelity line drawings from ancient Egyptian artifacts, addressing the twin challenges of limited training data and substantial stylistic variability. To overcome these obstacles, we introduce a novel data augmentation technique, Line-Density Aware Augmentation (LDAA), which can be integrated into standard generative frameworks like Pix2Pix and CycleGAN. As shown in Fig. 4, the pipeline comprises three stages: (1) data construction and preprocessing, (2) application of the LDAA strategy, and (3) model training and evaluation.

3.1 Data Construction and Preprocessing

A high-quality dataset is fundamental to the model's success. Our core dataset was derived from three ultra-high-resolution (8192×8192 pixels) scans of painted coffins from the Saqqara necropolis. To obtain precisely paired ground truth, we

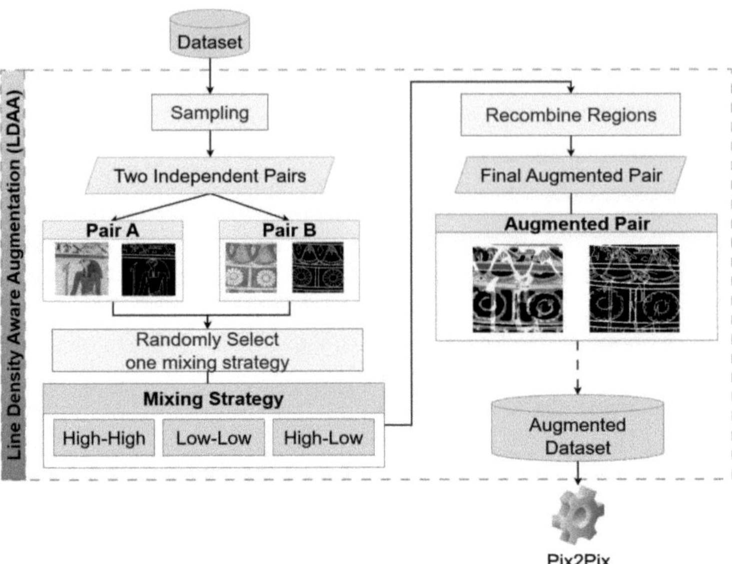

Fig. 4. Overview of the proposed integrated pipeline for automatic line-drawing generation.

utilized professional, hand-drawn line drawings created by an expert team[1] – a process that, while ensuring high accuracy, is exceptionally time-consuming. These drawings meet the rigorous standards required for archaeological catalog publications.

Since deep learning models cannot process such large images directly, we divided each scan–drawing pair into 256 × 256 pixel patches using a top-to-bottom, left-to-right tiling strategy. The initial 3,072 patches included many non-informative regions (e.g., blank wood or empty background), which were removed—over 60% of the total—yielding a focused set of 1,200 patches with significant visual content for fine-tuning.

For inference on the original 8192 × 8192 images, we applied a similar tiling approach with overlapping patches, later blended via masking to ensure seamless reconstruction and avoid edge artifacts. The main challenge is the limited size of this curated dataset, which increases the risk of overfitting. To address this, we augmented it with two large-scale public edge-detection benchmarks—BSDS500 [5] and BIPED [6] –to pretrain the model on abundant low-level line

[1] The expert team was led by Professor Liu Guan from the Center for Visual Studies (CVS), Peking University. To illustrate the labor-intensive nature of this manual work, according to the team's records, the creation of a single, relatively simple frontal view drawing of a coffin required approximately 27 h of expert labor. This highlights the significant efficiency bottleneck in traditional digital documentation methods and underscores the practical necessity for the automated approach explored in this paper.

and edge features. This transfer serves as a regularizer, enabling the network to generalize beyond the small Egyptian set while adapting to its distinctive style. All images were preprocessed via image registration, resizing to 512×512 pixels, and pixel-value normalization to the range $[-1, 1]$.

3.2 Line-Density Aware Augmentation (LDAA)

While conventional data augmentation techniques, such as random rotations or color jittering, enhance a model's generalization and invariance to minor transformations, they prove insufficient for the fine-grained precision demanded by our task. These methods primarily introduce global image variations without fundamentally altering the local structural complexity of the content; for instance, a rotated dense line pattern remains inherently challenging to disambiguate. Consequently, they fail to provide the model with novel discriminatory information critical for resolving the intricate, closely-spaced line structures characteristic of Egyptian coffin art.

Therefore, the motivation behind our proposed Line Density-Aware Augmentation (LDAA) strategy is to directly address this critical challenge of enhancing line parsing precision, particularly within high-density regions. By strategically synthesizing novel training samples—for example, by compositing two high-density areas or juxtaposing dense and sparse patterns—we explicitly compel the model to acquire more robust and discriminative feature representations of intricate linework. This targeted training on algorithmically synthesized complex scenarios significantly improves the model's capacity to generate highly precise and accurate outputs, representing a substantial advancement over generic augmentation methodologies.

Probabilistic Application of LDAA. To strike a balance between exposing the model to the original data distribution and our more challenging synthetic samples, our augmentation pipeline incorporates a probabilistic control mechanism. This approach is inspired by the established practice of stochastic regularization in modern data augmentation strategies, where the probabilistic application of transforms is crucial for achieving robust performance [25,26].

During each training iteration, our Line Density-Aware Augmentation (LDAA) pipeline is applied to the batch with a probability p. If triggered, the process initiates by sampling two independent image-lineart pairs and randomly selecting one of three predefined mixing strategies, outputting the newly augmented pair to the network. Conversely, with a probability of $(1-p)$, the original, unmodified batch is fed directly into the network.

This probabilistic process for generating the final training batch $\mathrm{B}_{\mathrm{out}}$ from an input batch B_{in} can be formally expressed as:

$$\mathrm{B}_{\mathrm{out}} = \begin{cases} \mathrm{LDAA}(\mathrm{B}_{\mathrm{in}}), & \text{if } u < p \\ \mathrm{B}_{\mathrm{in}}, & \text{if } u \geq p \end{cases} \tag{1}$$

where u is a random variable sampled from a uniform distribution $\mathcal{U}(0,1)$ and LDAA($\cdot$) denotes the application of our augmentation pipeline. In our experiments, we set $p = 0.6$ based on ablation studies (see **Ablation on Augmentation Probability** p in Sect. 4.4). This ensures the model maintains exposure to the ground-truth data distribution, a principle philosophically aligned with methods like AugMix, which explicitly blend original and augmented data [27].

Core Step: Density Analysis and Mask Generation. The cornerstone of the LDAA strategy is the precise spatial partitioning of "dense" and "sparse" regions within a line drawing. This sub-process involves three key steps, as detailed in Fig. 5.

Generating a Continuous Density Field (Gaussian Blur). The input ground-truth line art is initially a binary image. To quantify local line density, we first apply a Gaussian Blur to "diffuse" the discrete lines into a continuous grayscale *smooth density map*. In this map, each pixel's intensity is directly proportional to the local concentration of line features.

Establishing a Global Segmentation Standard (Calculating Global Threshold τ*).* To ensure a consistent and robust criterion for density across the entire dataset, we calculated the median of all pixel values from all generated density maps within the entire training set. The median is chosen due to its robustness against outliers—such as images with exceptionally high or very low line densities—compared to the mean. This approach guarantees a more balanced and representative threshold for effectively partitioning the data into "dense" and "sparse" regions. This robust statistical value is designated as the global threshold τ.

Binarization for Complementary Mask Generation (M_{high} *and* M_{low}*).* Each smooth density map is subsequently binarized using the global threshold τ. If a pixel's density value is greater than or equal to τ, its corresponding location in the high-density mask (M_{high}) is marked as 1 (white). Conversely, if the value is less than τ, its location in the low-density mask (M_{low}) is marked as 1. This meticulous process yields a pair of precise and complementary regional masks for each input image, which are then used in the subsequent LDAA operations.

Cross-Image Regional Recombination. With the density masks generated, we randomly select one of three distinct strategies to recombine regions, thereby creating challenging and structurally coherent synthetic samples. Visual examples of these strategies are presented in Fig. 6.

Specifically, we employ three mixing strategies, each designed to enhance different aspects of the model's learning capacity:

- **High-High Mixing:** This strategy merges high-density regions from both source images. Its primary aim is to improve the model's performance on fine-grained and complex structural details, forcing it to learn robust representations in highly intricate areas.

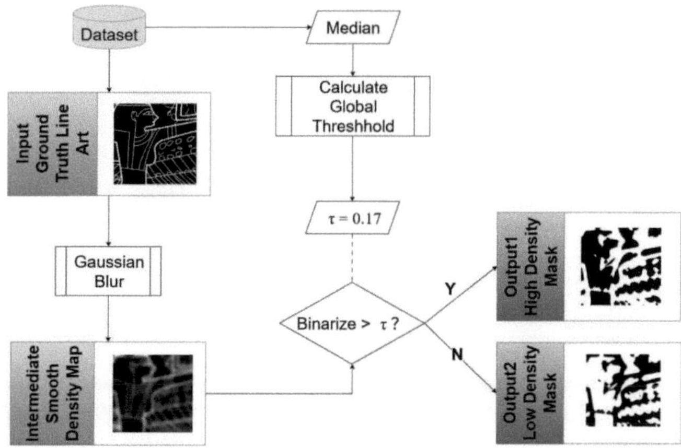

Fig. 5. The Density Analysis and Mask Generation pipeline. A ground-truth line art is converted into a smooth density map via Gaussian Blur. This map is then binarized using a global threshold (τ) to produce two complementary outputs: a high-density mask (M_{high}) and a low-density mask (M_{low}).

- **Low-Low Mixing:** This strategy fuses low-density regions from both sources. It strengthens the model's ability to handle sparse or underrepresented patterns, ensuring better generalization in simpler or less cluttered areas.
- **High-Low Mixing (Cross-Mixing):** This strategy combines a high-density region from one source with a low-density region from another. This cross-combination encourages the model to generalize across stylistic transitions and varying levels of detail, promoting robustness to diverse visual complexities.

This recombination process is applied synchronously to both the input artifact images, denoted as I, and their corresponding line drawings, L. The mathematical definition is as follows:

$$I_{\text{aug}} = (I_A \odot M) + (I_B \odot (1 - M)) \tag{2}$$

$$L_{\text{aug}} = (L_A \odot M) + (L_B \odot (1 - M)) \tag{3}$$

Here, $\odot$ represents the Hadamard Product (element-wise multiplication). M_A and M_B are the masks selected from source image A and source image B, respectively. These masks can be any from the set $\{M_{\text{high}}, M_{\text{low}}\}$, allowing for the construction of all three aforementioned mixing strategies (High-High, Low-Low, and High-Low). The resulting training pairs, $(I_{\text{aug}}, L_{\text{aug}})$, are structurally coherent yet stylistically chimeric by design, providing a rich learning signal for the model.

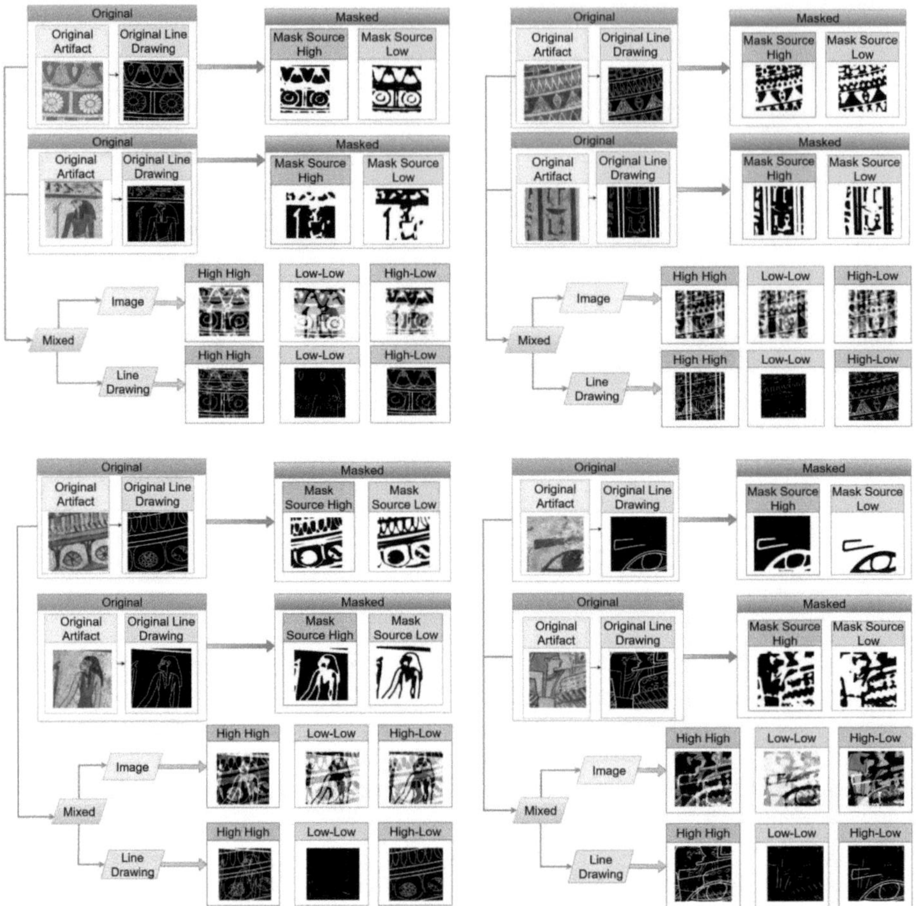

Fig. 6. Visualization of Line-Density Aware Augmentation (LDAA). For each source pair (e.g., in each of the four quadrants), we first analyze its line art to generate high- and low-density masks. The final "Augmentation" row demonstrates the results of applying one of three distinct mixing strategies: High-High Mix, Low-Low Mix, and High-Low Mixing.

3.3 Deep Neural Network Training and Evaluation

This research primarily employs the Pix2Pix [4] framework for image-to-image translation. Its generator utilizes a U-Net [28] architecture with skip connections. This specific structure effectively mitigates the loss of crucial low-level details, such as fine textures on artifact surfaces and minute strokes in hieroglyphs, during the encoding-decoding process. The discriminator adopts a 70×70 PatchGAN structure, which guides the generator to prioritize the synthesis of high-frequency details by independently evaluating the authenticity of local image patches.

The model's optimization objective is a weighted sum of a conditional adversarial loss, $L_{cGAN}(G, D)$, and an L1 reconstruction loss, $L_{L1}(G)$, with the total loss function defined as:

$$L_{total} = L_{cGAN}(G, D) + \lambda L_{L1}(G) \quad (4)$$

In this study, the hyperparameter λ was set to 100. This high weighting strongly enforces structural accuracy, aligning with the primary criterion for academic line drawings: fidelity to the original form. All experiments were conducted on an NVIDIA RTX 4090 Laptop GPU, utilizing the Adam [29] optimizer with a learning rate of 2×10^{-4}, a batch size of 8, and trained for 200 epochs.

To demonstrate the versatility and model-agnostic nature of our LDAA strategy, we also integrated it into a CycleGAN framework for comparative analysis. While CycleGAN is typically employed for unpaired image-to-image translation, for a fair comparison within this study, it was trained on the same paired dataset. This approach allows us to validate that the performance enhancements attributed to LDAA are not exclusive to the U-Net architecture of Pix2Pix but can generalize effectively to other generative models with differing architectures. This provides clear evidence for the robustness and broad applicability of our proposed data augmentation methodology.

4 Experiments and Results

This section presents a series of experiments designed to evaluate the effectiveness of the proposed method. The evaluation consists of three complementary parts: a qualitative comparison, which provides visual inspection of the generated line drawings; a quantitative comparison, which employs standard image-to-image translation metrics; and ablation studies, which assess the contribution of each component in the Line-Density–Aware Augmentation (LDAA) strategy.

4.1 Baselines and Evaluation Metrics

To ensure a comprehensive evaluation, our method is compared against both traditional and deep learning–based baselines. The traditional baseline is the Canny edge detection algorithm [2], which serves as a representative non-deep-learning approach. For deep learning comparisons, we employed two representative generative frameworks—Pix2Pix [3] and CycleGAN [4] –and configured each in three variants. The first variant is the vanilla model, trained without any data augmentation, to establish the baseline capability of the architecture. The second variant was trained with conventional geometric transformations, such as random flipping and cropping, in order to assess the benefits of generic augmentation. The third variant integrated the proposed LDAA strategy into Pix2Pix and CycleGAN, enabling direct evaluation of its impact on performance.

For quantitative assessment, we adopted three widely used metrics to measure the similarity between generated line drawings and ground truth. Peak Signal-to-Noise Ratio (PSNR) [30]measures pixel-wise reconstruction error. Higher values indicate lower noise and greater fidelity to the original image; Structural Similarity Index (SSIM) [31] evaluates similarity in structure, contrast, and luminance, aligning more closely with human visual perception than PSNR. Its value ranges from −1 to 1, with higher scores indicating a stronger structural match; Learned Perceptual Image Patch Similarity (LPIPS) [32] utilizes a deep neural network trained to predict human perceptual similarity, with lower LPIPS scores indicating that two images are more alike in terms of visual appearance, aesthetic quality, and perceptual coherence.

4.2 Qualitative Comparison

Visual quality is critical for the application of line drawings in archaeology and art history. Figure 7 presents a qualitative comparison between our method and the baselines on three representative types of Egyptian artifacts: dense decorative patterns, sparse hieroglyphic inscriptions, and heavily eroded surfaces.

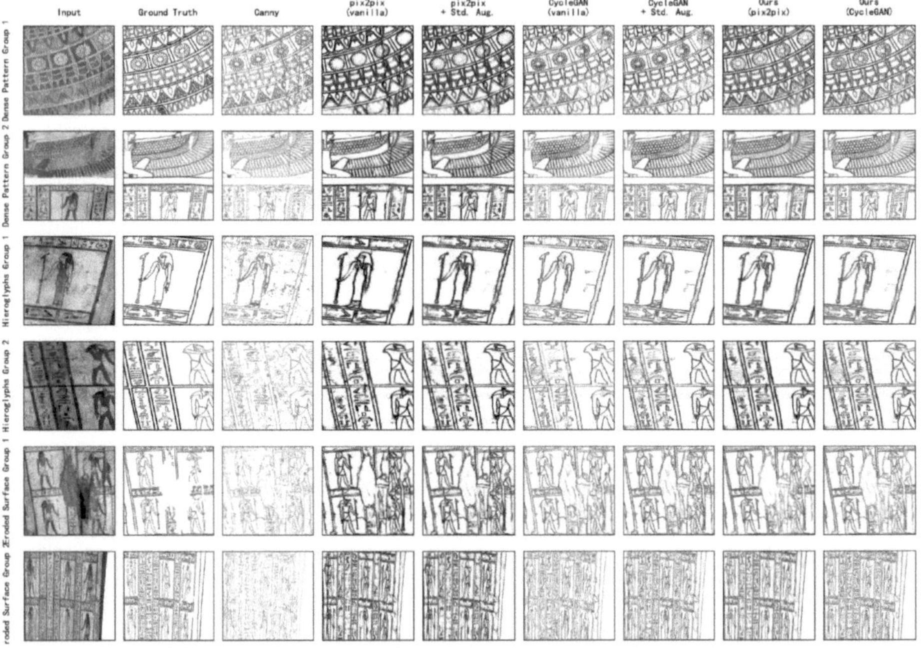

Fig. 7. Qualitative comparison of our method against baselines across representative artifact types. The Canny edge detector produces noisy and fragmented lines. The vanilla Pix2Pix [3] and CycleGAN [4] models, including their versions with standard augmentation, struggle with fine details and can produce blurry or incomplete results. Our method (Ours), enhanced by LDAA and applied to both Pix2Pix and CycleGAN, consistently generates the cleanest, most continuous, and structurally faithful line drawings, demonstrating superior performance and robustness.

Firstly, for dense decorative patterns, the primary challenge lies in resolving fine, closely spaced lines. The Canny [2] detector produces noisy and structurally incoherent results, while vanilla Pix2Pix [3] and CycleGAN [4] models, as well as their standard augmentation variants, tend to generate blurry, merged, or uncertain strokes. This is exemplified by the circular border in the first row of Fig. 7, where baseline outputs are faint, broken, or ambiguous. In contrast, LDAA-enhanced models produce crisp, continuous circles, indicating not only improved detail preservation but also greater decisiveness in geometric rendering. This effect is likely reinforced by the "High–High Mixing" strategy, as corroborated by the ablation study in Sect. 4.4.

Then, for hieroglyphic inscriptions, scholarly usage demands high legibility and precision. Baseline models often produce shaky, incomplete, or distorted strokes, undermining the academic value of the results and failing to preserve the sharp, calligraphic qualities of the script. Our method consistently generates clean, continuous, and accurate lines that faithfully reproduce the angularity and distinct strokes of each character. This improvement is particularly associated with the "Low–Low Mixing" strategy, which helps the model focus on sparse but semantically critical elements, as confirmed by later ablation experiments.

Finally, for eroded surfaces, the task is to reconstruct plausible line structures despite severe pigment loss and surface damage. Canny and baseline deep learning models fail to recover coherent shapes, instead tracing the contours of the damage and producing fragmented noise. Our LDAA-based models demonstrate robust generalization, producing continuous and logically connected lines that bridge missing regions. This capability arises from the combined effect of all LDAA components, which expose the model to a balanced mix of high-density, low-density, and transitional compositions during training. Through this process, the model learns the underlying stylistic rules of Egyptian art, enabling informed interpolation and reconstruction of missing details—achievements unattainable by simpler augmentation techniques.

4.3 Quantitative Comparison

To provide an objective assessment, we calculated the average PSNR, SSIM, and LPIPS scores for all methods across our entire test set. The results, encompassing the traditional Canny method alongside both the Pix2Pix and CycleGAN frameworks with various augmentation strategies, are consolidated in Table 1.

Based on the comprehensive analysis of Table 1 and Fig. 8, two key conclusions can be drawn:

Firstly, baseline methods exhibit significant limitations. The traditional Canny algorithm performs poorly across all metrics (PSNR: 15.34, SSIM: 0.68), with its particularly high LPIPS score of 0.451 quantitatively confirming that its noisy and fragmented output is perceptually distant from the ground truth. While vanilla deep learning models like Pix2Pix and CycleGAN offer substantial improvement over Canny, their performance remains modest (PSNR $\approx$ 20). This reflects their capacity to capture general forms but not the fine details or line confidence crucial for this domain, as corroborated by qualitative examples

Table 1. Quantitative Comparison with Baseline Methods. This table presents the performance evaluation using three standard metrics: Peak Signal-to-Noise Ratio (PSNR) [25], and Structural Similarity Index Measure (SSIM) [26], where higher scores indicate better performance (↑), and Learned Perceptual Image Patch Similarity (LPIPS) [27], where a lower score is preferred (↓).

Method	PSNR (↑)	SSIM (↑)	LPIPS (↓)
Canny [2]	15.34	0.68	0.451
pix2pix (vanilla) [3]	20.12	0.85	0.231
pix2pix + Standard Aug.	21.55	0.88	0.189
CycleGAN (vanilla) [4]	19.89	0.84	0.245
CycleGAN + Standard Aug.	21.03	0.87	0.208
Ours (pix2pix + LDAA)	**24.78**	**0.93**	**0.132**
Ours (CycleGAN + LDAA)	**24.21**	**0.91**	**0.146**

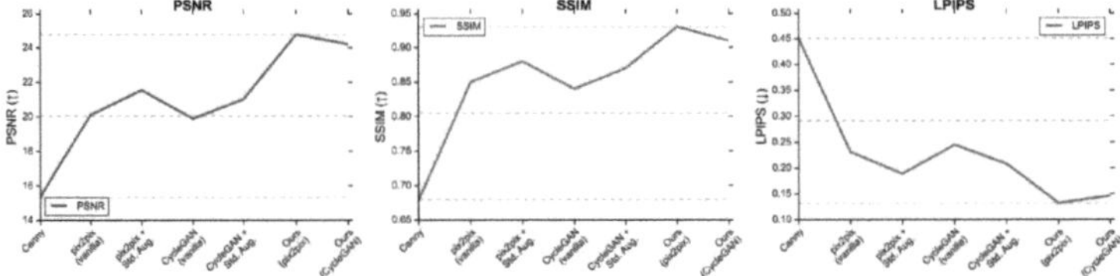

Fig. 8. Quantitative comparison of our method against baselines across three key metrics (PSNR [25], SSIM [26], LPIPS [27]). For PSNR and SSIM, higher scores are better (↑), while for LPIPS a lower score is better (↓). The trend lines clearly demonstrate that our proposed method (Ours + LDAA) achieves the best performance across both Pix2Pix and CycleGAN frameworks.

in Fig. 7. Notably, applying standard data augmentation yields only marginal benefits (PSNR $\approx$ 21), underscoring that simple geometric transformations are insufficient to teach models the complex stylistic grammar inherent in Egyptian art. This highlights the critical necessity for a more sophisticated, domain-aware augmentation strategy.

Secondly, a comparison between the two generative frameworks reveals that Pix2Pix consistently holds a slight edge over CycleGAN in this paired-data task. This is an expected outcome, as Pix2Pix's architectural design, particularly its direct L1 reconstruction loss, enforces stricter pixel-level correspondence, making it inherently well-suited for tasks demanding high structural fidelity. However, the most critical finding is the transformative impact of our Line-Density Aware Augmentation (LDAA) strategy. Applying LDAA triggers a dramatic performance leap across both architectures, pushing them far beyond the capabilities of the baseline models. For instance, LDAA boosts the PSNR score from a modest 21.55 to an impressive 24.78 for Pix2Pix, and similarly elevates CycleGAN's score from 21.03 to 24.21. This powerful and consistent improvement across two distinct model backbones robustly demonstrates that our LDAA is a model-agnostic and highly effective strategy. The superior LPIPS scores of 0.132 (Pix2Pix) and 0.146 (CycleGAN) are particularly noteworthy. This significant reduction in perceptual error confirms that the generated drawings are not only mathematically more accurate but also visually and aesthetically approach the quality of human-drawn ground truth, which represents the ultimate goal for cultural heritage applications.

4.4 Ablation Study

Ablation on LDAA Components. To further analyze the individual contribution of each component within our Line-Density Aware Augmentation (LDAA) strategy, we conducted a comprehensive ablation study by training three distinct variants of our full model, each with one of the specific mixing strategies disabled: Ours w/o Cross-Mixing excludes the combination of high-density and low-density regions, preventing the model from learning to generalize across stylistic transitions; w/o High-High Mixing removes the mixing of high-density regions, consequently limiting the model's ability to capture and reproduce fine-grained structural details; and w/o Low-Low Mixing disables the combination of low-density regions, which specifically impacts the model's capacity to effectively handle sparse or underrepresented content.

Table 2. Quantitative Results of the Ablation Study for LDAA. This table evaluates the individual contribution of each mixing strategy within our Line-Density Aware Augmentation (LDAA). We compare the full LDAA model against three ablated variants, each with one mixing strategy (Cross-Mixing, High-High Mixing, or Low-Low Mixing) disabled. The results consistently demonstrate that the full model achieves the best scores across all metrics, confirming the essential and positive contribution of all three components to the model's overall performance. Notably, the most significant performance degradation is observed when Cross-Mixing is removed, highlighting its critical role.

Method	PSNR (↑)	SSIM (↑)	LPIPS (↓)
Ours (Full Model)	**24.78**	**0.93**	**0.132**
w/o Cross-Mixing	22.51	0.89	0.175
w/o High-High Mixing	23.15	0.90	0.161
w/o Low-Low Mixing	23.42	0.91	0.158

The results presented in Fig. 9, Fig. 10, and Table 2 unequivocally demonstrate that each component of the Line-Density Aware Augmentation (LDAA) strategy is essential for achieving optimal performance. The removal of any of the three mixing strategies consistently leads to a degradation in both visual quality (as shown qualitatively in Fig. 9 and Fig. 10) and quantitative scores Table 2. Specifically, the model without "Cross-Mixing" exhibits a general deterioration in

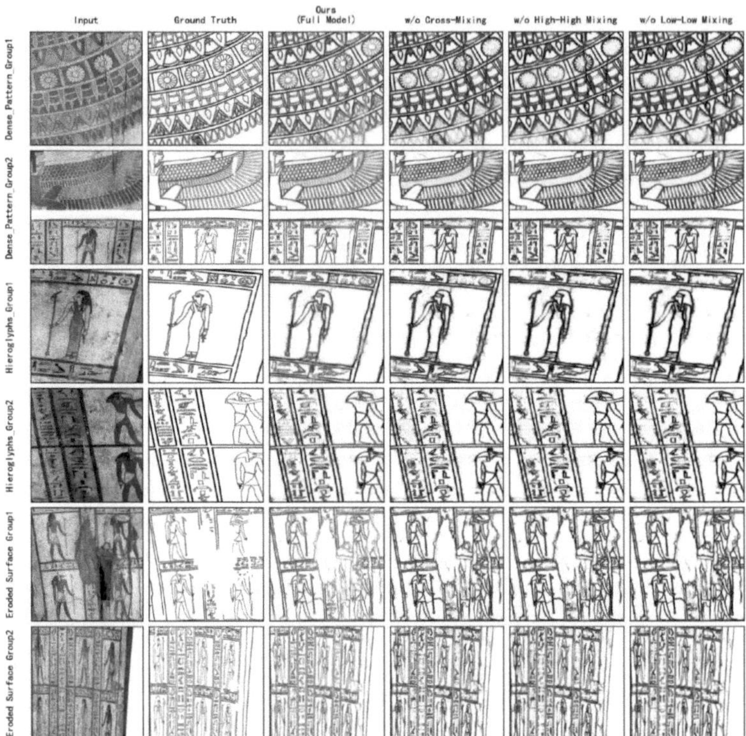

Fig. 9. Visual Results of the Ablation Study on LDAA Components. Column 3 (Full Model) serves as benchmark. Removing Cross-Mixing degrades overall line quality, while removing High-High or Low-Low Mixing reduces performance on dense or sparse patterns, respectively.

the overall line quality of the generated Egyptian images, with a particularly significant decline across all quantitative metrics. Conversely, models lacking "High-High Mixing" struggle with purely complex samples, such as dense sarcophagus patterns, while those without "Low-Low Mixing" show reduced performance on purely simple test samples like sparse hieroglyphs. Nevertheless, the performance decrease from removing either "High-High Mixing" or "Low-Low Mixing" is comparatively milder than that observed in the absence of "Cross-Mixing". The complete LDAA model, incorporating all three strategies, consistently yields the best results across all metrics and visual inspections, thereby validating our comprehensive augmentation design as both effective and necessary for robust line art generation in this challenging domain.

Ablation on Augmentation Probability. To validate our choice of the augmentation probability p and investigate its impact on model performance, we conducted an ablation study. Our model was trained with varying $p \in \{0.4, 0.6, 0.8, 1.0\}$, while all other hyperparameters remained constant. The quan-

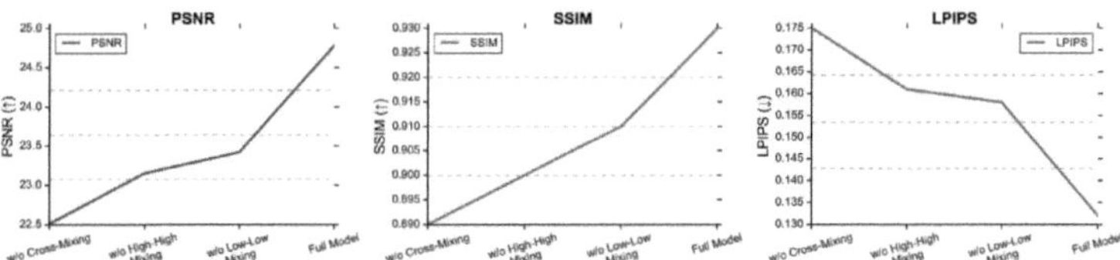

Fig. 10. Line charts of ablation study (Table 2). Each chart shows the performance trend for a specific metric (PSNR, SSIM, LPIPS) as key mixing strategies are disabled. The "Full Model" consistently achieves the best scores (highlighted in gold), with performance degrading as components are removed, most notably in the "w/o Cross-Mixing" variant. This visualization reinforces the conclusion that all three mixing strategies are essential for optimal performance.

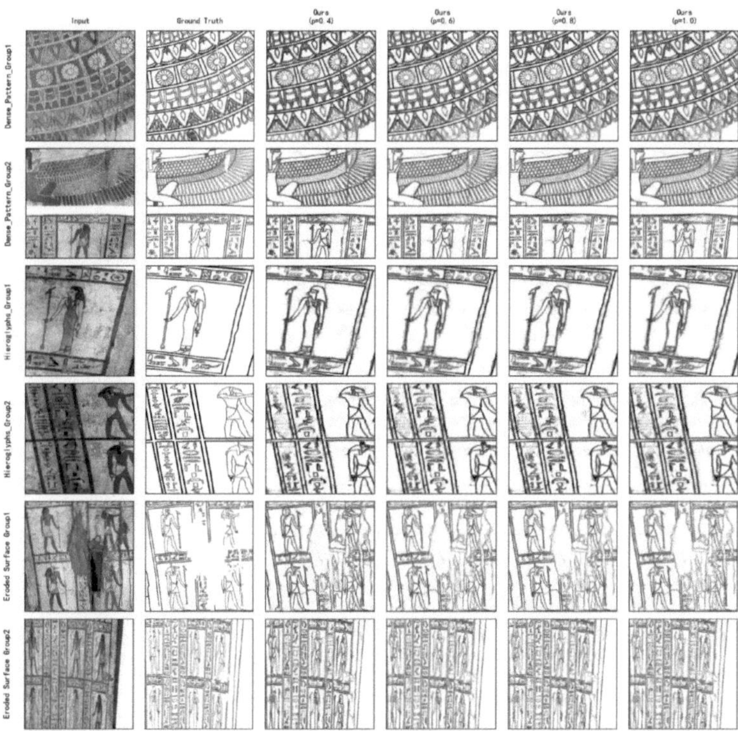

Fig. 11. Qualitative results of the ablation study on augmentation probability p. This figure compares line drawings generated by our model trained with different p values across various artifact types. While all settings produce high-quality results, subtle differences in line definition and sharpness are discernible upon close inspection. The model with $p = 0.6$ consistently produces the crispest and most coherent results.

titative results are summarized in Table 3 and visually illustrated in Fig. 12, with qualitative comparisons presented in Fig. 11.

Table 3. Quantitative results of the ablation study on augmentation probability p. This table presents the performance of our method across three standard metrics (PSNR, SSIM, LPIPS) for different values of p. The optimal balance is achieved at $p = 0.6$.

Method	PSNR (↑)	SSIM (↑)	LPIPS (↓)
Ours ($p = 0.4$)	23.95	0.91	0.151
Ours ($p = 0.6$)	**24.78**	**0.93**	**0.132**
Ours ($p = 0.8$)	24.62	0.92	0.139
Ours ($p = 1.0$)	24.08	0.90	0.148

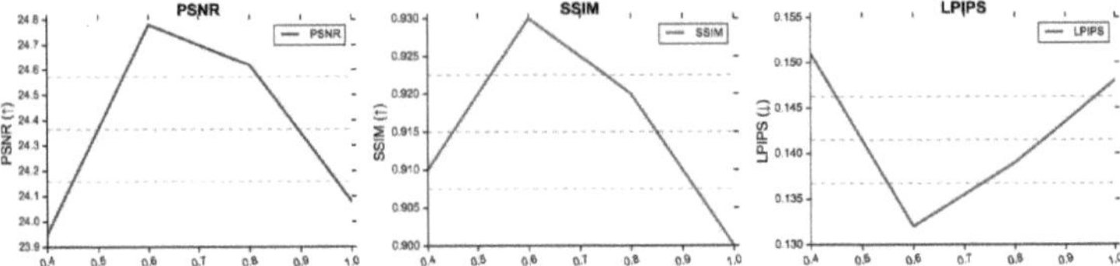

Fig. 12. Quantitative trends of augmentation probability p (Table 3). Performance peaks at $p = 0.6$, confirming the importance of balancing original and augmented data.

As shown in Table 3 and Fig. 12, the model achieves optimal performance when $p = 0.6$. Too little augmentation ($p = 0.4$) limits robustness, while too much ($p = 1.0$) omits ground-truth distribution and harms generalization. Visual differences (Fig. 11) are subtle, but objective metrics clearly favor $p = 0.6$.

5 Conclusion

In this work, we addressed a significant technical challenge in cultural heritage preservation: generating high-quality line drawings from ancient Egyptian artifact images, a task complicated by data scarcity and vast stylistic variance. We proposed a novel data augmentation strategy, termed Line-Density Aware Augmentation (LDAA), which intelligently synthesizes new training samples by analyzing and recombining regions of different line densities. By integrating LDAA with standard generative frameworks like Pix2Pix and CycleGAN, we created a more stable and effective pipeline for this image-to-image translation task.

Our extensive qualitative and quantitative experiments have demonstrated that our proposed method significantly outperforms traditional algorithms and baseline deep learning models. The generated line drawings exhibit higher line structural accuracy, superior image quality, and greater fidelity to the original images. This work not only provides a practical and efficient tool for archaeologists, art historians, and museum curators for the purpose of archiving, analysis, and restoration, but also presents a valuable data augmentation paradigm for other image translation tasks in the domain of cultural heritage where training data is limited and stylistically diverse.

Despite the promising results, our work has certain limitations that open avenues for future research. The output of our model is a raster image, while resolution-independent vector graphics are often more desirable for scholarly applications. Future work could explore generating vectorized line drawings directly, potentially by integrating LDAA with recent advancements in differentiable rendering or diffusion models. Furthermore, our current pipeline is fully automated and could benefit from a human-in-the-loop mechanism [33,34], where an expert could provide real-time feedback to refine the model's output, bridging the gap between automated generation and expert knowledge.

References

1. Xu, D.: Research and implementation on line drawing generation method for ancient Chinese frescoes. Tianjin University (2016)
2. Canny, J.: A computational approach to edge detection. IEEE Trans. Pattern Anal. Mach. Intell. **8**, 679–698 (1986)
3. Isola, P., Zhu, J.Y., Zhou, T., Efros, A.A.: Image-to-image translation with conditional adversarial networks. In: Proceedings of the IEEE Conference on Computer Vision and Pattern Recognition (CVPR) (2017)
4. Zhu, J.Y., Park, T., Isola, P., Efros, A.A.: Unpaired image-to-image translation using cycle-consistent adversarial networks. In: Proceedings of the IEEE International Conference on Computer Vision (ICCV) (2017)
5. Berkeley Segmentation Data Set and Benchmarks 500 (BSDS500). The Berkeley Computer Vision. http://gkaggle.com/datasets/balraj98/berkeley-segmentation-dataset-500-bsds500
6. Soria, X., Riba, E., Sappa, A.: Dense extreme inception network: towards a robust CNN model for edge detection. In: Proceedings of the IEEE/CVF Winter Conference on Applications of Computer Vision (WACV), pp. 1923–1932 (2020)
7. Sobel, I., Feldman, G.: A 3×3 Isotropic Gradient Operator for Image Processing. Stanford Artificial Intelligence Project (1968)
8. Wang, T.C., Liu, M.Y., Zhu, J.Y., Tao, A., Kautz, J., Catanzaro, B.: High-resolution image synthesis and semantic manipulation with conditional GANs. In: Proceedings of the IEEE Conference on Computer Vision and Pattern Recognition (CVPR) (2018)
9. Ho, J., Jain, A., Abbeel, P.: Denoising diffusion probabilistic models. In: Advances in Neural Information Processing Systems (NeurIPS) (2020)
10. Zhang, L., Rao, A., Agrawala, M.: Adding conditional control to text-to-image diffusion models. In: Proceedings of the IEEE/CVF International Conference on Computer Vision (ICCV) (2023)
11. Zhao, Y., Wang, C., Zhang, H., Zhang, J.: A deep learning-based method for the virtual restoration of Dunhuang murals. ACM J. Comput. Cultural Heritage (JOCCH) **14**(3), 1–20 (2021)
12. Wang, W., Li, Y., Ye, H., Ye, F., Xu, X.: DunhuangGAN: a generative adversarial network for Dunhuang mural art style transfer. In: IEEE International Conference on Multimedia and Expo (ICME) (2022)
13. Liu, B., He, F., Du, S., Zhang, K., Wang, J.: Dunhuang murals contour generation network based on convolution and self-attention fusion. Appl. Intell. **53**(19), 22073–22085 (2023)

14. Han, P., et al.: DiffuMural: restoring Dunhuang murals with multi-scale diffusion. arXiv preprint arXiv:2504.09513 (2025)
15. Shorten, C., Khoshgoftaar, T.M.: A survey on image data augmentation for deep learning. J. Big Data **6**(1), 60 (2019)
16. Yang, S., Xiao, W., Zhang, M., Guo, S., Zhao, J., Shen, F.: Image data augmentation for deep learning: a survey. arXiv preprint arXiv:2204.08610 (2022)
17. Srivastava, N., Hinton, G., Krizhevsky, A., Sutskever, I., Salakhutdinov, R.: Dropout: a simple way to prevent neural networks from overfitting. J. Mach. Learn. Res. **15**(1), 1929–1958 (2014)
18. Ioffe, S., Szegedy, C.: Batch normalization: accelerating deep network training by reducing internal covariate shift. In: International Conference on Machine Learning (ICML), pp. 448–456. PMLR (2015)
19. Torrey, L., Shavlik, J.: Transfer learning. In: Handbook of Research on Machine Learning Applications and Trends: Algorithms, Methods, and Techniques, pp. 242–264. IGI Global (2010)
20. Zhang, H., Cisse, M., Dauphin, Y.N., Lopez-Paz, D.: mixup: beyond Empirical Risk Minimization. In: International Conference on Learning Representations (ICLR) (2018)
21. Yun, S., Han, D., Oh, S.J., Chun, S., Choe, J., Yoo, Y.: CutMix: regularization strategy to train strong classifiers with localizable features. In: Proceedings of the IEEE/CVF International Conference on Computer Vision (ICCV), pp. 6023–6032 (2019)
22. Harris, E., Marcu, A., Painter, M., Niranjan, M., Prügel-Bennett, A., Hare, M.: Fmix: enhancing mixed sample data augmentation. arXiv preprint arXiv:2002.12047 (2020)
23. Hendrycks, D., Mu, N., Cubuk, E.D., Zoph, B., Gilmer, J., Lakshminarayanan, B.: Augmix: a simple data processing method to improve robustness and uncertainty. arXiv preprint arXiv:1912.02781 (2019)
24. Uddin, M.S., Li, S., Lung, B.: SaliencyMix: a saliency-guided data augmentation strategy for better generalization. arXiv preprint arXiv:2108.11859 (2021)
25. Cubuk, E.D., Zoph, B., Mané, D., Vasudevan, V., Le, Q.V.: AutoAugment: learning augmentation strategies from data. In: Proceedings of the IEEE/CVF Conference on Computer Vision and Pattern Recognition (CVPR) (2019)
26. Cubuk, E.D., Zoph, B., Shlens, J., Le, Q.V.: RandAugment: practical automated data augmentation with a reduced search space. In: Proceedings of the IEEE/CVF Conference on Computer Vision and Pattern Recognition Workshops (CVPRW) (2020)
27. Hendrycks, D., Mu, N., Cubuk, E.D., Zoph, B., Gilmer, J., Thulasidasan, S.: Augmix: a simple data processing method to improve robustness and uncertainty. In: International Conference on Learning Representations (ICLR) (2020)
28. Ronneberger, O., Fischer, P., Brox, T.: U-net: convolutional networks for biomedical image segmentation. In: Navab, N., Hornegger, J., Wells, W.M., Frangi, A.F. (eds.) MICCAI 2015. LNCS, vol. 9351, pp. 234–241. Springer, Cham (2015). https://doi.org/10.1007/978-3-319-24574-4_28
29. Kingma, D.P., Ba, J.: Adam: a method for stochastic optimization. arXiv preprint arXiv:1412.6980 (2014)
30. Gonzalez, R.C., Woods, R.E.: Digital Image Processing, 4th edn. Pearson (2018)
31. Wang, Z., Bovik, A.C., Sheikh, H.R., Simoncelli, E.P.: Image quality assessment: from error visibility to structural similarity. IEEE Trans. Image Process. **13**(4), 600–612 (2004)

32. Zhang, R., Isola, P., Efros, A.A., Shechtman, E., Wang, O.: The unreasonable effectiveness of deep features as a perceptual metric. In: Proceedings of the IEEE Conference on Computer Vision and Pattern Recognition (CVPR), pp. 586–595 (2018)
33. Licklider, J.C.R.: Man-computer symbiosis. IRE Trans. Hum. Factors Electron. **HFE-1**(1), 4–11 (1960)
34. Fagyal, Z., et al.: What determines what is relevant? Human or AI? Why not both? Commun. ACM **67**(4), 31–34 (2024)

Spatial Narrative Logic in Computational Vision: A Methodological Study of Depthmap Software in Artistic Generation

Yuzhao Liu and Shijun Yue(✉)

Xi'an University of Architecture and Technology, Xi'an 710000, Shanxi, China
17661529223@163.com

Abstract. Within the context of artificial intelligence-driven expansion of visual arts boundaries, the transformation of spatial structural information into visual representations constitutes a significant research focus in computational art studies. This study employs Depthmap spatial analysis software as the core computational tool for artistic research. By integrating methodologies from space syntax theory, visual narrative theory, and parametric generation theory, an experimental framework for image generation is established through a four-step pathway: spatial structure analysis, parameter extraction, semantic mapping, and artistic generation. The process is primarily driven by three key metrics derived from Depthmap: integration, connectivity, and visible area. This provides novel perspectives for the visualization of future urban concepts, the reconstruction of cultural heritage, and the implementation of immersive spatial installations. This study endeavors to integrate the structural logic of programming languages with the perceptual dimensions of artistic expression, thereby exploring novel possibilities for spatial language representation in computational art.

Keywords: Computer Art · Spatial Analysis · Space Syntax Theory · Artificial Intelligence

1 Introduction

The rapid advancement of artificial intelligence has enabled computational art—an artistic form integrating algorithmic thinking, data logic, and aesthetic approaches—to continually transcend the expressive boundaries of traditional art. The interdisciplinary development between art and technology has permeated the contemporary art sphere, where the synthesis of artistic practices and the deepening of cross-media domains have become an inevitable trajectory for multidimensional creative advancement [1]. Within this context, "space" as a medium no longer exists merely as a physical entity in the traditional sense, but is progressively transforming into a "data carrier" that can be computationally processed and analytically examined. This "data carrier" possesses the capacity to facilitate artistic creation. A pivotal research direction in computational art involves the integration of structural characteristics of urban spaces with visual language systems.

X. Li et al. (Eds.): CCAC 2025, CCIS 2886, pp. 68–84, 2026.
https://doi.org/10.1007/978-981-95-8256-3_4

Depthmap is widely employed in fields such as architecture, urban design, and cognitive geography due to its robust computational capabilities among numerous spatial analysis software platforms. It serves as a vital tool for understanding the relationship between humans and space through quantitative computation of spatial parameters such as accessibility, integration, and visual connectivity. Its core is to use mathematical methods to describe and analyze the relationships between topology, geometry, and actual distances in space [2]. This paper takes Depthmap as a starting point to explore how it provides methodological foundations for artistic generation, thereby constructing a "spatial visualization-computation-narration" pathway.

Current explorations in computational art primarily focus on image recognition, machine learning-based artwork generation, and artificial intelligence generated content (AIGC). The sole reliance on spatial parameters as a defining element lacks substantive consideration. The integration of visual interpretations of spatial parameters within Processing facilitates the transformation of Depthmap analytical data into visually articulated artistic imagery. This largely represents an expansion of the pre-existing boundaries of artistic creation, as well as an exploration into diverse modes of spatial perception representation.

2 Theoretical Framework: Space, Narrative, and Computational Vision

2.1 The Narrative Dimension of Space and Its Structural Logic

Within the framework of postmodern spatial theory, space has long transcended the concept of a mere physical container, evolving instead into a socially, culturally, and linguistically constructed "narrative field".

Henri Lefebvre posits in *The Production of Space* that space constitutes a "socially constructed entity produced through practice," wherein every spatial configuration inherently embodies an "encoded system" of power, behavior, and cognition. Space possesses a grammatical structure, capable of narrating stories through its constituent elements (such as axes, nodes, and interfaces). The theory of space syntax was developed in the 1970s, and in 1984, B. Hillier and J. Hanson co-authored The Social Logic of Space, Marks the formal establishment of the theory of spatial syntax [3]. At its core, this approach conceptualizes space as a dynamic system for the generation of movement and sightlines. This theory employs visualized network diagrams and metric calculations to reveal spatial characteristics such as integration and connectivity, thereby reflecting the underlying organizational logic of space. This logic not only influences people's behavioral patterns but also constitutes a kind of "implicit narrative mechanism".

2.2 The Construction Logic of Visual Narrative

"Narrative" refers to the structured process of organizing information in a coherent sequence. In the realm of visual arts, narrative expression can be achieved through spatial composition, chromatic cues, morphological variations, and perspectival movement. Narrative imagery does not merely serve as a straightforward documentation of temporal events; rather, it employs spatial organization to guide viewers through a process of logical interpretation.

The three dimensions emphasized by visual narrative theory are the syntactic dimension, the semantic dimension, and the pragmatic dimension (see Fig. 1).

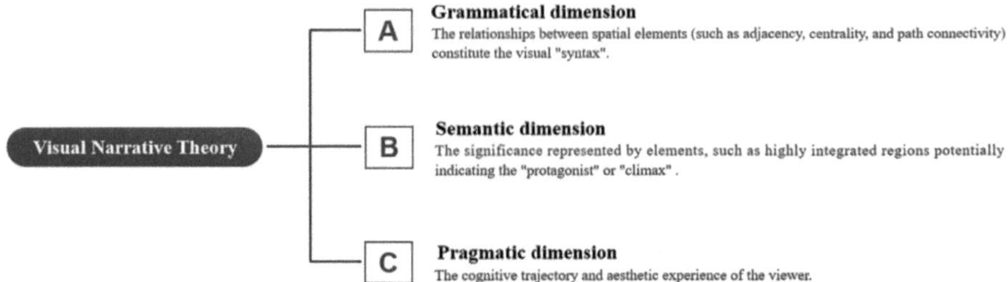

Fig. 1. The three dimensions emphasized by visual narrative theory

On this basis, the parametric maps generated by Depthmap (such as integration maps and isovist maps) can be regarded as a form of "structural atlas," which may facilitate the development of novel narrative compositional approaches and even evolve into interactive, dynamic mechanisms for artistic narration.

2.3 Computational Vision: From Perceptual Simulation to Aesthetic Generation

"Computational Vision" originally falls within the domain of computer vision, focusing on the simulation of human cognitive processes pertaining to image and spatial perception. From experimental aesthetics to computational aesthetics, the field has evolved from employing scientific methods to elucidate human aesthetic phenomena to utilizing machines to simulate human aesthetic processes [4]. In recent years, the rapid advancement of artificial intelligence (AI) technology has catalyzed transformative innovations in the field of artistic creation. Cutting-edge technologies such as Generative Adversarial Networks (GANs) and deep learning have been extensively applied across diverse artistic domains, including music, visual arts, and literature [5]. In the field of generative art, it serves as a bridge that integrates data, rules, and visual language.

Depthmap functions as a "perceptual simulator" that reflects human visual experiences in spatial environments, primarily through computational analyses of spatial visibility (e.g., Isovist analysis) and the integration of pedestrian pathways (e.g., Axial Analysis). Such experiences can serve as a foundational basis for artistic creation, being transformed into visual elements such as lines, color blocks, and motion trajectories. The application of "computational vision" in art extends beyond mere "representation" to constitute a form of "reconstruction," transforming spatial logic into an artistic expression characterized by rhythmic vitality, dynamic momentum, and formal aesthetics. This mode of expression can be realized through parametric mapping mechanisms (Table 1).

Table 1. Parameter mapping mechanism

Spatial Parameters	Artistic Features	Possible Visual Expressions
Integration	Attention/Focus	Increased brightness and color saturation
Connectivity	Rhythm	Dense patterns and repetitive structures
Visibility	Spatial Flow	Curvilinear shapes and dynamic paths

2.4 Theoretical Integration: An Artistic Generation Model for Spatial Data

Drawing upon the interdisciplinary integration of the aforementioned three theoretical frameworks, this paper constructs the following logical model for "Artistic Visualization of Spatial Data (see Fig. 2)".

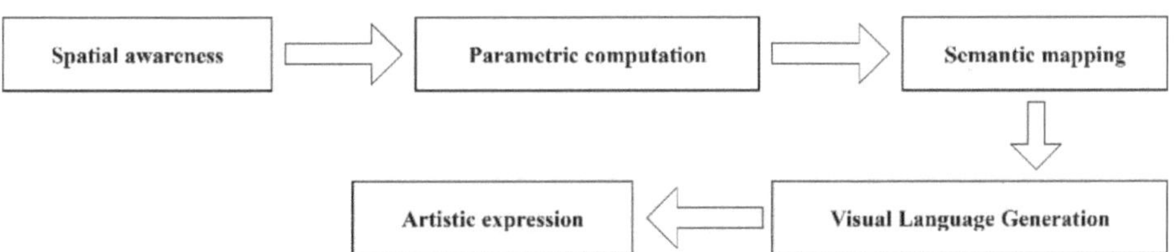

Fig. 2. Logic model for the "Artistic Representation of Spatial Data".

This model emphasizes a five-step translation pathway from "physical space" to "visual representation." As the core tool in the first stage (Perception-Parametrization), Depthmap bridges the computability of spatial structures with the expressibility of artistic representation.

Within this pathway, narrative is not superimposed upon visual imagery but rather organically "emerges" from the spatial structure itself. This model not only provides theoretical underpinnings for subsequent artistic generation, but also offers artists, urban designers, and architects a creative paradigm of "space as script."

3 Methodological Framework: Application Pathway of Depthmap in Artistic Generation

3.1 Overview of Depthmap Operations and Spatial Analysis Workflow

Overview of Software Functions. In today's era of highly advanced technology, the role of computer model analysis in spatial structure analysis is increasingly recognized by a wide range of scholars [6]. Depthmap is a visualization analysis tool developed by the Space Syntax Laboratory at University College London (UCL), grounded in the theoretical framework of space syntax. The core modules comprise: Axial Analysis, which extracts the minimal set of covering paths in spatial networks to assess accessibility and connectivity; Isovist Analysis, which quantifies the total visible space from specific vantage points; Visibility Graph Analysis, which constructs point-based visibility graphs in two-dimensional planes to compute metrics such as integration and connectivity; and Agent Simulation, which employs virtual pedestrian modeling to investigate path selection and spatial behavioral patterns (see Fig. 3).

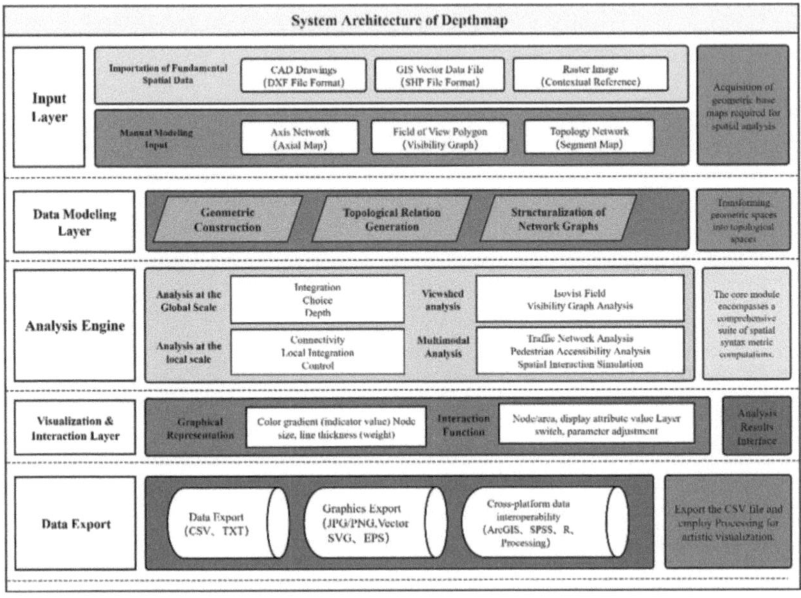

Fig. 3. Depthmap system architecture diagram.

Analysis Workflow Description. The workflow encompasses the importation of architectural floor plans or urban block layouts in DXF format, followed by modeling procedures and culminating in data export operations (see Fig. 4).

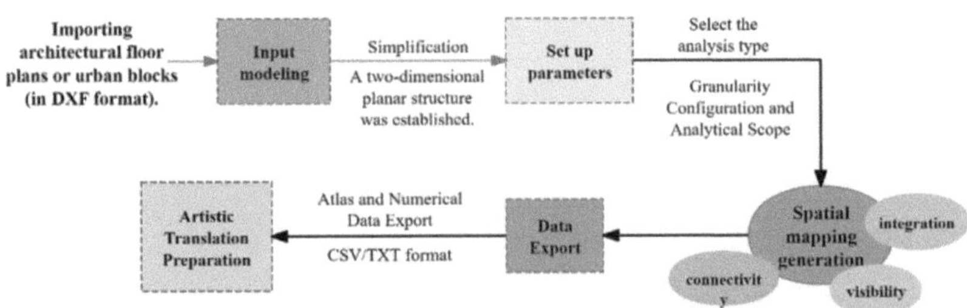

Fig. 4. Flowchart of Depthmap analysis process.

3.2 The Correspondence Mechanism Between Spatial Parameters and Visual Language.

The transformation of spatial parameters into visual elements constitutes a critical component in achieving computational art generation. This study establishes the following correspondence relationships (Table 2).

Table 2. Spatial parameter to visual element mapping table.

Parameter	Meaning	Artistic mapping dimension	Visualization representation
Integration	Accessibility	Composition focus, brightness/tone center	Center is bright and has high contrast
Connectivity	connectivity	Structural density, rhythm sense	Repeated patterns, densely populated grid areas
Isovist Area	Field of vision breadth	Spatial openness, color distribution	Transparency, gradient color blocks
Agent Flow	Path frequency	Movement locus	Streamline composition, dynamic blur

These parameters can be semantically applied to art generation systems—such as through color channels, shape formation, and motion trajectories—thereby transforming spatial analytical maps into a "grammatical foundation" for narrative imagery.

3.3 Transformation Mechanism: The Generative Pathway from Data to Imagery

Mapping spatial parameters such as integration, connectivity, and visibility to artistic elements (e.g., brightness, density, transparency) based on Processing's computational language. A fundamental mapping function is established where the original parameters I, C, and V denote Integration, Connectivity, and Visibility, respectively.

Integration degree primarily reflects the overall accessibility level of spatial configurations, with its numerical values mapped to brightness values (ranging from 0 to 255).

$$Color\_Intensity = round\,(255 * Norm\,(I)) \tag{1}$$

Connectivity denotes the direct linkage of nodes within a local spatial network, with its numerical value mapped to either graphical dimensions or point density. To preclude mechanistic monotony in representation, minor stochastic perturbations are introduced alongside fundamental linear scaling.

$$Shape\_Size = max\,(1.0, C * S + rand\,(0,\ \delta)) \tag{2}$$

where S is the scaling factor (e.g., S = 2.0), and δ is the magnitude of random perturbation (e.g., δ = 2.0)).

Viewshed represents the spatial visibility range of a node. To accentuate the salience of low-visibility areas, an inverse linear mapping with defined upper and lower bounds is employed to regulate the continuity of visual effects.

$$Alpha = clamp\ (\alpha_{min} + (1 - Nrom\ (V) * (\alpha_{max} - \alpha_{min}), 0.1) \tag{3}$$

3.4 Cross-Platform Collaboration Methodology

To effectively transform Depthmap outputs into artistic content, a cross-platform workflow integration is required (Table 3).

Table 3. Cross-platform workflow integration table.

Tool	Functional orientation	Uses
Depthmap	Data generation	Generate integration degree and connectivity diagrams
Rhino + Grasshopper	Modeling and Visualization Platform	Extract the spatial contour and structural elements
Processing/p5.js	Artistic image generation	Parameter-driven graphic visual generation
TouchDesigner	Dynamic visualization	Interactive or music-driven dynamic spatial presentation

This multi-tool collaborative strategy not only elevates the quality of visual output but also introduces enhanced cross-sensory integration (such as auditory, kinetic, and haptic feedback), thereby expanding the medium boundaries of computational art.

4 Experimental Study on Depthmap Analysis and Processing-Based Image Generation

4.1 Research Context and Case Overview

Ullens Center for Contemporary Art (see Fig. 5), situated in the core zone of Beijing's 798 Art District. Since its official opening in 2007, it has undergone three spatial renovations [7]. It stands as one of China's most representative contemporary art institutions, featuring a spatial design that integrates industrial heritage characteristics with contemporary modes of expression. The diverse spatial configurations resulting from the adaptive reuse of the original factory building provide robust empirical samples for this research.

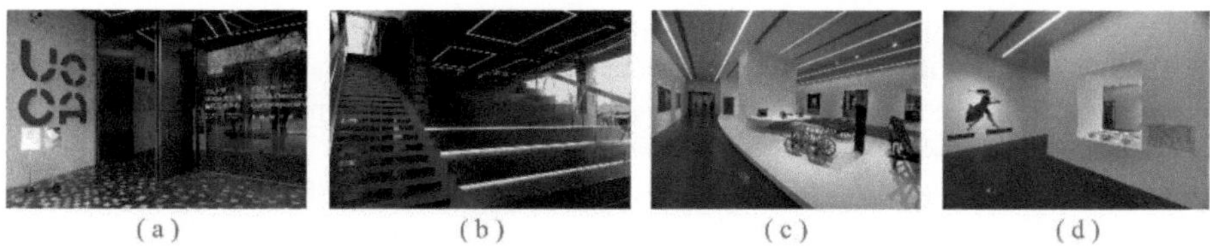

Fig. 5. Ullens Center for Contemporary Art.

4.2 Spatial Syntax Analysis: Visual Representation of Structural Parameters

Analysis Workflow Description. The spatial layout of the main exhibition area on the first floor of the UCCA was analyzed using visibility graph analysis through Depthmap software, following the procedural sequence outlined below (see Fig. 6).

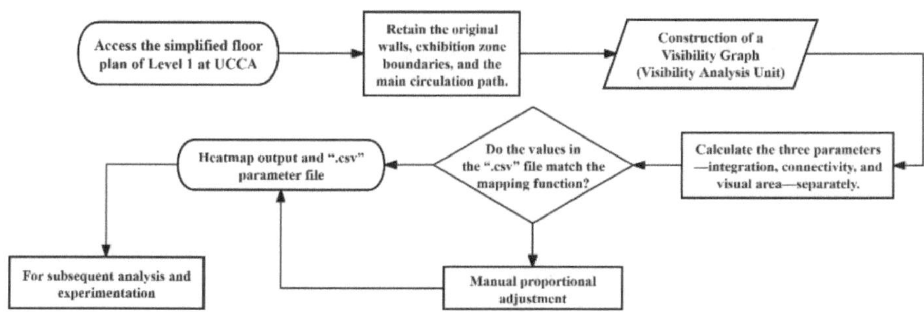

Fig. 6. Flowchart of Depthmap analysis.

Parameter Diagram Results and Structural Interpretation. After conducting spatial integration, connectivity, and visibility area analyses using Depthmap software, the following heatmap of metric values was generated (see Fig. 7).

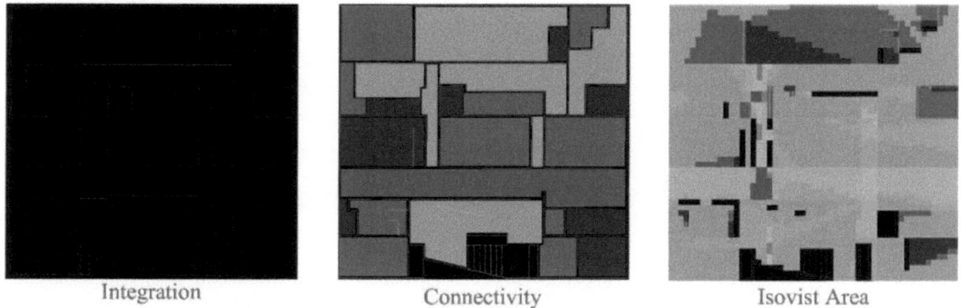

Fig. 7. Thermal analysis Value Map.

The central axis area of the main exhibition hall exhibits the highest spatial integration, with prominent centrality and accessibility; the entrance and secondary exhibition halls demonstrate moderate integration, playing a clearly auxiliary role in visitor flow distribution. Areas with high node connectivity are concentrated at the intersection nodes of the exhibition zones, particularly at the corners of the eastern and western halls and the central atrium, where they frequently intersect with visitor circulation routes. The main north-south exhibition hall offers expansive sightlines with a broad visual range, whereas corners and smaller gallery sections exhibit markedly constricted sightlines and pronounced spatial compression.

4.3 Visual Simulation in Processing Environment: An Experimental Study on Image Generation

Experimental Platform and Interaction Relationship. To achieve the simulation and generation from spatial structures to visual imagery, this study develops an experimental model based on Processing, which attempts to translate space syntax parameters into control variables for image generation.

Processing was originally developed in 2001 by Casey Reas and Ben Fry at the MIT Media Laboratory. Designed specifically for electronic arts and visual interaction design, it supports cross-platform operation. The system architecture diagram of Processing is presented below (see Fig. 8).

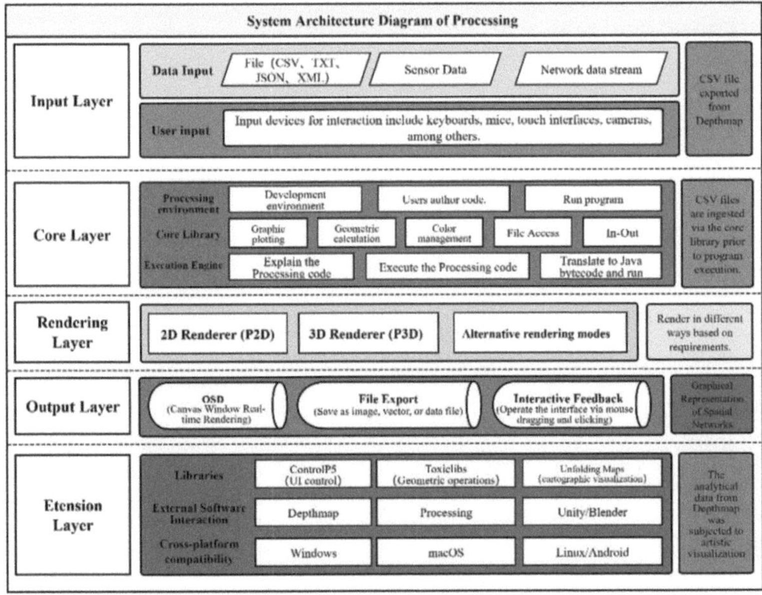

Fig. 8. Processing system architecture diagram.

Depthmap and Processing exhibit a specific data interoperability (see Fig. 9), which establishes the foundation for artistic generation.

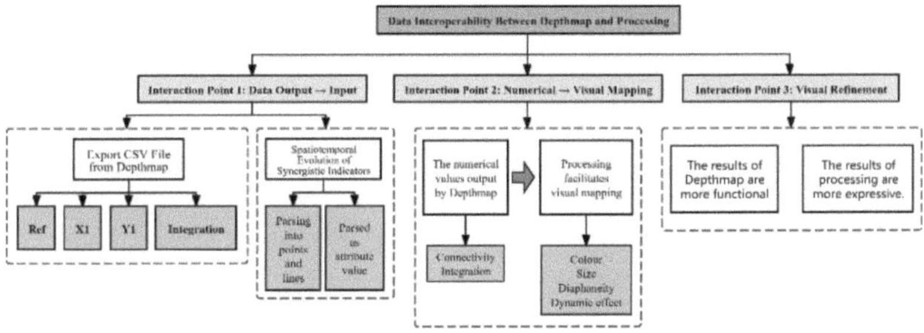

Fig. 9. Data interaction diagram between Depthmap and Processing.

The Artistic Creation Process. The node data exported from Depthmap was imported using the Processing platform, where integration values control point brightness, isovist values regulate image transparency, and connectivity determines graphic density. The overall image exhibits a "center-outward radial" visual structure, corresponding to the perceptual experience of highly integrated spatial cores. The generation process is illustrated in the following diagram (see Fig. 10).

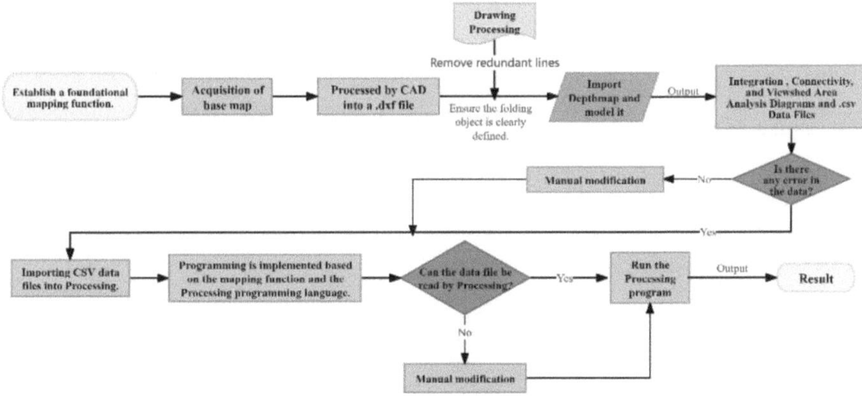

Fig. 10. Complete generation flowchart.

Structural Mapping Summary. Preliminary experimental results have validated the control efficacy of spatial structural parameters on image generation. This transduction mechanism can serve as a parameter input source for future AI prompt-based image generation systems (Table 4).

Table 4. Escape mechanism cross-reference table.

Result display	Characteristic	Result
High integration	The focus is clear and centered	Facilitates the establishment of a narrative framework

(continued)

Table 4. (*continued*)

Result display	Characteristic	Result
High connectivity	The composition has a dense rhythm	Representing event switching or information flow variation
Low field of vision	Fuzzy compression processing	Creating emotional tension or an atmosphere of mystery

5 Computational Aesthetic Evaluation of Generated Images

5.1 Establishment of Index System

This paper adopts a "three-level evaluation system" (namely: formal aesthetics, structural aesthetics, and narrative aesthetics), and combines quantifiable indicators to analyze the experimental results, and establishes a multi-dimensional evaluation framework from low-level visual features to spatial structure mapping and then to narrative logic.

Formal aesthetic level: Focuses on perceptual attributes such as contrast, color harmony, and symmetry to ensure fundamental visual readability and aesthetic coherence of the image.

Structural Aesthetics Layer: Emphasizes the structural mapping between Depthmap data (integration, connectivity, visibility) and visual representation, highlighting spatial focus, rhythm, and balance.

Narrative Aesthetics Layer: Focuses on the semantic-logical transformation of images, evaluating whether a narrative framework of "introduction—transition—climax" is established, with emphasis on the salience of introduction, coherence of transition, and integrity of narrative structure.

5.2 Evaluation Methodology and Calculation Formula

To ensure the operational feasibility of the metrics, this study converted all indicators into a five-point Likert scale, with scores obtained through subjective evaluations from 20 audience members (Table 5).

Table 5. Evaluation system table.

Level	Name of index	Sample survey questions	Score
Aesthetics of form	Contrast	Is the contrast in brightness clear?	1–5 Likert
	Color harmony	Do the colors coordinate well?	1–5 Likert
	Symmetry	Does it have a sense of symmetry?	1–5 Likert
Structural aesthetics	Focus	Is there a visual center?	1–5 Likert
	Rhythmicity	Does it have rhythm?	1–5 Likert

(*continued*)

Table 5. (*continued*)

Level	Name of index	Sample survey questions	Score
	Balance	Is the overall structure stable?	1–5 Likert
Narrative layer	Inceptive salience	Can one perceive the "starting point"?	1–5 Likert
	Consistency	Can one perceive the turning point?	1–5 Likert
	Narrative integrity	Is the whole complete?	1–5 Likert

Each is marked as I_{ij}, where i represents the level (formal aesthetics = 1, structural aesthetics = 2, narrative aesthetics = 3), and j indicates the jth indicator under that level. The scoring range for each indicator is established on a 1-to-5 Likert scale. Each level can be assigned a weight ω_i, and the internal weights ω_{ij} of the indicators can also be defined.

Based on this, computational formulas for three aesthetic dimensions are constructed. Formal aesthetics layer:

$$F = \sum_{j=1}^{5} \omega_{1j} * I_{1j} \tag{4}$$

Structural aesthetics layer:

$$S = \sum_{j=1}^{5} \omega_{2j} * I_{2j} \tag{5}$$

Narrative aesthetics layer:

$$N = \sum_{j=1}^{5} \omega_{3j} * I_{3j} \tag{6}$$

The final comprehensive aesthetic index:

$$CAI = \omega_1 * F + \omega_2 * S + \omega_3 * N \tag{7}$$

When the weights are equal ($\omega_1 = \omega_2 = \omega_3 = \frac{1}{3}$), the overall evaluation value can be directly obtained through the three-level mean.

5.3 Investigation and Data Analysis

Based on the aforementioned evaluation metrics and computational formulae, the following statistical data table has been generated (Table 6).

Table 6. Survey data statistics table.

Level	Index	Average score	Weight	Final score
Aesthetics of form	Contrast	4.2	0.33	1.39

(*continued*)

Table 6. (*continued*)

Level	Index	Average score	Weight	Final score
	Color harmony	3.8	0.33	1.25
	Symmetry	4.0	0.33	1.32
Subtotal (F)	—	—	—	3.96
Structural aesthetics	Focus	4.3	0.33	1.41
	Rhythmicity	3.7	0.33	1.22
	Balance	4.2	0.33	1.39
Subtotal (S)	—	—	—	4.02
Narrative aesthetics	Inceptive salience	4.0	0.33	1.32
	Consistency	3.6	0.33	1.19
	Narrative integrity	3.9	0.33	1.29
Subtotal (N)	—	—	—	3.80
Comprehensive index	—	—	—	3.93

Note. 1.0–2.0: Low aesthetic quality, characterized by a lack of coherence between form and semantics; 2.0–3.0: Moderate aesthetic quality with partial indicators showing inconsistency; 3.0–4.0: Intermediate aesthetic quality, exhibiting favorable visual attributes yet requiring improvement in narrative logic; 4.0–5.0: High aesthetic quality, demonstrating strong visual appeal and coherent narrative logic.

The results show that the comprehensive index (CAI) is 3.93, indicating that the overall level is at a medium to high level. In the "three-level evaluation system", the structural aesthetics layer (4.02) has the highest score, suggesting that the structural features of the Depthmap spatial analysis are more prominent in visual representation. However, the narrative aesthetics layer (3.80) is relatively low, indicating that "semantic transformation and narrative logic" need further optimization, which is precisely the focus of the future development of this method system.

6 Methodological Reflection and Applicability

This study establishes a generative framework integrating spatial syntax, visual narrative, and computational art with Depthmap-based spatial analysis at its core. Case studies validate the operational feasibility and expressive capacity of this methodology in artistic creation. However, the efficacy of any approach in generative art applications is constrained not only by its technical logic but also by artistic concepts, expressive media, and audience perception.

6.1 Subjectivity and Generalization Issues in Parameter Conversion

Artists may exhibit significant variations in their interpretation of integration and "visual centrality," while parameter mapping decisions—such as scale adjustments and color selections—are likewise influenced by individual experience and aesthetic preferences. Certain spatial parameters (such as agent path flow) inherently possess uncertainty, which tends to generate "explanatory noise." This method demonstrates superior efficacy in urban spaces compared to natural, hybrid, or non-geometric spatial contexts. This indicates that the approach is suitable for architectural/urban spaces with clear structures and defined pathways, yet it struggles to accommodate non-linear configurations (such as natural mountainous terrains), randomly generated forms (e.g., algorithmically grown spaces), or installations that operate beyond geometric logic.

6.2 Cross-Media Adaptability and Extensibility of the Methodology

This methodology emphasizes visual image output, yet its underlying mechanism possesses inherent potential for cross-media translation, particularly in the following dimensions.

Audio Synthesis. By converting spatial integration into pitch and connectivity into rhythmic density, a "sonic representation of space" can be generated.

Interactive Experience. Integration with engines such as Unity and Unreal enables the construction of interactive spatial experience installations, where viewer interactions dynamically alter parametric visual representations.

AI Collaborative Creation. Leveraging tools such as Stable Diffusion and Runway ML, the base spatial parameter maps undergo stylistic refinement to achieve diverse expressive styles.

6.3 The Potential for Visual-Poetic Transformation of Spatial Parameters

Current approaches primarily employ basic visual elements such as color, luminance, rhythm, and form for parametric interpretation. However, from an artistic linguistic perspective, there exists a broader spectrum of visual dimensions yet to be explored (Table 7).

Table 7. Potential visual dimension comparison table.

Spatial Semantics	Translation direction	Potential visual expression
Sense of enclosure	Atmosphere building	The boundaries are blurred and the density increases
Sense of openness	Spatial deconstruction	Gradient, transparency, deformation expansion
Rhythm change	Dynamic enhancement	Dynamic composition, motion blur
Social space	Emotional enhancement	Layer superposition and semantic image integration

Future research could integrate AI image generation (e.g., diffusion models) and affective computing to advance from geometric data translation to affective imagery generation, further progressing through spatial narrative construction toward higher-order expression in visual poetics.

7 Epilogue

Amidst the growing integration of artificial intelligence and art, investigating the relationship between "data structures" and "aesthetic expression" constitutes a challenging yet highly promising research endeavor. This study employs Depthmap, a spatial analysis tool, to transform sterile spatial data into illuminating thermal insights, convert structural logic into narrative threads, and explore the potential for algorithmic tools to achieve poetic expression.

Future research could incorporate Depthmap parameters as semantic guidance factors, integrating generative artificial intelligence and large-scale model algorithms for style transfer and creative generation, thereby enhancing the expressive power and complexity of artistic works. In 2024, the Shandong Art Museum also installed an art installation utilizing algorithmic technology (see Fig. 11). Professor Casey Reas from the Department of Design Media Arts at the University of California showcased works utilizing Processing in a solo exhibition held at the Digital Art Museum (DAM) in Berlin (see Fig. 12).

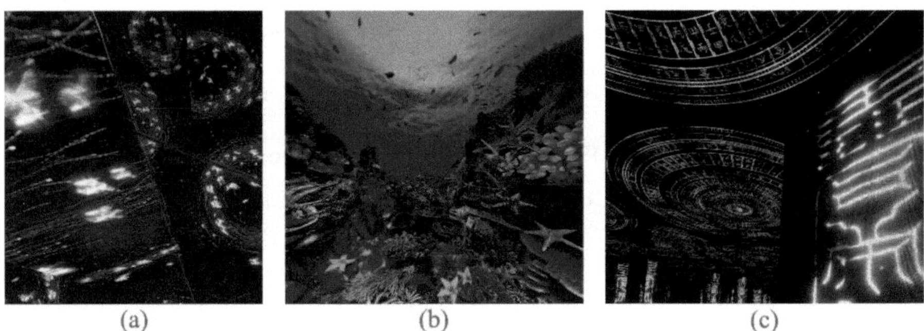

(a) (b) (c)

Fig. 11. Art installation pictures of Shandong Art Museum.

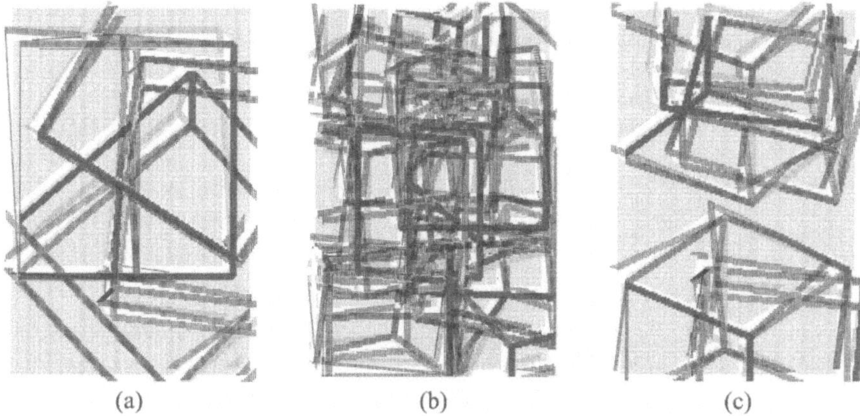

(a) (b) (c)

Fig. 12. Professor Casey Reas's Processing Artwork.

In the future, the application of computational art, AI-generated art, and similar forms is expected to become more widespread. Computer art is a brand-new art form formed by the integration of computers and art, and it is a technological expression approach for art forms. Meanwhile, the diverse demands of human beings for the forms of expressing beauty have further promoted the development of computer art [8]. Future computational art may no longer merely serve as a showcase for technical virtuosity, but rather evolve into a convergence point integrating spatial experience, somatic perception, cultural memory, and algorithmic intelligence.

Acknowledgments. I would like to express my sincere gratitude to my advisor, Professor Yue Shijun, for his intellectual guidance and inspiration. My appreciation also extends to the China Computer Federation for providing this valuable opportunity. As a student specializing in the arts, computational art has revealed to me the expanding frontiers of artistic practice. I anticipate that future research in this domain will continue to broaden in scope and depth.

Disclosure of Interests. The authors, Yuzhao Liu and Shijun Yue, have no competing interests to disclose in relation to the content of this article.

References

1. Zhou, S.: Cross-media development of artistic integration and technological convergence. Art Mag. (09), 145–147 (2023). https://doi.org/10.13864/j.cnki.cn11-1311/j.007197
2. Liu, X., Luo, B., Cao, C., et al.: Research on spatial update of urban old districts based on spatial syntax - taking the central commercial street of Zhangjiajie City as an example. Urban Archit. **22**(14), 28–30 (2025). https://doi.org/10.19892/j.cnki.csjz.2025.14.08
3. "The Social Logic of Space" marks the official establishment of spatial grammar theory. By Hillier. Space is a Machine. China Building Industry Press (2008)
4. Lu, Y., Guo, C., Lin, Y., Zhuo, F., et al.: Computational aesthetics of artistic images: research frontiers and perspectives. Acta Automatica Sinica **46**(11), 2239–2259 (2020). https://doi.org/10.16383/j.aas.c200358

5. Ma, S.: Artificial intelligence in music composition: thoughts on intervention methods and human-machine relationships. J. Central Conservatory Music (02), 84–100 (2024). https://doi.org/10.16504/j.cnki.cn11-1183/j.2024.02.001
6. Hu, B., Ni, Z., Lv, Y.: Optimization design of transfer space wayfinding in metro stations based on depthmap. Urban Rapid Rail Transit **29**(01), 30–34 (2016). CNKI:SUN:DSKG.0.2016-01-015
7. Lu, M., Fu, Y.: Daily life and landscape - research on the spatial renovation design of ullens contemporary art center. In: China Institute of Interior Design. 2021 Interior Design Paper Collection. Central Academy of Fine Arts, pp. 131–135 (2021). https://doi.org/10.26914/c.cnkihy.2021.047332
8. Zhang, Y., Xu, Y.: The driving forces of computational art and its developmental prospects following the emergence of computer technology. West China Acad. J. (01), 36–38 (2015). https://doi.org/10.16721/j.cnki.issn2095-6916.2015.01.020

Computatinal Music Art

ChordCrafter: Learning Stylistic Distributions for Chord Progression with Monte Carlo Sampling

Xinyi Tong[1,2,3,4], Tianle Wang[1,2,4,5], Peiyang Yu[1,2,4,5], Jishang Chen[1,2,4,5], Sirui Zhang[1,2,4,5], Liangke Zhao[1,2,4,5], Yuqing Lu[2], Haoxin Zhang[1,2,4,5], Duo Xu[2,7], Feng Yu[1,2,4,5], Song-Chun Zhu[2,3], and Xin Jin[2,6](✉)

[1] Department of AI Music and Music Information Technology, Central Conservatory of Music, Beijing, China
tongxinyi@mail.ccom.edu.cn

[2] Beijing Institute for General Artificial Intelligence, Beijing, China
jinxinbesti@foxmail.com

[3] Peking University, Beijing, China

[4] Key Laboratory of Music and Brain Science, Central Conservatory of Music, Ministry of Education, Beijing, China

[5] Laboratory of AI Music, Central Conservatory of Music, Laboratory of Philosophy and Social Sciences, Ministry of Education, Beijing, China

[6] Beijing Electronic Science and Technology Institute, Beijing, China

[7] Tianjin Conservatory of Music, Tianjin, China

Abstract. Harmony, primarily embodied by chord progressions, forms the structural and stylistic foundation of diverse musical genres, ranging from Classical and Jazz to Pop, etc. Harmony-precedence music composition often begins with establishing a fundamental chord progression, upon which melody, accompaniment, texture, and instrumentation are developed. To mimic this chord precedence in human composition, chord constraints are commonly utilized in the music generation task within the field of Artificial Intelligence. However, there remains a notable gap in explicitly modeling the stylistic richness inherent in chord progression sequences. In this paper, we propose ChordCrafter, a novel framework for learning stylistic distributions of chord progressions, emphasizing interpretability and controllability. We conceptualize chord progressions on a high-dimensional musical feature manifold, characterized by musically-informed filters that capture harmonic properties such as consonance, tension, voice-leading smoothness, and root motion statistics. Monte Carlo sampling is employed to estimate the probabilistic model of the stylistic distributions and generate diverse chord progressions from the learned style-conditioned distribution. Experiments on both objective and subjective evaluations demonstrate the superiority of ChordCrafter, indicating the generated chord progressions are stylistically faithful, musically coherent, and diverse.

Keywords: Music Generation · Harmony and Chord Progression · Probabilistic Modeling

X. Li et al. (Eds.): CCAC 2025, CCIS 2886, pp. 87–102, 2026.
https://doi.org/10.1007/978-981-95-8256-3_5

1 Introduction

Harmony, primarily represented through the sequence of chords known as the chord progression, serves as the fundamental structure and stylistic indicator in music theory [24,27,28,32]. Chord progressions are not arbitrary; they are characterized by diverse patterns, such as specific chord transitions, preferred harmonic functions, tension and resolution properties, which are key determinants of musical style. These characteristics differentiate genres like Baroque counterpoint, Jazz improvisation, or Pop songwriting.

In human composition, a harmony-precedence approach is often adopted: a foundational chord progression is first established, and melodies, rhythms, accompaniments, textures, and instrumentation are developed subsequently. This highlights the chord progression as a significant carrier of musical intent. To mimic this chord precedence in human music composition, chord constraints are commonly utilized in the music generation tasks within the field of Artificial Intelligence. Across various methodologies in music generation, harmonic conditioning is consistently prioritized as a fundamental constraint (e.g., chord-conditioned melody generation) [4,8,9], thereby supporting coherence, structural, and stylistic consistency throughout the generation process. However, there remains a significant gap in comprehensively analyzing the diversity of chord arrangements. While some efforts explore the regularity of chord sequence arrangements [7,20,30], rule-based and simple probabilistic models neglect the musical characteristics of various chord patterns, failing to explicitly model the stylistic richness inherent within chord progression sequences.

In this paper, we propose ChordCrafter, a novel probabilistic framework for explicitly learning the stylistic distributions over chord progressions, emphasizing interpretability and controllability and integrating fundamental music-theoretic knowledge. We conceptualize a chord progression not merely as a sequence of symbolic labels (e.g., C, G, Am, F) but on a high-dimensional musical feature manifold. Each dimension of the manifold corresponds to a quantifiable musical attribute defined by a comprehensive set of interpretable, musically-informed feature filters. Monte Carlo sampling is employed to estimate the probabilistic model of the stylistic distributions and generate diverse chord progressions from the learned style-conditioned distribution. Meanwhile, the stylistic difference of genres can be captured by a probability distribution defined over the musical feature manifold. We learn the parameters for distinct musical styles sourced from the Choco Chord Corpus [2] and generate diverse chord progressions from the learned style-conditioned distribution. This approach inherently prioritizes interpretability (the filters define the controllable dimensions) and controllability (sampling can be guided or constrained on the manifold). The main contributions of this work are:

- A novel probabilistic framework for stylistic chord progression generation, emphasizing interpretability and controllability
- A comprehensive set of musically-informed filters, defining the dimensions of musical feature manifold.

- An effective method for learning stylistic probability distributions of chord progressions with Monte Carlo techniques.
- Experiments on objective evaluation and subjective human study demonstrate the superiority of ChordCrafter.

The remainder of this paper is organized as follows: Sect. 2 reviews related work on music generation, chord-conditional music generation, and harmonic modeling. Section 3 provides a detailed description of the ChordCrafter framework, including the formulation of the musical feature manifold, the probabilistic model, and the Monte Carlo-based learning and sampling procedures. Section 4 describes our experimental setup, datasets, baselines, objective and subjective evaluation metrics, and presents a thorough analysis of the results. Section 5 discusses the implications of our findings, limitations, and promising future works. Finally, Sect. 6 concludes the paper.

2 Related Work

2.1 Controllable Music Generation

The task of controllable music generation is fundamentally concerned with enabling creators to explicitly specify musical parameters or to perform fine-grained modifications during the generative process. Such control facilitates the creation of outputs that meet particular stylistic, structural, or expressive requirements. A substantial body of research has explored symbolic-domain approaches, with MIDI serving as a compact and interpretable representation that allows individual musical attributes to be decoupled and manipulated [10,17,29,31,33,36]. For example, MusicVAE [29] disentangles high-level attributes such as pitch, rhythm, and style within a latent space, enabling targeted changes to specific components of a musical phrase. Similarly, EC2-VAE [36] adopts an explicit separation of pitch and rhythm representations, paving the way for independent yet coherent manipulation of these musical dimensions. Building upon these principles, subsequent work has allowed customization via reference inputs—such as melodies, chord progressions, or rhythmic patterns—to guide the generative model [8,39]. Notably, ComMu [14] extends controllability by integrating a diverse combination of metadata, including pitches, velocities, and key chords, thereby offering a richer parameter space for generation. However, while these symbolic approaches excel in controlling melodic content, they tend to focus predominantly on single-instrument or monophonic melodies and thus struggle with the inherent complexity of multi-instrument, multi-track compositions. In parallel, recent text-to-music methods have sought to impose high-level semantic control by conditioning the generative process on natural language descriptions at the audio waveform level [1,5,9,12,13,21,26,38]. Although large-scale models exhibit strong capability in mapping textual prompts to audio content, they frequently treat music purely as an acoustic signal, overlooking crucial symbolic structures such as harmonic relationships and melodic contours. Consequently, the outputs from these models remain challenging to control or revise at a granular symbolic level, limiting their utility for fine-structured compositional tasks.

2.2 Chord-Conditional Music Generation

The importance of harmonic context as a guiding factor in generative music systems has long been recognized. Early approaches [22,40] demonstrated that chord-conditioned generation not only yields more coherent musical outputs but also provides a robust foundation for melodic development. The introduction of Transformer-based architectures has markedly advanced this domain, owing to their ability to capture long-range dependencies and align harmonic context with specific musical features, such as chord tone ratios [4]. Recent work has explored hybrid architectures. MelodyDiffusion [19], for instance, integrates Transformers with diffusion processes to achieve robust chord conditioning on discrete symbolic data, preserving harmonic integrity throughout generation. PopMNet [34] highlights the significance of modeling structural relationships—especially those dictated by harmonic progression—in producing realistic and convincing melodies. Building upon these foundations, Dai et al. [8] introduce a hierarchical decomposition approach that grants fine-grained control over harmonic content by applying explicit chord conditioning at multiple compositional layers. Similarly, Zhang et al. [37] propose a harmony-aware learning framework that quantitatively models harmonic relationships, yielding outputs of greater stylistic consistency and coherence. Recent trends have expanded the scope from monophonic to polyphonic generation, where chord conditioning plays an even more critical role. For example, Wu et al. [35] focus on chorale harmonization, generating rich four-part textures directly from chord symbols, while Gao et al. [11] present an end-to-end system capable of synthesizing both singing and instrumental accompaniment by leveraging cross-attention between chords and associated lyrics. Comanducci et al. [6] employ variational autoencoders to capture distributions of harmonic complexity, whereas Jiang et al. [15] introduce a unified sequence modeling paradigm that generalizes across diverse chord-conditioned generation tasks. In a more interactive setting, Jung et al. [16] enhance large-scale music language models by incorporating explicit chord progression features, thereby supporting user-guided generation. As observed by Kong et al. [18], the field has evolved from early LSTM-based methods towards modern diffusion models, yet harmonic conditioning remains a persistent and central theme. Despite these advances, open challenges include extending stylistic diversity and engineering computationally efficient architectures capable of accurately managing complex harmonic contexts.

2.3 Harmonic Modeling

Modeling harmonic structure—particularly the generation of chord sequences—has been approached through a diverse range of computational paradigms, reflecting the intrinsic complexity and stylistic variability of harmonic progressions. Early work by Pachet et al. [25] casts Markov sequence generation as a constraint satisfaction problem, enabling interactive refinement of output sequences according to user-specified rules. Conklin [7] formalizes a semiotic representation of chord sequences tailored to electronic dance music, allowing generative systems to depart from fixed key signatures and thereby fostering creative harmonic modulation. From a different perspective, Shukla et al. [30] utilize reinforcement learning to embed music-theoretical constraints directly into the reward signal, resulting in chord progressions that are both theoretically sound and stylistically convincing. Beyond stand-alone generative models, recognizing and preserving structural regularities within sequences is critical for producing musically coherent behaviors. Transformer-based architectures have emerged as powerful tools in this space, effectively modeling long-range dependencies and context alignment. Li et al. [20] propose a sequence-to-sequence Transformer specifically for chord progression generation, addressing limitations in effective sequence length while maintaining harmonic coherence across intertwined melody and chord lines. This body of work consistently emphasizes controllability and long-term coherence as essential factors in harmonic sequence modeling. In our framework, harmonic modeling is realized via an energy-based formulation, where filter functions define the energy landscape governing generative decisions. This structured and interpretable approach allows precise control over harmonic outcomes, avoiding the complexity inherent in overparameterized deep network architectures or reward-shaping schemes. By maintaining a transparent link between model parameters and musical features, this design retains both flexibility and analytical clarity.

3 Method

As illustrated in Fig. 1, ChordCrafter conceptualizes chord progressions within a high-dimensional musical feature manifold, leveraging filters informed by music theory to capture harmonic properties. To derive the stylistic distribution of these progressions, we employ Monte Carlo sampling to estimate the probabilistic model and generate diverse chord progressions from the learned style-conditioned distribution.

3.1 Preliminary

Given a chord progression sequence with L chords that exemplifies a particular musical style S:

$$C = \{c_1, c_2, \ldots, c_L\} \in \mathcal{D}^{12 \times Q} \tag{1}$$

$\mathcal{D}$ represents the complete chord dictionary, encompassing 12 root pitches and Q chord qualities (e.g., major, minor, dominant-seventh, etc.), which delineates the characteristics within chords. Our approach involves learning a style-conditioned probability distribution $P(C|S)$, from which samples can be drawn.

For the purpose of model training, all chord progressions within the corpus are transposed to a common reference key (C major/A minor) to ensure representational consistency. This facilitates model to focus on the relative harmonic function rather than absolute keys, enhancing its generalization across different musical contexts.

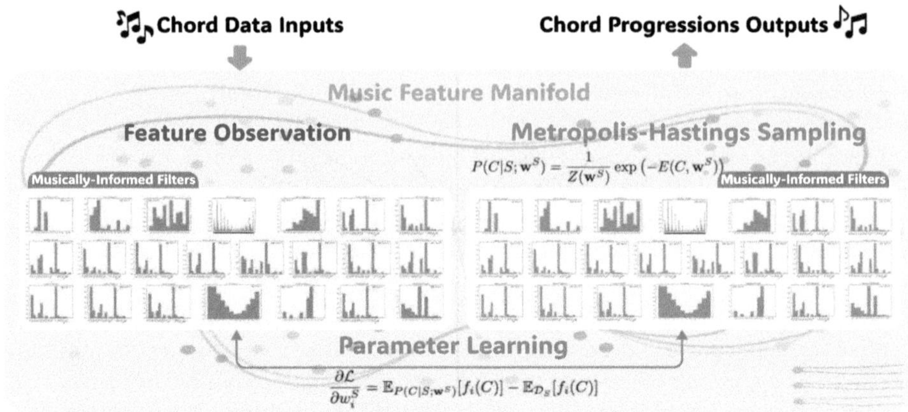

Fig. 1. A figure caption is always placed below the illustration. Please note that short captions are centered, while long ones are justified by the macro package automatically.

3.2 Probabilistic Formulation

The Musical Feature Manifold. We conceptualize the space of all possible chord progressions as a high-dimensional manifold. We navigate the space through a set of 22 musically-informed feature filters, instead of navigating it by symbolic transitions. Each filter $f_i(C)$ assigns a scalar value to a progression C, rendering the progression as a point $\mathbf{f}(C) = (f_1(C), \ldots, f_{22}(C))$ on this 22-dimensional manifold. In essence, the features extracted from chord progression sequences are grounded in music theory, presenting a novel form of musical interpretability.

Energy-Based Model. Following the maximum entropy principle [41], we define the probability of a chord progression C for a style S using an energy-based model (Gibbs distribution):

$$P(C|S;\mathbf{w}^S) = \frac{1}{Z(\mathbf{w}^S)} \exp\left(-E(C,\mathbf{w}^S)\right) \tag{2}$$

where the energy function $E(C, \mathbf{w}^S)$ is expressed as a weighted linear combination of the feature filter responses:

$$E(C,\mathbf{w}^S) = \sum_{i=1}^{N} w_i^S \cdot f_i(C) = (\mathbf{w}^S)^\top \mathbf{f}(C) \tag{3}$$

Here, $\mathbf{f}(C)$ is the vector of $N = 22$ filter values for progression C, and $\mathbf{w}^S$ is the vector of style-dependent parameters. $\langle \cdot, \cdot \rangle$ denotes inner product. A lower energy corresponds to a higher probability. The weights w_i^S encode the preferences of style S on the feature manifold. $Z(\mathbf{w}^S) = \sum_{C'} \exp(-E(C', \mathbf{w}^S))$ is the partition function, a normalization constant that is generally intractable. To seek the optimal parameters, the learning process adopts Maximum Likelihood Estimation (MLE) to minimize the divergence between the probabilistic model $p(C; \Lambda|S)$ and the distribution of chord progression groundtruth:

$$p^* = \arg\max_{p \in \Omega_p} \frac{1}{N} \sum_{i=1}^{N} \log p(c_i|S; \mathbf{w}^S) \tag{4}$$

$$\Omega_p = \left\{p(C) : \mathrm{E}_{p(C;\mathbf{w}^S)} \left[f^i(C)\right] = h_i, i = 1, \ldots, K\right\} \tag{5}$$

where, $\mathrm{E}_{p(C;\mathbf{w}^S)} \left[f^i(C)\right]$ is the marginal distribution of p corresponding to observed features from groundtruth. h_i denotes the histogram vectors of the i-th feature. The features are extracted by filtering the entire chord progression. The optimization process adjusts the sampling probabilities of the individual chords c_i that comprise the entire chord progression C, aiming to minimize the difference between the expected histogram features of the filtered C and those of the observed data.

3.3 Musical Feature Filters

The core of our model's musical intelligence resides in a comprehensive suite of feature filters, which serve as the primary mechanism for encoding harmonic knowledge. These filters are grounded in established principles from harmony theory, psychoacoustics, and computational musicology [3,23,27], functioning as quantitative descriptors that map any symbolic chord progression onto a high-dimensional feature manifold. The design philosophy behind these filters is to deconstruct the abstract concept of "style" into a rich tapestry of measurable harmonic properties. These properties can be broadly organized into four conceptual categories:

Psychoacoustic Properties aim to quantify the perceptual and emotional experience of the harmony. This involves modeling the fundamental push-and-pull between consonance and dissonance, which dictates the sensory pleasantness of chords, as well as profiling the progression's overall harmonic tension curve—a crucial element in creating musical narrative and emotional arcs.

Voice-Leading Qualities assess the logical and smooth flow of harmony from one chord to the next. While our model does not explicitly generate individual note lines, we use proxies, such as the distance between chordal vector representations, to infer the parsimony of motion, a hallmark of effective voice leading that minimizes awkward leaps.

Functional and Structural Patterns analyze the harmonic syntax of the progression. This includes tracking the statistical prevalence of specific root movements (e.g., the cycle of fifths, a cornerstone of Western tonal music), quantifying the degree of diatonicity versus chromaticism (a key differentiator between folk music and bebop jazz), and identifying the presence of core chord functions that establish or release tonal stability, such as tonic and dominant chords.

Tonal Coherence evaluates how strongly a progression affirms a central key. By relating all pitches back to a unified tonal center, these filters measure key stability and the tendency towards modulation, capturing how a style either reinforces or deliberately subverts listener expectations of a "home" key.

Operationally, each filter processes a full progression C and outputs either a statistical distribution (represented as a normalized histogram) or a single scalar value. The specific implementation of each filter is detailed below:

- **Root Distribution:** This filter computes the frequency distribution of root notes across the 12 chromatic pitch classes. It provides a foundational summary of the progression's tonal focus, revealing which scale degrees are emphasized and thus indicating the underlying tonal hierarchy and centricity.
- **Quality Distribution:** This computes the histogram of all chord qualities (e.g., major, minor, dominant 7th, half-diminished) present in the progression. This feature characterizes the "harmonic palette" of a style—whether it relies on a simple triadic vocabulary or employs a richer set of complex, extended, or altered chords.
- **Bass Distribution:** Distinct from the root distribution, this filter computes the histogram of the bass notes—the actual lowest-sounding pitch of each chord. By accounting for chord inversions, it captures the melodic contour of the harmonic foundation, which is a critical stylistic element in genres like walking-bass jazz or classical counterpoint.
- **Key-Relative Pitch Distribution:** This constructs a histogram of all constituent pitches within the progression, with each pitch represented as its scale degree relative to the established tonal center. This offers a fine-grained view of the overall tonal landscape, moving beyond abstract chord symbols to the actual notes in use.
- **Root Movement:** This filter computes the frequency distribution of melodic intervals between the roots of adjacent chords. It quantifies the syntax of harmonic motion, capturing the prevalence of functional movements (e.g., the $+7$ semitone V-I cadence) and other characteristic patterns of root succession.
- **Intra-Chord Intervals:** This calculates the histogram of vertical harmonic intervals formed between the root and all other notes within each chord. This feature is crucial for capturing characteristic voicings and sonorities, distinguishing, for example, a close-voiced four-part chorale from a widely-spaced, open jazz piano voicing of the same chord symbol.
- **Harmonic Tension:** This filter measures the distribution of tension values throughout the progression. Each chord is assigned a pre-defined tension score based on its quality, reflecting its inherent dissonance and complexity (e.g., diminished 7th $>$ dominant 7th $>$ major). This allows the model to learn the typical dynamic arc of tension and release for a given style.
- **Root-Scale Relationship:** This computes the histogram of the scale degrees of the root notes themselves. It directly measures the diatonicity of the harmonic foundation, quantifying how frequently the progression utilizes chords built on diatonic versus chromatic scale steps.
- **Note-Scale Relationship:** A global counterpart to the above, this filter is applied to all non-root chord tones. It provides a comprehensive measure of

the progression's overall diatonicism, answering the question: "To what extent do the notes in this harmony adhere to the established key?"

- **Sequential Chord Distance:** This filter computes the average distance (e.g., cosine or Euclidean) between the vector embeddings of consecutive chords. It serves as a robust proxy for harmonic smoothness and local coherence, capturing the degree of stepwise versus disjunct motion in the harmonic space.
- **Conditional Chord Quality (12 filters):** This powerful set comprises 12 distinct filters, with each dedicated to one of the 12 chromatic pitch classes as a root. For a given root K, its corresponding filter measures the probability distribution of chord qualities built upon it. This captures the context-dependent nature of functional harmony—for instance, the high probability that a G root will manifest as a dominant 7th chord within a C major context—providing a detailed map of a style's harmonic grammar.

3.4 Parameter Learning via MCMC

For each musical style S, we learn the weight vector $\mathbf{w}^S$ from a corpus of example progressions $\mathcal{D}_S$ using Maximum Likelihood Estimation. The gradient of the log-likelihood with respect to a weight w_i^S is given by:

$$\frac{\partial \mathcal{L}}{\partial w_i^S} = \mathbb{E}_{P(C|S;\mathbf{w}^S)}[f_i(C)] - \mathbb{E}_{\mathcal{D}_S}[f_i(C)] \tag{6}$$

This gradient intuitively represents the difference between the observed expected feature and the groundtruth, with the learning process aiming to align these expectations.

The data expectation $\mathbb{E}_{\mathcal{D}_S}[f_i(C)]$ is straightforward to compute by averaging $f_i(C)$ over the training corpus. However, the model expectation $\mathbb{E}_{P(C|S;\mathbf{w}^S)}[f_i(C)]$ is intractable. We approximate it using samples generated from the current model $P(C|S;\mathbf{w}^S)$ via Markov Chain Monte Carlo (MCMC). Specifically, we use Metropolis-Hastings sampling to generate a chain of progressions. These samples are used to estimate the model expectation, , which informs updates to the weights $\mathbf{w}^S$ via stochastic gradient ascent. For each sampled chord progression, we perform feature extraction using the same filters to obtain another statistical feature f_i^{gen}. The coefficient $\mathbf{w}^S$ is updated according to $\mathbf{w}_{t+1}^S = \mathbf{w}_t^S - \eta\,(\mathbf{f}(C)^{gen} - \mathbf{f}(C)^{gt})$, where t denotes the optimization time step and η is the learning rate. By the optimization of $\mathbf{w}^S$, the sampling probabilities of the chords are effectively refined. The entire procedure is detailed in Algorithm 1.

3.5 Generation and Musical Realization

Once weights $\mathbf{w}^S$ are determined for a target style S, the generation process becomes straightforward: we employ a new MCMC sampler to generate samples from the final learned distribution $P(C|S;\mathbf{w}^S)$. We initialize with a random

Algorithm 1 Parameter Learning for a Style S

Input: Style corpus $\mathcal{D}_S$, filters $\{f_i\}$, learning rate η.
Initialize weights $\mathbf{w}^S \leftarrow \mathbf{0}$.
Pre-compute data expectation $\mathbf{E}_{\text{data}} \leftarrow \mathbb{E}_{\mathcal{D}_S}[\mathbf{f}(C)]$.
for each training iteration **do**
  Generate a batch of M progressions $\{C'_j\}_{j=1}^{M}$ by running M parallel MCMC chains using the current model $P(C|S; \mathbf{w}^S)$.
  Compute model expectation $\mathbf{E}_{\text{model}} \leftarrow \frac{1}{M}\sum_{j=1}^{M} \mathbf{f}(C'_j)$.
  Compute gradient $\nabla\mathcal{L} \leftarrow \mathbf{E}_{\text{model}} - \mathbf{E}_{\text{data}}$.
  Update weights $\mathbf{w}^S \leftarrow \mathbf{w}^S - \eta\nabla\mathcal{L}$.
end for
Output: Learned weights $\mathbf{w}^S$.

progression and iteratively propose changes (e.g., substitute a random chord at a random position). Each proposed change is either accepted or rejected based on the Metropolis-Hastings criterion, which considers the change in energy, ΔE. After a burn-in period, the samples collected represent high-probability progressions in the target style. To produce listenable audio, the symbolic chord progression is converted into a multi-track MIDI file using a predefined orchestration template specific to each style. For instance, Pop style employs arpeggiated piano, block synth pads, and a simple bassline; Jazz utilizes four-note shell voicings on piano, a walking bassline, and ride cymbal; Classical features four-part SATB-style block chords performed by a string quartet. These orchestration templates map the generated chord sequences to MIDI notes, creating complete musical pieces.

4 Experiments

In this section, we present experiments designed to evaluate the effectiveness of chord progression generation, focusing on both objective and subjective criteria.

4.1 Dataset and Settings

Dataset. For our experiments, we utilize Choco, the Chord Corpus [2], a comprehensive dataset containing chord progressions sourced from over 2,000 songs spanning more than 80 genres. Our analysis focuses on 13 common and musically distinct styles: Ballad, Blues, Country, Disco, Electro Pop, Folk, Funk, Latin, Pop, Rock, RnB, Classical, and Jazz. For each style, we select a curated set of 50 to 100 representative progressions, each typically consisting of 16 to 64 chords.

Baselines. We evaluate our model, **ChordCrafter**, by comparing it to three baselines that represent distinct modeling paradigms:

- **HMM-based**: A first-order Hidden Markov Model trained on the chord sequences for each style, exemplifying a classic statistical approach.

- **LSTM-based**: A 2-layer Long Short-Term Memory network with 256 hidden units and 256-dimensional chord embeddings, trained on a next-chord prediction task.
- **MusicVAE-based**: We adapt the widely-used MusicVAE model [29] for this task. A single VAE is trained across all styles, utilizing style-specific one-hot vectors for conditioning to generate style-controlled progressions.
- **Transformer-based**: A transformer-based sequence-to-sequence model [20] adapted for generating chord progressions, trained using style-specific one-hot vectors for conditioning rather than melodies.

Implementation Details. The Metropolis-Hastings sampler employs a proposal function that randomly selects a position within the progression and replaces the chord with a new one from the overall vocabulary. For parameter learning, as detailed in Algorithm 1, we utilize a batch size of $M = 64$ and a learning rate of $\eta = 0.01$, optimized with the Adam optimizer. During generation, MCMC chains are executed for 2000 steps with a 500-step burn-in period.

4.2 Evaluation Metrics

To assess stylistic similarity between generated and groundtruth, we employ the Overall Distance (OD) and the Earth Mover Distance (EMD) to evaluate the distributional similarity in four dimensions. Lower EMD values indicate better similarity.

- **Overall Distance (OD)**: Calculated as the mean squared error between the average 22-dimensional feature vectors of the generated and test sets. This metric evaluates how effectively a model captures the high-level stylistic properties defined by our filters.
- **Pitch Histogram (PH-EMD)**: the EMD between the pitch class distributions, assessing tonal content.
- **Interval Histogram (IH-EMD)**: the EMD between the interval distributions measures the similarity of the melodic contours.
- **Chord Histogram (CH-EMD)**: the EMD between distributions of chord types (e.g., major, minor, dominant 7th), reflecting harmonic vocabulary.

4.3 Quantitative Results

Table 1 presents the average metric scores across all 13 styles. The proposed ChordCrafter consistently exhibits superior performance in most metrics, especially excelling in capturing explicit stylistic features, as indicated by the Overall Distance (OD).

The results demonstrate that ChordCrafter outperforms others significantly in Overall Distance (OD), a predictable outcome since it directly optimizes its

Table 1. Objective Evaluation: Average Metrics Across 13 Styles.

Metric	HMM	LSTM	MusicVAE	Transformer	ChordCrafter (Ours)
OD (↓)	0.351	0.203	0.189	0.093	**0.054**
PH-EMD (↓)	0.188	0.115	0.124	0.104	**0.091**
IH-EMD (↓)	0.243	0.167	0.155	0.117	**0.128**
CH-EMD (↓)	0.152	0.098	**0.089**	0.095	0.093

internal model to align with these feature statistics. This performance in handling high-level features translates into superb control over tonal and interval content, as evidenced by the low Pitch Histogram EMD (PH-EMD) and Interval Histogram EMD (IH-EMD). The Transformer, VAE and LSTM baselines are competitive in chord vocabulary due to their capabilities as strong density estimators. Nonetheless, their lack of explicit modeling of the target features results in greater stylistic drift. The HMM, constrained by its Markov assumption, performs poorest across all distributional metrics. ChordCrafter achieves an effective balance between adhering to stylistic statistics and generating innovative, plausible combinations.

4.4 Subjective Evaluation

While objective metrics provide a quantitative measure of stylistic similarity, they cannot fully capture the perceived musicality and aesthetic quality of the generated outputs. To assess these crucial human-centric dimensions, we conducted a comprehensive subjective evaluation.

Study Design and Participants. The study involved a diverse cohort of 25 individuals, deliberately structured to capture a range of perceptual perspectives. The first group consisted of 12 participants with formal music training (e.g., musicians, composers, or advanced music students), whose expert knowledge would allow for a critical assessment of harmonic structure and stylistic nuance. The second group comprised 13 casual listeners without such a background, providing valuable insight into the general appeal and coherence of the generated music for a non-specialist audience.

The study was administered via a web-based interface in a double-blind, randomized fashion. For each of the three target styles—Pop, Jazz, and Classical—participants listened to a set of musical excerpts generated by each of the five models. The presentation order of all excerpts was randomized for each participant to mitigate order effects and potential learning biases. This design ensures that neither the sequence of stimuli nor any prior knowledge of the models could influence the participants' judgments.

Evaluation Criteria. For each audio excerpt, participants were asked to provide ratings on a 1-to-5 Likert scale across three distinct criteria, which were clearly defined to guide their assessment:

- **Musical Coherence**: This criterion assessed the internal logic and structural integrity of the chord progression. Participants were asked to rate how musically sensible and well-formed the progression felt, and whether it conveyed a clear sense of harmonic direction, as opposed to sounding random or disjointed.
- **Stylistic Consistency**: This measured how authentically the excerpt fit the conventions of the target genre. Participants rated how well the harmonic language matched their expectations for Pop, Jazz, or Classical music, focusing on whether the progression felt idiomatic and characteristic of the style.
- **Overall Quality**: This served as a holistic, summative judgment of the excerpt 's aesthetic value. Participants were asked to provide their overall artistic impression, considering factors like pleasantness, creativity, and general listenability.

Table 2. Subjective Evaluation: Average Scores (1–5 Scale)

Criterion	Model	Pop	Jazz	Classical
Musical Coherence (↑)	HMM	2.6	2.4	2.7
	LSTM	3.6	3.4	3.5
	MusicVAE	3.5	3.5	3.6
	Transformer	3.8	3.5	3.9
	ChordCrafter	**4.3**	**4.1**	**4.2**
Stylistic Consistency(↑)	HMM	2.4	2.1	2.5
	LSTM	3.4	3.2	3.3
	MusicVAE	3.6	3.4	3.5
	Transformer	4.1	4.3	3.9
	ChordCrafter	**4.6**	**4.4**	**4.5**
Overall Quality(↑)	HMM	2.5	2.3	2.6
	LSTM	3.5	3.3	3.4
	MusicVAE	3.6	3.4	3.5
	Transformer	3.9	3.7	4.0
	ChordCrafter	**4.4**	**4.2**	**4.3**

Results and Analysis. The aggregated results, presenting the mean scores across all participants, are detailed in Table 2. The findings reveal a clear and consistent preference for the progressions generated by our proposed method.

Across all three styles and all three evaluation criteria, our model not only achieved the highest average scores but did so by a substantial margin. Statistical analysis confirmed that these differences were highly significant (e.g., paired t-tests against the next-best performing model yielded $p < 0.01$).

This strong subjective validation indicates that our feature-guided approach successfully produces music that is not only statistically faithful but is also perceived by human listeners as more intentional, stylistically authentic, and musically satisfying than the outputs from the comparative models. The high ratings, from both expert and non-expert listeners alike, underscore the effectiveness of our method in capturing the perceptually salient qualities that define musical style and quality.

5 Conclusion

In this paper, we introduce a novel framework for generating stylistic chord progressions by learning and sampling from a probability distribution defined on a musical feature manifold. By leveraging a set of 22 musically-informed feature filters, our model emphasizes an interpretable, controllable generative process. The energy-based formulation based on Markov Chain Monte Carlo provides a flexible way to estimate the probabilistic model of the stylistic distributions and generate diverse chord progressions. Our experiments demonstrate the superiority in both objective and subjective evaluations. For future work, the framework can be expanded to include filters for rhythmic and melodic features. We aim to replace the template-based realization with a learned orchestration module.

Acknowledgments. This study was funded by Special Program of National Natural Science Foundation of China (Grant No. T2341003), Advanced Discipline Construction Project of Beijing Universities, Major Program of National Social Science Fund of China (Grant No. 21ZD19).

References

1. Agostinelli, A., Denk, T.I., et al.: Musiclm: Generating music from text. arXiv preprint arXiv:2301.11325 (2023)
2. de Berardinis, J., Meroño-Peñuela, A., Poltronieri, A., Presutti, V.: Choco: a chord corpus and a data transformation workflow for musical harmony knowledge graphs. Sci. Data **10**(1), 641 (2023)
3. Bowling, D.L., Purves, D., Gill, K.Z.: Vocal similarity predicts the relative attraction of musical chords. Proc. Natl. Acad. Sci. **115**(1), 216–221 (2018)
4. Choi, K., Park, J., Heo, W., Jeon, S., Park, J.: Chord conditioned melody generation with transformer based decoders. IEEE Access **9**, 42071–42080 (2021)
5. Cideron, G., Girgin, S., Verzetti, M., et al.: Musicrl: aligning music generation to human preferences. arXiv preprint arXiv:2402.04229 (2024)
6. Comanducci, L., Gioiosa, D., Zanoni, M., Antonacci, F., Sarti, A.: Variational autoencoders for chord sequence generation conditioned on western harmonic music complexity. EURASIP J. Audio Speech Music Process. **2023**(1), 24 (2023)

7. Conklin, D.: Chord sequence generation with semiotic patterns. In: Machine Learning and Music Generation, pp. 6–20. Routledge (2018)
8. Dai, S., Jin, Z., Gomes, C., Dannenberg, R.B.: Controllable deep melody generation via hierarchical music structure representation. arXiv preprint arXiv:2109.00663 (2021)
9. Ding, S., et al.: Songcomposer: a large language model for lyric and melody composition in song generation. arXiv preprint arXiv:2402.17645 (2024)
10. Dong, H.W., Hsiao, W.Y., Yang, L.C., Yang, Y.H.: Musegan: multi-track sequential generative adversarial networks for symbolic music generation and accompaniment. In: Proceedings of the AAAI Conference on Artificial Intelligence, vol. 32 (2018)
11. Gao, S., et al.: An end-to-end approach for chord-conditioned song generation. arXiv preprint arXiv:2409.06307 (2024)
12. Huang, Q., Park, D.S., Wang, T., Denk, T.I., et al.: Noise2music: text-conditioned music generation with diffusion models. arXiv preprint arXiv:2302.03917 (2023)
13. Huang, R., Huang, J., Yang, D., et al.: Make-an-audio: text-to-audio generation with prompt-enhanced diffusion models. arXiv preprint arXiv:2301.12661 (2023)
14. Hyun, L., Kim, T., Kang, H., Ki, M., et al.: Commu: dataset for combinatorial music generation. arXiv preprint arXiv:2211.09385 (2022)
15. Jiang, J., Chin, D., Lin, L., Liu, X., Xia, G.: Versatile symbolic music-for-music modeling via function alignment. arXiv preprint arXiv:2506.15548 (2025)
16. Jung, J., Jansson, A., Jeong, D.: Musicgen-chord: advancing music generation through chord progressions and interactive web-ui. arXiv preprint arXiv:2412.00325 (2024)
17. Kawai, L., Esling, P., Harada, T.: Attributes-aware deep music transformation. In: ISMIR, pp. 670–677 (2020)
18. Kong, X.: Deep learning in music generation: a comprehensive investigation of models, challenges and future directions. In: ITM Web of Conferences, vol. 70, p. 04027. EDP Sciences (2025)
19. Li, S., Sung, Y.: Melodydiffusion: chord-conditioned melody generation using a transformer-based diffusion model. Mathematics **11**(8), 1915 (2023)
20. Li, S., Sung, Y.: Transformer-based seq2seq model for chord progression generation. Mathematics **11**(5), 1111 (2023)
21. Liu, H., Chen, Z., Yuan, Y., Mei, X., et al.: Audioldm: text-to-audio generation with latent diffusion models. arXiv preprint arXiv:2301.12503 (2023)
22. Ma, D., Liu, B., Qiao, X., Cao, D., Yin, G.: Coarse-to-fine framework for music generation via generative adversarial networks. In: Proceedings of the 2020 4th high performance computing and cluster technologies conference & 2020 3rd international conference on big data and artificial intelligence, pp. 192–198 (2020)
23. Masina, I., Presti, G.L., Stanzial, D.: Dyad's consonance and dissonance: combining the compactness and roughness approaches. The Eur. Phys. J. Plus **137**(11), 1254 (2022)
24. Navarro-Cáceres, M., Caetano, M., Bernardes, G., Sánchez-Barba, M., Merchán Sánchez-Jara, J.: A computational model of tonal tension profile of chord progressions in the tonal interval space. Entropy **22**(11), 1291 (2020)
25. Pachet, F., Roy, P.: Markov constraints: steerable generation of Markov sequences. Constraints **16**(2), 148–172 (2011)
26. Parker, J.D., Spijkervet, J., Kosta, K., et al.: Stemgen: a music generation model that listens. arXiv preprint arXiv:2312.08723 (2023)
27. Perone, J.: Harmony Theory: a bibliography. Music Reference Collection, Bloomsbury Academic (1997). https://books.google.co.jp/books?id=e-X2KGyq4ZgC

28. Reybrouck, M.: Musical Sense-Making: Enaction, Experience, and Computation. Routledge (2020)
29. Roberts, A., Engel, J., Raffel, C., Hawthorne, C., Eck, D.: A hierarchical latent vector model for learning long-term structure in music. In: International conference on machine learning, pp. 4364–4373. PMLR (2018)
30. Shukla, S., Banka, H.: An automatic chord progression generator based on reinforcement learning. In: 2018 international conference on advances in computing, communications and informatics (ICACCI), pp. 55–59. IEEE (2018)
31. Tan, H.H., Herremans, D.: Music fadernets: controllable music generation based on high-level features via low-level feature modelling. arXiv preprint arXiv:2007.15474 (2020)
32. Vuust, P., Heggli, O.A., Friston, K.J., Kringelbach, M.L.: Music in the brain. Nat. Rev. Neurosci. **23**(5), 287–305 (2022)
33. Wang, Z., Wang, D., Zhang, Y., Xia, G.: Learning interpretable representation for controllable polyphonic music generation. arXiv preprint arXiv:2008.07122 (2020)
34. Wu, J., Liu, X., Hu, X., Zhu, J.: Popmnet: generating structured pop music melodies using neural networks. Artif. Intell. **286**, 103303 (2020)
35. Wu, S., Li, X., Sun, M.: Chord-conditioned melody harmonization with controllable harmonicity. In: ICASSP 2023–2023 IEEE International Conference on Acoustics, Speech and Signal Processing (ICASSP), pp. 1–5. IEEE (2023)
36. Yang, R., Wang, D., Wang, Z., Chen, T., Jiang, J., Xia, G.: Deep music analogy via latent representation disentanglement. arXiv preprint arXiv:1906.03626 (2019)
37. Zhang, X., Zhang, J., Qiu, Y., Wang, L., Zhou, J.: Structure-enhanced pop music generation via harmony-aware learning. In: Proceedings of the 30th ACM International Conference on Multimedia, pp. 1204–1213 (2022)
38. Zhang, Y., Ikemiya, Y., Xia, G., Murata, N., et al.: Musicmagus: zero-shot text-to-music editing via diffusion models. arXiv preprint arXiv:2402.06178 (2024)
39. Zhao, J., Xia, G., Wang, Y.: Domain adversarial training on conditional variational auto-encoder for controllable music generation. arXiv preprint arXiv:2209.07144 (2022)
40. Zhu, H., et al.: Xiaoice band: A melody and arrangement generation framework for pop music. In: Proceedings of the 24th ACM SIGKDD International Conference on Knowledge Discovery & Data Mining, pp. 2837–2846 (2018)
41. Zhu, S.C., Wu, Y.N., Mumford, D.: Minimax entropy principle and its application to texture modeling. Neural Comput. **9**(8), 1627–1660 (1997)

MusicMamba: A Mamba-Based Automatic Singing Transcription Model

Mengqiao Chen[1], Tianrui Li[1], Qikai He[1], Qian Huang[2], and Wei Xu[1(✉)]

[1] School of Electronic Information and Communications, Huazhong University of Science and Technology, Hubei Provincial Key Laboratory of Smart Internet Technology, Wuhan, China
xuwei@hust.edu.cn

[2] Composition Department, Wuhan Conservatory of Music, Wuhan, China

Abstract. Automatic singing transcription (AST), which refers to the process of inferring the onset, offset, and pitch from the singing audio, is of great significance in music information retrieval. In recent years, methods based on deep neural networks have made significant progress in the field of AST. CNNs, RNNs, transformers, and even object detection methods have all demonstrated excellent performance in the AST domain. It is found that spectrum note detection has obvious two-dimensional long sequence features in AST scenarios. Therefore, Mamba is introduced into AST tasks for the first time, and the Mamba-based AST model, MusicMamba, is proposed. We specifically modify the 2D Selective Scan (SS2D) structure to achieve better model performance. We conducted comparative tests with mainstream AST models on the SSVD3.0, ISMIR2014, and MIR-ST500 datasets, and MusicMamba demonstrated outstanding performance across all datasets.

Keywords: AST · note object detection · mamba

1 Introduction

Automatic singing transcription is a task that automatically estimates the sequence of notes from a singing recording, with each note including onset, offset, and pitch. It plays a crucial role in various applications such as music analysis, search, and generation. The traditional approach in the AST field is to use signal processing methods for fundamental frequency tracking and note segmentation [24,26].

In recent years, methods based on deep neural networks have made significant progress in the field of AST. Typically, spectrograms are used as input, and neural networks are employed to predict the probabilities of the onset, offset, and pitch of each frame, which are then converted into note-level results through post-processing. For example, in Wang [36], convolutional neural networks (CNN) are first used to extract high-dimensional features from the spectrogram, followed by fully connected layers to obtain frame-level transcription results. In FU&SU [8],

X. Li et al. (Eds.): CCAC 2025, CCIS 2886, pp. 103–116, 2026.
https://doi.org/10.1007/978-981-95-8256-3_6

residual networks and RNN are employed for note segmentation, combined with pitch detection to complete the transcription task. CFT [44] uses a transformer model to leverage harmonic sequences in sound for transcription, while Yong [31] integrates phoneme information into traditional spectral inputs to obtain onset/offset, then uses a pitch algorithm to determine pitch.

In addition to frame-level AST methods, note-level AST methods have also emerged. T3MS [17] proposed a complete end-to-end transcription framework based on the transformer model, while MusicYOLO [38] directly detects the temporal boundaries (onset/offset) of note objects in spectral images based on object detection methods, and then searches for the pitch of notes based on the bottom edge of the note bounding box.

Mamba [10] is an innovative state space model (SSM) [11] [15] that effectively addresses the efficiency bottleneck of Transformers in long sequence modeling, demonstrating strong performance in both language modeling and vision tasks.The Mamba state space model is integrated into the YOLO framework to address the limitations of traditional YOLO models in handling complex scenes and long-range dependencies. Spectrum note detection in AST scenarios exhibits distinct two-dimensional image long sequence features. Therefore, this paper introduces Mamba into AST tasks for the first time, proposing the Mamba-based AST model MusicMamba. We specifically modify the 2D Selective Scan (SS2D) [43] structure to focus the Mamba SSM on perceiving vertical harmonic features and horizontal pitch features of notes, thereby achieving better model performance.

This paper evaluated the performance of the MusicMamba model on the SSVD3.0, ISMIR2014, and MIR-ST500 datasets. The experimental results show that the MusicMamba model achieved an F1 score of 94.57% (COnP) and 93.25% (COnPOff) on SSVD3.0, outperforming other existing algorithms. It also performed well on other datasets and validated the effectiveness of each part of the model through ablation experiments.

2 Related Work

2.1 Singing Transcription

Singing Transcription refers to the task of identifying the onset time, offset time, and pitch of monophonic vocal melodies from musical recordings. Traditional methods typically rely on frame-based operations in the time domain, followed by post-processing to convert frame-level results into note-level results (onset, offset, pitch). [30] designed two deep neural networks to perform fundamental frequency (F0) extraction and note segmentation, respectively. Merging the outputs of these networks yielded the final transcription results. Compared to the state-of-the-art method at the time [32], the system achieved significant improvements by utilizing DNNs to distinguish different F0s, with an average raw fundamental frequency accuracy gain of 20%. [18] explicitly represented pitch curve features as observations on f_0 and Δf_0 using HMMs, enhancing note recognition performance through post-processing heuristics. Similarly, TONY [22] employed

HMMs to track pitch via the pYIN algorithm, followed by Viterbi decoding for note-level transcription. Subsequently, [29] proposed a Bayesian hierarchical hidden semi-Markov model (HHSMM) to generate a note sequence. This model comprises three submodels describing local key, pitch, and onset time. [28] comprised a semi-Markov language model and an acoustic model based on convolutional recurrent neural networks (CRNNs). It employed the Viterbi algorithm to estimate the most probable notes from musical signals, demonstrating improved AST performance over HSMM-based approaches.

Recently, several note-level transcription algorithms have emerged. To avoid the cumulative errors inherent in multi-stage approaches, [17] integrates note values, pitch, and temporal information. MusicYOLO [38] leverages the YOLOX [46] object detection model to detect onset and offset points, then employs a spectral peak search algorithm to determine pitch values. This innovation offers a fresh perspective for vocal transcription.

Additionally, several multimodal approaches have been applied to singing transcription tasks. Considering the linguistic characteristics of singing voices, Yong [31] incorporated supplementary phonetic posterior graph (PPG) information to enhance accuracy. However, the PPG extractor requires an additional training process and hinders the cross-language generalization of AST models. Singing voice transcription (SVT) research [40,41] leverages self-supervised pretraining models [1,2] and multimodal learning techniques utilizing both audio and video inputs to tackle singing transcription tasks. In ROSVOT [27], note boundary prediction is formulated as one-dimensional semantic segmentation guided by word boundaries, while pitch prediction employs an attention-based decoder.

2.2 Note Detection Vision Model

Building on the concept of note-level transcription, the YOLO architecture can be prioritized when developing visual models for note detection. YOLOv1 [14], as the first CNN-based single-stage object detector, has undergone years of continuous development, surpassing other single-stage detectors and being widely adopted in various practical applications. Early improvements in YOLO performance were closely tied to enhancements in its backbone network, leading to the widespread adoption of DarkNet. YOLOv7 [34] introduced the E-ELAN structure, which enhances model capability without disrupting the original gradient paths. YOLOv8 [9] integrates strengths from previous generations, employing CSPDarknet53 with a two-stage feature pyramid network (C2f) that offers richer gradient flow. This lightweight design balances accuracy and adaptability across diverse scenarios. More recently, Gold YOLO [37] proposed a Gather-and-Distribute (GD) mechanism based on self-attention operations, addressing information fusion challenges in traditional Feature Pyramid Networks [19] and Rep-PAN [4], thereby achieving state-of-the-art performance.

Based on SSM [11,15], Mamba [10] achieves linear complexity in input size, addressing the computational efficiency issue of Transformers when modeling long sequences in the state space.In the field of generalized visual backbone models, common approaches are structured state models designed to efficiently handle long-range dependencies while maintaining linear complexity, such as S5 [13], H3 [6], and GSS [3]. Recently, Mamba [10] introduced an input-dependent SSM layer and leveraged a parallel selective scanning mechanism (S6). Within the vision domain, several studies have also explored SSM performance on two-dimensional structured visual data. VMamba [20] employs a bidirectional scanning Mamba across two spatial dimensions within a hierarchical Swin-Transformer [21] style architecture to efficiently construct a global receptive field. In contrast, Vision Mamba (Vim) [47] proposes a holistic design that performs a single bidirectional scan across the entire image, outperforming traditional vision transformers like DeiT. LocalVMamba [33] addresses the challenge of capturing detailed local information by introducing scanning methods across different windows and dynamic scanning directions across network layers.

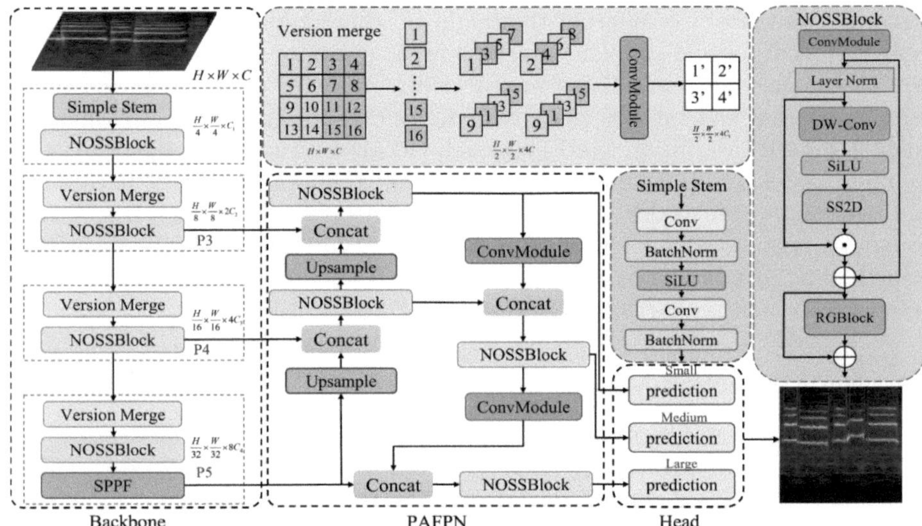

Fig. 1. Illustration of the overall architecture.

3 Method

3.1 Model Overview

The MusicMamba model architecture is shown in Fig. 1. This architecture follows the layered structure of the YOLO [4,9] architecture, consisting of Backbone, Neck, and Head. The Backbone component extracts multi-scale features, the Neck component is responsible for feature pyramid fusion, and the Head is a decoupled detection head that directly outputs the boundary information of the target (note), which is then converted into onset, offset, and pitch. Within these structures, there are three core modules: Simple Stem, Version Merge, and NOSSBlock. Among these, NOSSBlock is the core component of the MusicMamba model, responsible for modeling the feature relationships within the spectrum in AST tasks. By improving the SS2D structure in the Mamba algorithm, the SSM focuses on perceiving the vertical harmonic features and horizontal pitch features of notes.

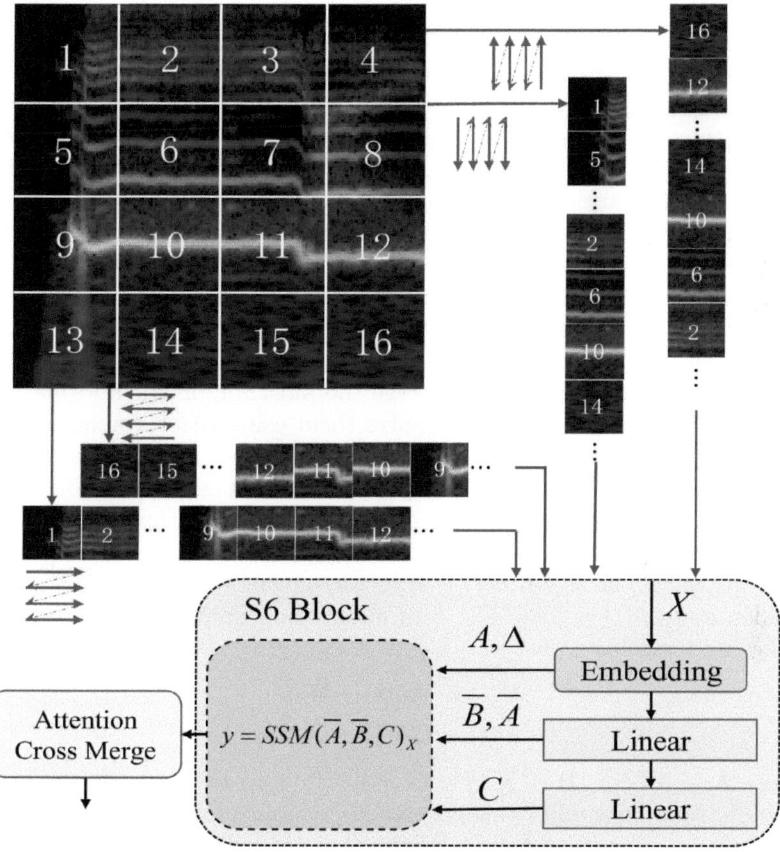

Fig. 2. Illustration of 2D-Selective-Scan (SS2D).

Simple Stem is configured based on the research by [42], using two convolutions with a stride of 2 and a kernel size of 3, without using non-overlapping patches. The Version merge module does not use traditional convolution downsampling, as traditional CNNs and ViTs typically use 3×3 convolutions with stride of 2, but this approach disrupts the sequence structure required by Mamba. To address this issue, Version merge splits the input feature map along the channel dimension into multiple groups (e.g., splitting the C channel into [C1, C2, C3, C4]), directly concatenates the split sub-feature maps along the channel dimension, temporarily expands the channel count (e.g., from C to 4C), and finally uses a 1×1 convolution to compress the channel count back to the target size (e.g., 4C→C), achieving downsampling. This method avoids the fragmentation of scan paths caused by traditional downsampling, ensuring that SSM can correctly handle global dependencies.

3.2 SS2D

SS2D is a key component of NOSSBlock. In the task of detecting harmonic notes, SS2D decomposes image features into multi-directional sequences and then merges them into global features, addressing the limitations of SSM in modeling local image features. In the AST scenario, spectrum note detection exhibits distinct two-dimensional image long sequence features (as shown in the spectrogram in Fig. 2). The spectrogram of a song typically forms a long image, where notes follow harmonic characteristics and are arranged sequentially. These notes exhibit distinct features in both the horizontal and vertical directions of the spectrum. In the horizontal direction, changes in pitch over time can be observed (e.g., blocks 9–12), while in the vertical direction, harmonic frequency relationships and note onset segmentation can be seen (e.g., blocks 1, 5, 9, 13). SS2D naturally adapts to the AST task by decomposing image features into multi-directional sequences. It can merge the most important information from the spectrum into features and then solve them using the Mamba method.

The SS2D structure is shown in Fig. 2, consisting of scan expansion, S6block, and Attention Cross Merge (ACM). It scans the image in multiple directions and expands it into a sequence, which is then processed by the SSM formula and merged back into 2D features. SSM originates from the Kalman filter [16], which maps the input signal $u(t) \in \mathbb{R}$ to the output response $y(t) \in \mathbb{R}$ through the hidden state $h(t) \in \mathbb{R}^N$. The continuous-time SSM can be represented by the following formula:

$$h'(t) = \mathbf{A}h(t) + \mathbf{B}u(t), \tag{1}$$

$$y(t) = \mathbf{C}h(t) + Du(t), \tag{2}$$

where $\mathbf{A} \in \mathbb{R}^{N \times N}$, $\mathbf{B} \in \mathbb{R}^{N \times 1}$, $\mathbf{C} \in \mathbb{R}^{1 \times N}$, and $\mathbf{D} \in \mathbb{R}^1$ are the weighting parameters. Mamba applies this continuous system to discrete time series data by converting parameters A and B into their discrete counterparts A and B, respectively, using fixed discretization rules, thereby better integrating the system into deep learning architectures. The discretized SSM formula is as follows:

$$\overline{\mathbf{A}} = \exp(\Delta\mathbf{A}) \tag{3}$$

$$\overline{\mathbf{B}} = (\Delta\mathbf{A})^{-1}(\exp(\Delta\mathbf{A}) - I)\Delta\mathbf{B} \tag{4}$$

where Δ represents a time scale parameter that adjusts the temporal resolution of the model, exp(.) is the exponential matrix that preserves the dynamic characteristics of continuous systems.

$$h_t = \overline{\mathbf{A}}h_{t-1} + \overline{\mathbf{B}}u_t \tag{5}$$

$$y_t = \mathbf{C}h_t \tag{6}$$

The SSM mechanism can use the hidden state h(t) to remember historical information and control information flow through matrices **A**, **B**, and **C** to efficiently process sequential data.

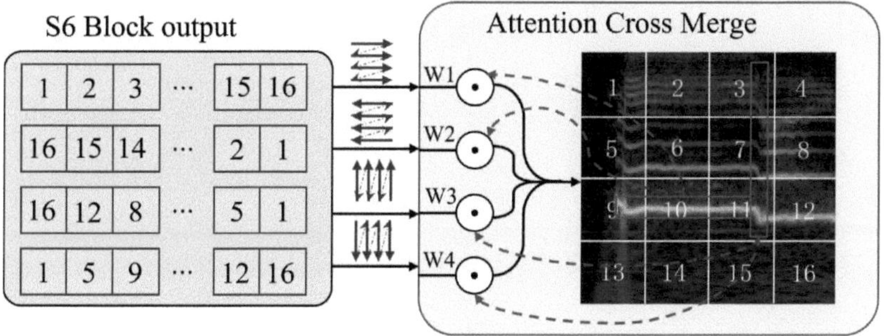

Fig. 3. Illustration of Attention Cross Merge.

Unlike simple sequence reshape and summation, our Attention Cross Merge(ACM) dynamically merges the outputs of the S6 Block (as shown in Fig. 3). The output of the S6 Block is a sequence obtained by scanning and expanding the spectral image along four directions: top-down, bottom-up, left-right, and word-right-to-left . These four sequences not only comprehensively cover all information in the spectral image but also enhance the expression of both horizontal and vertical features of the spectrum. Horizontal features are beneficial for expressing the temporal information of notes, while vertical features are beneficial for expressing the harmonic information and onset information of notes. As marked by the red rectangular box in Fig. 3, attention Cross Merge dynamically merges to increase the weights of $w1$ and $w2$ when scanning pitch information (horizontal direction) within the note duration, and increases the weights of $w3$ and $w4$ when scanning harmonic information (vertical direction) at the note boundaries, thereby obtaining more distinguishable merged features.

3.3 RGBlock

In singing transcription tasks, global features of the spectrogram (such as the temporal arrangement regularity between notes) reflect the macro-level information of music, while local features (such as the instantaneous energy boundaries of individual notes) capture micro-level details. To address the challenge of balancing global context modeling with local precision, we replace the traditional MLP with a residual gated block (RGBlock): its residual connections transmit global spectrum patterns, while the local gating mechanism focuses on instantaneous spectrum changes (The structure is shown in detail in Fig. 4). The RGBlock balances global and local features through a multi-branch and gating mechanism without significantly increasing computational complexity.

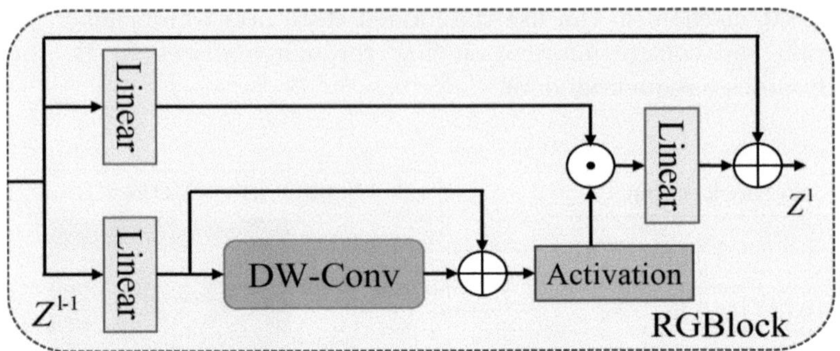

Fig. 4. Arthitecture of RGBlock.

RGBlock divides the input into local branches (Eq. 7) and global branches (Eq. 8). Global branches use linear layers to extract detailed features, while local branches additionally add the DWConv (depth-wise convolutional [25]) to retain note position information.

$$R_{\text{local}}^{l-1} = T_{\text{local}}^{l-1}(f_A') \tag{7}$$

$$R_{\text{global}}^{l-1} = T_{\text{global}}^{l-1}(f_B') \tag{8}$$

Gate fusion includes local enhancement (Eq. 9) and dynamic weighting (Eq. 10). Local enhancement performs DWConv on local branch results and connects them with residual connections to enhance detail features. Dynamic weighting uses element-wise multiplication ($\odot$) to distribute global information as "weights" to local features.

$$\mathcal{Y}(x) = GELU(DWConv(x) + x) \tag{9}$$

$$R_{\text{fusion}}^{l} = R_{\text{global}}^{l-1} \odot \mathcal{Y}(R_{\text{local}}^{l-1}) \tag{10}$$

Residual connections add the fused features to the original input to prevent information loss (Eq. 11). Overall, RGBlock is able to globally learn note spacing features and clarify note edges in our task, resulting in more accurate transcription results.

$$f_{\text{RG}} = T_{\text{fusion}}^{l}(R_{\text{fusion}}^{l}) + f_A' \tag{11}$$

4 Experiment and Result

4.1 Dataset and Metrics

The datasets used in this paper include:

- SSVD3.0 is a sight-singing dataset that we expanded based on the SSVD2.0 [39] dataset. The training set was expanded from 67 songs to 300 songs, and the original test set of 127 songs was split and expanded into a validation set of 100 songs and a test set of 100 songs. It can be found on our GitHub page[1].

[1] https://github.com/hust-itec2/SSVD3.0.

- MIR-ST500 [36] is the largest public dataset used in AST. It consists of 500 Chinese pop songs.
- ISMIR2014 [23] contains 38 English pop vocal clips sung by both untrained adults and children.

We use the library `mir_eval` [5] to calculate the precision, recall, and F1 values. We used the metrics proposed in [7]: F1-measure of COn (correct onset), COff (correct offset), COnOff (correct onset and offset), COnP (correct onset and pitch), and COnPOff (Correct onset, offset and pitch). We used the default parameters of `mir_eval`, which sets the onset tolerance to 50 ms, the offset tolerance to larger value between 50 ms and 0.2 of note duration, and the 50 cents for the pitch tolerance.

This paper compares several mainstream AST algorithms: TONY [22], FU&SU [8], Wang [36], Phoneme [31], and MusicYOLO [38] on the above-mentioned test datasets. The MusicMamba algorithm proposed in this paper is trained using the SSVD3.0 training set.

4.2 Onset and Offset Analysis

First, we conducted a comparative analysis of onset/offset detection performance on both the ISMIR2014 and SSVD3.0 datasets. The mainstream models participating in the comparison include note transcription software TONY, Omnizart [12,45], transcription model FU&SU, Phoneme, MusicYOLO, and the MusicMamba model proposed in this paper. All models requiring training were trained using the SSVD3.0 training set. The comparison results are shown in Table 1.

Table 1. Onset/offset detection results on ISMIR2014 and SSVD3.0(%).

	ISMIR2014		SSVD3.0	
	COn	COff	COn	COff
TONY	67.63	74.47	79.28	93.54
FU&SU	78.76	75.87	83.87	86.03
omnizart	79.51	78.52	78.47	79.01
Phoneme	**93.05**	85.76	94.82	96.56
MusicYOLO	90.01	84.96	95.18	97.95
MusicMamba	92.51	**87.77**	**96.09**	**98.58**

The MusicMamba proposed in this paper achieved the best results, except for onset detection on the ISMIR2014 dataset, where it ranked second. This distinction arises because the Phoneme model is specifically designed for onset detection, lacking end-to-end transcription capabilities. In contrast, the proposed MusicMamba operates as a fully end-to-end transcription model, demonstrating superior performance across onset, offset, and pitch detection tasks.

4.3 Note Transcription Analysis

Next, we conduct a comparative analysis of note transcription. Table 2 shows the results of COnP, and Table 3 shows the results of COnPOff, where the models that need to be trained all use the SSVD3.0 training set. In addition to the existing models mentioned above, this experiment also conducted a special discussion on Wang's transcription algorithm. Since Wang's transcription algorithm has a special compatibility relationship with the MIR-ST500 training set he proposed, this paper additionally adds a comparison with Wang's results on the MIR-ST500 dataset. Notably, MusicMamba* was trained on the MIR-ST500 dataset rather than the SSVD3.0 dataset.

The results show that the proposed MusicMamba achieves the best results in both COnP and COnPOff comparison tests, outperforming existing state-of-the-art models. On the relatively special dataset MIR-ST500 , a significant lead can also be achieved with the same training set as Wang.

Table 2. COnP results on ISMIR2014, SSVD3.0 and MIR-ST500. The model marked with * was trained by MIR-ST500(%)

	ISMIR2014			SSVD3.0			MIR-ST500		
	P	R	F	P	R	F	P	R	F
TONY	65.69	58.60	61.70	75.56	73.02	74.27	38.92	43.29	40.78
FU&SU	77.81	70.62	73.80	65.02	60.14	62.48	36.46	38.55	37.33
Phoneme	83.06	84.36	82.00	88.47	87.46	87.92	50.69	53.88	51.73
MusicYOLO	83.65	81.38	82.50	85.21	84.97	85.45	42.99	46.75	44.79
MusicMamba(ours)	87.79	84.43	**85.92**	94.52	94.63	**94.57**	47.97	42.46	44.72
Wang*	66.79	68.15	67.33	57.19	61.19	58.95	66.09	70.88	68.18
MusicMamba* (ours)	82.82	81.85	82.29	86.12	87.42	86.75	73.95	72.40	**72.52**

4.4 Ablation Study

This section conducts ablation studies on the three modules: NOSSBlock, ACM, and RGBlock. The experiments were conducted on the ISMIR2014 and SSVD3.0 datasets (as shown in Table 4). Instead of using NOSSBlock, The baseline experiment **(I)** use the traditional CSPLayer [35] for spectrum note detection. for spectrum note detection, experiment **(II)** uses the NOSSBlock with the Mamba architecture, experiment **(III)** replaces the conventional direct addition with ACM based on experiment (II), and experiment **(IV)** replaces the conventional MLP with RGBlock based on experiment (III). The experimental results show that the three core modules of MusicMamba all improve the transcription accuracy of AST, with NOSSBlock contributing the most.

Table 3. COnPOff results on ISMIR2014, SSVD3.0 and MIR-ST500. The model marked with * was trained by MIR-ST500(%)

	ISMIR2014			SSVD3.0			MIR-ST500		
	P	R	F	P	R	F	P	R	F
TONY	49.99	44.87	47.10	67.96	66.84	67.39	24.98	27.98	26.27
FU&SU	62.52	56.87	59.40	58.32	57.26	57.79	22.69	24.03	23.25
Phoneme	73.46	71.62	72.44	86.09	85.12	85.56	32.32	34.38	33.02
MusicYOLO	73.06	70.64	71.56	82.75	82.51	82.99	30.71	31.37	31.03
MusicMamba(ours)	73.8	71.72	**72.74**	93.2	93.31	**93.25**	32.60	30.07	31.28
Wang*	53.09	54.09	53.49	40.59	46.32	43.26	46.61	50.04	48.12
MusicMamba* (ours)	63.74	63.01	63.34	65.57	66.53	66.03	59.57	57.56	**58.45**

Table 4. Ablation study on key components of proposed model

	NOSSBlock	ACM	RGBlock	SSVD3.0			ISMIR2014		
				COn	COnP	COnPOff	COn	COnP	COnPOff
I				88.90	86.05	85.08	87.92	82.57	70.23
II	✓			94.62	92.80	91.74	90.96	85.08	71.14
III	✓	✓		95.86	94.32	92.91	91.13	85.43	71.96
IV	✓	✓	✓	**96.09**	**94.57**	**93.25**	**92.51**	**85.92**	**72.74**

5 Conclusion

This paper is based on the fact that spectrum note detection in the AST scenario has distinct two-dimensional image long sequence features. It introduces Mamba into the AST task for the first time and proposes the MusicMamba model based on Mamba. This model fully leverages Mamba's strengths in handling complex scenes and long-range dependencies, specifically improving its 2D Selective Scan (SS2D) structure to focus Mamba's SSM on perceiving vertical harmonic features and horizontal pitch features of notes, thereby achieving better model performance. Comparison experiments with mainstream AST algorithms and ablation experiments demonstrate the effectiveness of the MusicMamba model. In the future, we will continue to optimize SS2D to make it more suitable for AST issues.

Acknowledgments. This work is supported by the National Natural Science Foundation of China (No. 62277019).

References

1. Baevski, A., Zhou, Y., Mohamed, A., Auli, M.: wav2vec 2.0: a framework for self-supervised learning of speech representations. Adv. Neural Inf. Process. Syst. **33**, 12449–12460 (2020)
2. Shi, B., Hsu, W. N., Lakhotia, K., Mohamed, A.: Learning audiovisual speech representation by masked multimodal cluster prediction. arXiv preprint arXiv:2201.02184 (2022)
3. Mehta, H., Gupta, A., Cutkosky, A., Neyshabur, B.: Long range language modeling via gated state spaces. arxiv preprint, arXiv:2206.13947 (2022)
4. Li, C., et al.: Yolov6 v3.0: a full-scale reloading. arXiv preprint arXiv:2301.05586 (2023)
5. Raffel, C., et al.: `mir_eval`: a transparent implementation of common mir metrics. In: Proceedings of the 15th International Society for Music Information Retrieval, pp. 367–372 (2014)
6. Fu, D.Y., Dao, T., Saab, K.K., Thomas, A.W., Rudra, A., Ré, C.: Hungry hungry hippos: towards language modeling with state space models. In: International Conference on Learning Representations (ICLR) (2023)
7. Molina, E., Barbancho, A.M., Tardón, L.J., Barbancho, I.: Evaluation framework for automatic singing transcription. In: Proc. of the 15th International of Society for Music Information Retrieval Conference, pp. 567–572 (2014)
8. Fu, Z.S., Su, L.: Hierarchical classification networks for singing voice segmentation and transcription. Proc. Int. Soc. Music Inf. Retrieval Conf. pp. 900–907 (2019)
9. Glenn, J.: Yolov8 (2023). https://github.com/ultralytics/ultralytics/tree/main . https://github.com/ultralytics/ultralytics/tree/main
10. Gu, A., Dao, T.: Mamba: linear-time sequence modeling with selective state spaces. arXiv preprint arXiv:2312.00752 (2023)
11. Mehta, H., Gupta, A., Cutkosky, A., Neyshabur, B.: Long range language modeling via gated state spaces. In: International Conference on Learning Representations (ICLR) (2023)
12. Hsu, J.Y., Su, L.: Vocano: a note transcription framework for sining voice in polyphonic music. In: Proc. of the 22nd Int. Society for Music Information Retrieval, pp. 293–300 (2021)
13. Jimmy T.H., Smith, A.W., Linderman, S.W.: Simplified state space layers for sequence modeling. In: International Conference on Learning Representations (ICLR) (2023)
14. Redmon, J., Divvala, S., Girshick, R., Farhadi, A.: You only look once: unified, real-time object detection. In: Proceedings of the IEEE/CVF Conference on Computer Vision and Pattern Recognition. pp. 779–788 (2016)
15. Jue W., et al.: Selective structured state-spaces for long-form video understanding. In: IEEE Conference on Computer Vision and Pattern Recognition (CVPR), pp. 6387–6397 (2023)
16. Kalman, R.E.: A new approach to linear filtering and prediction problems. J. Basic Eng. **82**(1), 35–45 (1960)
17. Kim, L., Jeon, S., Heo, W., Park, J.: Note-level singing melody transcription for time-aligned musical score generation. IEEE Trans. Audio Speech Lang. Process. **33**, 1088–1102 (2025)
18. Yang, L., Maezawa, A., Smith, J.B., Chew, E.: Probabilistic transcription of sung melody using a pitch dynamic model. In: Proc. IEEE Int. Conf. Acoust., Speech, Signal Process, pp. 301–305 (2017)

19. Lin, T.Y., Dollár, P., Girshick, R., He, K., Hariharan, B., Belongie, S.: Feature pyramid networks for object detection. In: Proceedings of the IEEE conference on computer vision and pattern recognition, pp. 2117–2125 (2017)
20. Liu, Y., et al.: Vmamba: Visual state space model. In: The Thirty-eighth Annual Conference on Neural Information Processing Systems (2024)
21. Liu, Z., et al.: Swin transformer: Hierarchical vision transformer using shifted windows. In: 2021 IEEE/CVF International Conference on Computer Vision (ICCV), pp. 9992–10002 (2021)
22. Mauch, M., et al.: Computer-aided melody note transcription using the tony software: accuracy and efficiency. In: Proceedings of Sound and Music Computing (2015)
23. Molina, E., Barbancho-Perez, A.M., Tardon-Garcia, L.J., Barbancho-Perez, I., et al.: Evaluation framework for automatic singing transcription. In: Proceedings of the International Society for Music Information Retrieval Conference (ISMIR), pp. 567–572. IEEE (2014)
24. Emanuele, P.: An audio front end for query-by-humming systems. In: International Symposium/Conference on Music Information Retrieval, pp. 65–72 (2001)
25. Han, Q. et al.: On the connection between local attention and dynamic depth-wise convolution. In: ICLR (2021)
26. McNab, R.J., Smith, L.A., Witten, I.H.: Signal processing for melody transcription. In: Proceedings of 19th Aust. Computer Science Conference, pp. 301–307 (1997)
27. Li, R., Zhang, Y., Wang, Y., Hong, Z., Huang, R., Zhao, Z.: Robust singing voice transcription serves synthesis. In: Proceedings of the 62nd Annual Meeting of the Association for Computational Linguistics (Volume 1: Long Papers). Association for Computational Linguistics, pp. 9751–9766 (2024)
28. Nishikimi, R., Nakamura, E., Goto, M., Yoshii, K.: Audio-to-score singing transcription based on a crnn-hsmm hybrid model. APSIPA Trans. Signal Inf. Process. **10**(e7) (2021)
29. Nishikimi, R., Nakamura, E., Goto, M., Itoyama, K., Yoshii, K.: Bayesian singing transcription based on a hierarchical generative model of keys, musical notes, and f0 trajectories. IEEE/ACM Trans. Audio Speech Lang. Process. **28**, 1678–1691 (2020)
30. Rigaud, F., Radenen, M.: Singing voice melody transcription using deep neural networks. In: Proceedings of International Soc. Music Inf. Retrieval Conference, pp. 737–743. IEEE (2016)
31. Yong, S., Su, L., Nam, J.: A phoneme-informed neural network model for note-level singing transcription. In: 2023 IEEE International Conference on Acoustics, Speech and Signal Processing (ICASSP), pp. 1–5 (2023)
32. Salamon, J., Gomez, E.: Melody extraction from polyphonic music signals. In: Ph.D. dissertation, Universitat Pompeu Fabra, Barcelona, Spain (2013)
33. Huang, T., Pei, X., You, S., Wang, F., Qian, C., Xu, C.: Localmamba: Visual state space model with windowed selective scan. arxiv preprint, arXiv:2403.09338 (2024)
34. Wang, C.Y., Bochkovskiy, A., Liao, H.Y.M.: Yolov7: trainable bag-of-freebies sets new state-of-the-art for real-time object detectors. In: 2023 IEEE/CVF Conference on Computer Vision and Pattern Recognition (CVPR), pp. 7464–7475 (2023)
35. Wang, C.Y., Mark Liao, H.Y., Wu, Y.H., Chen, P.Y., Hsieh, J.W., Yeh, I.H.: Cspnet: A new backbone that can enhance learning capability of cnn. In: 2020 IEEE/CVF Conference on Computer Vision and Pattern Recognition Workshops (CVPRW), pp. 1571–1580. IEEE (2020)

36. Wang, J., Jang, J.: On the preparation and validation of a large-scale dataset of singing transcription. In: IEEE International Conference on Acoustics, Speech and Signal Processing (ICASSP). pp. 276–280. IEEE (2021)
37. Wang, C. et al.: Gold-yolo: Efficient object detector via gather-and-distribute mechanism. Adv. Neural Inf. Process. Syst. (36) (2024)
38. Wang, X., Tian, B., Yang, W., Xu, W., Cheng, W.: Musicyolo: a vision-based framework for automatic singing transcription. IEEE/ACM Trans. Audio Speech Lang. Process. **31**, 229–241 (2022)
39. Wang, X., Xu, W., Yang, W., Cheng, W.: Musicyolo: a sight-singing onset/offset detection framework based on object detection instead of spectrum frames. In: IEEE International Conference on Acoustics, Speech and Signal Processing (ICASSP), pp. 396–400. IEEE (2022)
40. Gu, X., Zeng, W., Zhang, J., Ou, L., Wang, Y.: Deep audio-visual singing voice transcription based on self-supervised learning models. arXiv preprint arXiv:2304.12082 (2023)
41. Gu, X., Ou, L., Zeng, W., Zhang, J., Wong, N., Wang, Y.: Automatic lyric transcription and automatic music transcription from multimodal singing. ACM Trans. Multimedia Comput. Commun. Appl. **20**(7), 1–29 (2024)
42. Li, L., et al.: Rethinking vision transformers for mobilenet size and speed. In: Proceedings of the IEEE international conference on computer vision (2023)
43. Liu, Y., et al.: Vmamba: Visual state space model. In: The Thirty-eighth Annual Conference on Neural Information Processing Systems (2024)
44. Wu, Y., Ju, Y., Lui, S., Yang, J., Fan, F., Du, X.: Cycle frequency-harmonic-time transformer for note-level singing voice transcription. In: 2024 IEEE International Conference on Multimedia and Expo (ICME), pp. 1–6 (2024)
45. Wu, Y.-T., et al.: Omnizart: a general toolbox for automatic music transcription. J. Open Source Softw. **6**(68), 3391 (2021)
46. Ge, Z., Liu, S., Wang, F., Li, Z., Sun, J.: Yolox: Exceeding yolo series in 2021. arXiv:2107.08430 (2021)
47. Zhu, L., Liao, B., Zhang, Q., Wang, X., Liu, W., Wang, X.: Vision mamba: efficient visual representation learning with bidirectional state space model. arxiv preprint, arXiv:2401.09417 (2024)

A Web-Based DAW for AI-Generated Music Workflow

Di Lu, Yan Gao, Yuan Zhang, Xiaoqing Wang, and Qingwen Zhou(✉)

Central Conservatory of Music, Beijing, China
{ld,gyan,zhang_yuan,wxiaoqing,zqingwen}@ccom.edu.cn

Abstract. The rapid advancement of artificial intelligence has led to significant breakthroughs in AI-generated music, enabling the production of high-quality audio at 48kHz sampling rates. However, a fundamental challenge persists in current AI music generation technologies: while end-to-end audio generation models produce high-fidelity music, their black-box nature makes musical elements (e.g., pitch, duration) difficult to edit. Conversely, symbolic generation methods (e.g., MIDI) retain structured and editable representations of music, yet rely heavily on professional post-production to achieve high-fidelity audio quality. To address this gap, this paper introduces a user-editable web-based **D**igital **A**udio **W**orkstation (DAW) specifically designed for music generated by symbolic generation methods. The main contributions include: an intuitive visual interface supporting direct manipulation of musical elements, a browser-based real-time audio renderer, and a standardized API that integrates symbolic music generation systems, enabling a seamless end-to-end workflow from AI-generated content to user refinement. Experimental results demonstrate that the sound quality is improved and nearly 97% of users have a positive intention to use our DAW.

Keywords: AI music generation · digital audio workstation · web-based DAW · editability · AI-generated music workflow · audio rendering

1 Introduction

Recent breakthroughs in artificial intelligence have fundamentally reshaped the landscape of music creation. Commercial AI music generation applications such as Suno [1], Udio [2], and Mureka [3] have demonstrated remarkable capabilities in producing high-fidelity musical audio, while open-source alternatives such as YuE [4] and SongGeneration [5] have emerged as viable options for researchers and developers. This rapid technological evolution has enabled both commercial and academic communities to achieve realistic music generation. However, these end-to-end generation models exhibit critical limitations that hinder practical music creation. Their inherent black-box architecture limits note-level musical refinement (e.g. note pitch, duration, velocity). This fundamental gap between generation and refinement has become the primary bottleneck in AI-generated music workflow, particularly for professional creators requiring precise artistic control.

X. Li et al. (Eds.): CCAC 2025, CCIS 2886, pp. 117–131, 2026.
https://doi.org/10.1007/978-981-95-8256-3_7

Symbolic music generation offers a distinct alternative to end-to-end music generation by focusing on musical symbolic formats rather than audio waveforms. This approach models music as structured sequences of musical events, including precise note parameters (e.g. pitch, duration, velocity) and higher-level musical constructs. Recent advancements like NotaGen [6], XMusic [7], and SongComposer's LLM-based system [8] demonstrate the capability to generate coherent symbolic compositions directly from text prompts. While symbolic methods preserve crucial musical structure and enable detailed editing, they introduce significant limitations. Most notably, the lack of inherent timbre representation requires an extra symbol-to-audio conversion process, known as audio rendering. Furthermore, producing professional-quality results demands specialized Digital Audio Workstation (DAW) software, substantial computing resources, and expert music production skills. These requirements establish a quality-editability trade-off: symbolic approaches provide note-level musical editability at the expense of audio fidelity, while end-to-end models deliver high-quality audio outputs but restrict editing possibilities. For most music creators, neither solution is ideal as they need both high-quality audio and flexible editing capabilities.

Commercial AI music platforms such as AIVA [9] and Tianyin [10] have developed web-based Digital Audio Workstations (DAWs) to address this technical challenge. These systems support basic editing of AI-generated music while improving audio output quality via built-in audio rendering and automated mixing algorithms. However, since the audio rendering is server-based, every parameter modification, including note adjustments or instrument changes, requires data transmission to remote servers for re-rendering. This architectural approach inevitably introduces latency that disrupts the creative workflow, making real-time interaction between editing and playback impossible.

Recent advances in web-based DAWs have confirmed the technical feasibility of real-time online audio rendering. Commercial applications [11–14] and open-source solutions [15–17] have successfully implemented this capability. However, these existing systems face several limitations when applied to AI-generated music workflow. First, commercial applications fail to provide accessible APIs for integration with existing AI music generation models. Second, open-source alternatives lack professional-grade audio rendering capabilities due to insufficient virtual instrument libraries and audio effects. Third, current solutions fail to support AI-specific musical elements including chord progressions and song structure. These shortcomings highlight the need for specialized tools designed for AI-generated music workflow.

This research presents a user-editable web-based DAW optimized for AI-generated music workflow. The main contributions of this paper are summarized as follows:

- An intuitive visual interface enables direct manipulation of musical elements (pitch, duration, velocity), instrument selection, multi-track arrangements, chord progressions, and song structure.
- A web-based rendering engine utilizes sample-based synthesis to achieve professional audio quality. The optimized processing pipeline integrates full virtual instruments and effects while maintaining low latency and 48kHz/16bit fidelity entirely client-side.

- Standardized API integration with an existing symbolic music generation system creates a complete generation-to-refinement workflow.

2 Related Works

Symbolic music generation aims to autonomously produce music in symbolic formats. Among existing formats, MIDI has become the major choice for both research and practical applications [18]. As an industry-standard protocol, MIDI employs an event-based representation by encoding the performance data and control information of notes in a compact binary format [19]. Table 1 summarizes common event types used in symbolic music generation studies [18, 20]. As the generated symbolic output (in MIDI format) directly feeds into our proposed web-based DAW, the implementation must fully support the visualization, modification, and audio rendering of all musical event types.

Table 1. Common event types used in symbolic music generation

Event type	Detail
Metadata	Tempo, time signature, key and scale
Instrument	Instrument used in a track
Note	Note onset, duration, pitch, velocity
Chord progression	Chord of each bar or beat
Song structure	Sections (verse, chorus, bridge, etc.)

Web-based DAWs operate entirely within web browsers without requiring local installation, providing core music production capabilities including audio/MIDI recording, multi-track editing, mixing, and support for effects processors and virtual instruments as well as traditional desktop DAWs. In addition, commercial applications [11–14] offer comprehensive production environments with collaborative features and plugin support. However, these systems are designed as general-purpose audio production environments and are not structurally optimized for AI-generated music workflow. In parallel, AI music platforms like AIVA [9] and Tianyin [10] excel in symbolic music generation but offer only limited or non-real-time rendering capabilities. As systematically compared in Table 2, there is a gap between AI-generated music and user-driven refinement.

To address this gap, our proposed web-based DAW is specifically tailored for handling AI-generated symbolic music. Guided by the functional priority analysis presented in Table 3, our system emphasizes MIDI editing, real-time rendering, and mixing capabilities as core requirements, while intentionally deprioritizing functions identified as low-priority for AI-generated music workflow—such as audio recording and extensive plugin hosting.

The Web Audio API is a powerful JavaScript programming interface for processing and controlling audio in web browsers. It features a modular graph-based architecture that supports various audio operations including synthesis, processing, mixing, and playback.

Table 2. Comparison of web-based DAW

	AI-generated music specialized	MIDI Editing	Realtime Rendering	Commercial
Soundtrap [11]		√	√	√
Bandlab [12]		√	√	√
AmpedStudio [13]		√	√	√
Soundation [14]		√	√	√
GridSound [15]		√	√	
OpenDAW [16]		√	√	
WAM-Studio [17]		√	√	
AIVA [9]	√	√		√
Tianyin [10]	√	Singing Voice only	Singing Voce only	√
Ours	√	√	√	

Table 3. Prioritization of functions of web-based DAW in this paper

Function type	Priority
Audio recording	Low
MIDI recording	Medium
Audio editing	Low
MIDI editing	**High**
Mixing	**High**
Effect / Virtual Instrument	**High**
Collaborative	Low
Open plugins support	Medium

With its low-latency performance and smooth integration with web technologies, this API has become the preferred solution for most web-based DAWs, outperforming alternative browser audio methods like the HTML5 Audio element.

AudioWorklet [21], a key component of the Web Audio API, enables custom low-latency audio processing by executing JavaScript code directly in the audio rendering thread. This bypasses main thread delays, ensuring reliable audio processing. The open plugin standard WAM 2.0 [22] utilizes AudioWorklet, demonstrating its suitability for real-time audio tasks like custom effects and sound synthesis. In this paper, we employ AudioWorklet as the core audio processing engine for our proposed web-based DAW.

3 System Overview

3.1 System Architecture

As shown in Fig. 1, the proposed web-based DAW engine features a layered modular architecture that decouples conventional DAW functionality into three vertically integrated layers while maintaining full system capability. This design enables intuitive music editing and real-time audio rendering directly within the browser environment. The architecture consists of three principal components:

The Presentation Layer constructs an interactive visual interface based on web front-end, incorporating specialized visualization components for musical metadata, multi-track arrangements, and note editing, thereby providing an intuitive user experience for music element manipulation.

The Logic Layer, serving as the core of the system, performs critical functions including symbolic music interpretation, symbol-to-audio rendering, and low-latency audio streaming.

The Data Layer implements an efficient localized storage solution leveraging advanced browser caching mechanisms, facilitating seamless management of timbre sample libraries and user data.

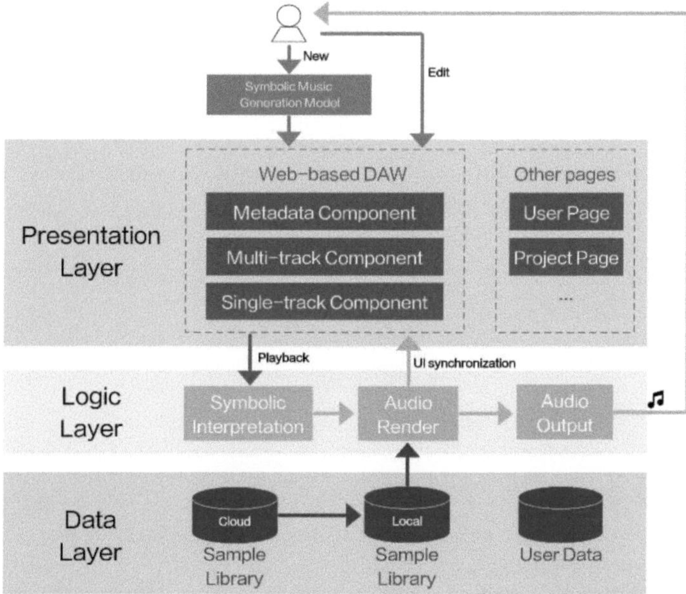

Fig. 1. Architecture of proposed web-based DAW, which consists of Presentation Layer, Logic Layer, and Data Layer.

The working process of the system is as follows: Initially, symbolic music data (e.g., MIDI format) is received and visually displayed through the Presentation Layer's interactive interface, enabling intuitive user editing. Upon playback initiation, the edited symbolic data is transmitted to the Logic Layer for processing. The symbolic interpretation module then analyzes and identifies required timbre resources, which are subsequently retrieved through the Data Layer's efficient loading mechanism. The audio rendering module subsequently converts the processed data into high-fidelity audio streams for output. Meanwhile, the system maintains precise synchronization between interface responses and audio output through a state synchronization mechanism.

3.2 Presentation Layer Design

The presentation layer implements an interface architecture specifically optimized for AI-generated music workflow. As shown in Fig. 2, the system uses a simple and clean interface style, which is different from conventional DAWs that have many complex features. This focused design provides the essential functionality while ensuring smooth performance in web browsers.

It mainly includes the following core components:

Metadata Area: Displays basic musical attributes such as tempo, time signature, key, and scale.

Multi-track Workspace:

- Ruler panel: Timeline ruler, chord progression ruler, and song structure ruler.
- Instrument panel: Instrument selection, volume faders, pan knobs, and mute/solo switches.
- Note panel: preview of notes in a track.
- Effect panel: Insert effect slots, parameter controls, and audio routing.
- Parameter panel: Automation curve editor.

Single-track Workspace: A piano roll component provides detailed note-level manipulation such as onset, duration, pitch, velocity, and so on.

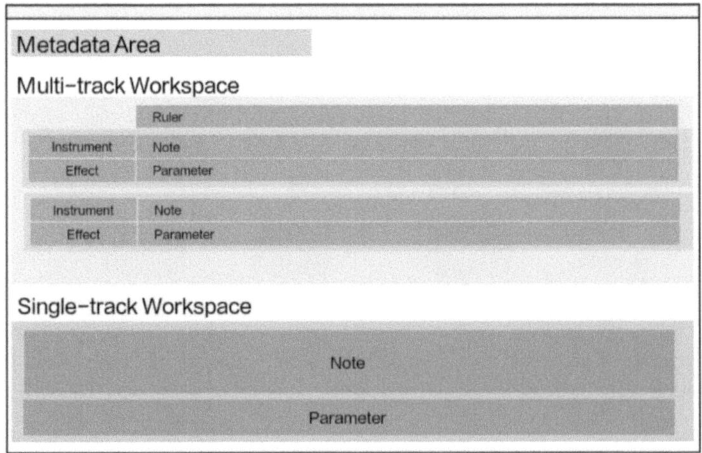

Fig. 2. The presentation layer interface layout consists of three main components: the metadata area, multi-track workspace, and single-track workspace.

The presentation layer offers purpose-built visual tools tailored for AI-generated music workflow, including an interactive chord progression display, song structure markers (verse/chorus/bridge), and other key symbolic elements from Table 1. This streamlined interface combines essential music editing functions with intuitive controls optimized for both professional and casual users.

3.3 Logic Layer Design

The logic layer functions as the core processing engine of the system, primarily responsible for real-time symbol-to-audio rendering and audio output processing. At the technical implementation level, the module utilizes the AudioWorklet mentioned Sect. 2 to construct an independent rendering thread, effectively mitigating the main thread blocking issues inherent in traditional Web Audio API.

As shown in Fig. 3, the audio graph comprises a core node module and two dedicated buses. **The audio rendering node**, leveraging AudioWorklet, enables sample - based waveform synthesis and supports audio effects such as Gain, EQ, Pan, and Compressor. **The reverb bus**, functioning as an auxiliary processing bus, receives the signals from the audio rendering node and applies spatial effect processing. **The master bus** integrates the dry signal path and the wet signal from the reverb bus, optimizes the signal through master processing units (compressor, EQ, and limiter), and then outputs it to the audio output device.

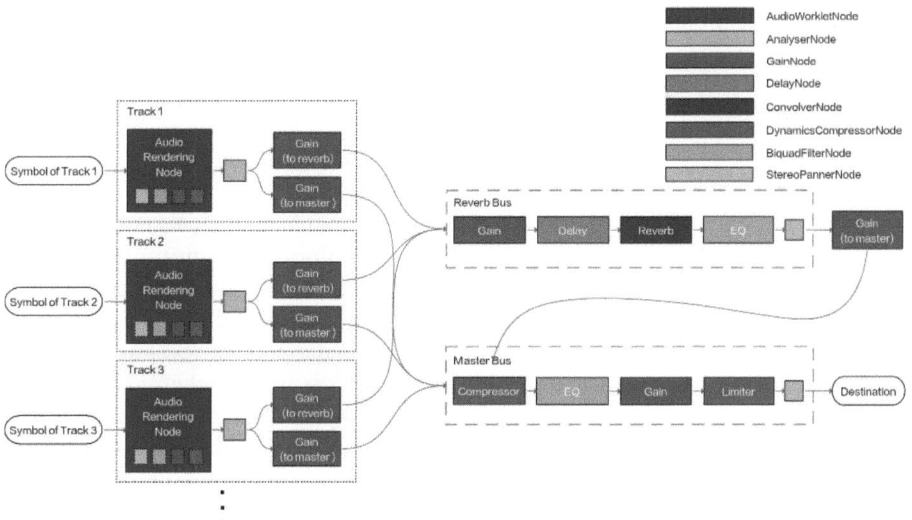

Fig. 3. The audio graph of our web-based DAW. The colored blocks represent different types of Web Audio API nodes. The audio rendering node is implemented using AudioWorklet, which operates in a separate thread, and incorporates four configurable effects: Pan, EQ, Gain, and Compressor.

This design offers several technical advantages: First, the independent bus design simplifies mixing operations while maintaining clear structure for easy maintenance and extensibility. Second, the reverb bus applies spatial effects for multiple nodes, which not only ensures acoustic coherence but also optimizes resource utilization. Third, multiple adjustable gain nodes provide flexible control over signal send levels.

3.4 Data Layer Design

The data layer in this paper was meticulously designed to support high-quality audio rendering. For sample data, we adopted the GM2.0 standard as the foundation, incorporating 128 instrument sounds, complemented by 8 traditional Chinese instruments and 8 extended drum kits. A multi-grained sampling strategy was implemented: (a) pitch intervals were set at semitone increments; (b) dynamic layers (4–8 levels) covered the full *ppp-fff* range; and (c) sample durations included short, medium, and sustained notes. Post-processing involved spectral analysis for timbral equalization, frequency response normalization, and precise loop point placement for seamless sustain in longer samples.

The sample organization and cloud implementation employed several key techniques. A mapping table was constructed to associate MIDI messages (e.g. program change number) with corresponding samples. Samples were managed in a hierarchical tree structure with embedded metadata describing instrument type, sampling parameters, and other relevant attributes. This organized collection was ultimately hosted on a cloud platform. During DAW operation in the browser, the system proactively loads potentially required samples based on the user's current editing context. To optimize performance, client-side caching is employed for frequently accessed samples, effectively reducing loading latency and improving loading speed.

4 Implementation

4.1 Web-Based DAW Implementation

This system utilizes a frontend-backend separation architecture. The backend, developed using Django, offers RESTful APIs specifically for handling and storing project metadata and sound library metadata. The frontend acts as the technical foundation, employing a modular design to construct a high-performance audio application.

The presentation layer takes Canvas 2D as the rendering core and implements the hierarchical drawing mechanism: the bottom layer renders static backgrounds and track grids with low redraw frequency; the middle layer dynamically renders note blocks which are updated in real-time based on track data; the top layer overlays interactive controls (e.g. effect knobs, volume sliders). The system enables note-level interaction (creating, moving, modifying, and deleting notes) by listening to mouse events (e.g. clicks, drags). To prevent interface lag during playback, visual updates are handled via `requestAnimationFrame()` method.

The logic layer enables multi-threaded audio processing through AudioWorklet. Each track corresponds to an independent AudioWorkletProcessor instance, integrating a sample playback engine and effects chain: it directly manipulates loaded instrument sample data as AudioBuffer within AudioWorkletProcessor's `process()` method to achieve sample-based synthesis and pitch adjustment (via resampling); real-time effects such as EQ, compression, and panning are implemented inside the AudioWorkletProcessor using native AudioNodes and JavaScript DSP algorithms. The symbolic music interpretation module uses FileReader to parse input MIDI files into raw events. A unified time reference is established via the AudioContext clock, enabling millisecond-level synchronization between symbol-to-audio rendering in AudioWorklet thread and MIDI events from main thread.

The data layer adopts a cloud-local collaborative storage solution. Cloud object storage provides 16bit/48kHz WAV sample files, organized into folders by instrument, pitch, duration, and velocity. Locally, IndexedDB is used to cache decoded AudioBuffer objects, a format directly usable by Web Audio API, thus eliminating real-time decoding overhead. When launching the DAW or switching instruments, a background thread fetches sample files via fetch, decodes them using `AudioContext.decodeAudioData()`, stores them in IndexedDB, and updates cache metadata (last used time, frequency). An LRU (Least Recently Used) caching strategy is adopted to periodically check IndexedDB size and evicts the least recently used or least frequently accessed AudioBuffer objects.

4.2 Integration with Symbolic Music Generation Model

The integration of web-based DAW and symbolic music generation models is achieved through a scenario-based API framework. Four core APIs are implemented:

- POST /api/ai/import: Imports a complete AI-generated symbolic music, which should be in standard MIDI format to ensure direct compatibility with the DAW's parsing engine.
- POST /api/ai/regenerate_bar: Regenerates the musical notes for a specific bar when triggered by a chord-change event initiated by the user.
- POST /api/ai/regenerate_section: Regenerates all notes within a structural section (e.g., verse, chorus) in response to a section-change event.
- POST /api/ai/regenerate_track: Regenerates the entire content of a single instrument track triggered by a track-change event.

This API architecture enables seamless coupling between DAW editing and AI generation capabilities. It maintains creative dominance for the user while leveraging AI for efficient, localized content regeneration.

5 Experiment

5.1 Performance Testing

Performance testing aims to verify the maximum number of polyphonic tones supported by web-based DAW during real-time playback and measure the associated audio rendering latency. A gradual load-increasing approach was adopted using a set of specially designed MIDI files. A total of 32 test files were used, each containing 1 to 32 tracks. Each track was designed to trigger 16 notes of different pitches simultaneously, thereby creating a controllable load gradient ranging from 16 to 512 polyphony tones.

Given that the AudioWorklet thread operates under strict real-time constraints and high priority, any failure to deliver audio samples on time results in audible glitches. Therefore, the occurrence of audible glitches was marked as the critical point indicating the system's performance limit. To quantify the impact of audio effects processing on performance, system behavior was tested both with and without the reverb bus enabled.

The test was conducted on two Windows-based devices: Device A equipped with an Intel i5-8250U processor and 8 GB RAM, and Device B equipped with an Intel i7-9750H processor and 16GB RAM. Both devices used the Chrome (v138) browser to ensure consistency in the testing environment. The results are shown in Fig. 4.

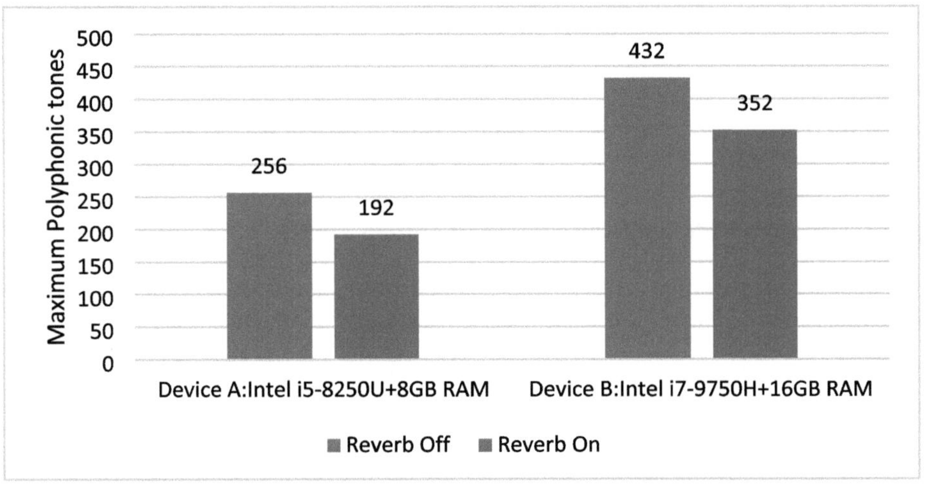

Fig. 4. The maximum polyphonic tones supported by web-based DAW during real-time playback. Tests were conducted on two different devices, with and without reverb bus enabled.

Experimental data indicate that Device A could stably handle 256 polyphonic tones (i.e., 16 tracks each playing 16 notes simultaneously) without reverb enabled, while its capacity decreased to 192 polyphonic tones (12 tracks) with reverb enabled. Device B demonstrated stronger performance: it supported 432 polyphonic tones (27 tracks) without reverb and maintained stable processing of 352 polyphonic tones (22 tracks) even with reverb enabled.

To further quantify real-time performance, we measured end-to-end audio rendering latency by inserting high-precision timestamps before MIDI event dispatch and detecting the first appearance of the test signal in the AudioWorkletProcessor's `process()` method. The test covered varying load conditions from 16 to 432 polyphonic tones, with each condition measured 100 times repetitively. The results are summarized in Table 4.

The performance testing results demonstrate that our web-based DAW's polyphony support capability is positively correlated with device specifications, and the processing of reverb effects introduces approximately 5–25% performance overhead in terms of both maximum polyphony and latency. The audio rendering latency remains below 100ms even at the maximum supported polyphony of 432 tones, well within acceptable

Table 4. Audio Rendering Latency Test Results (ms)

Polyphony	Device A (Reverb off)	Device A (Reverb on)	Device B (Reverb off)	Device B (Reverb on)
64	16.3 ± 2.1	18.3 ± 2.4	14.3 ± 2.8	16.3 ± 2.0
128	32.1 ± 2.6	38.7 ± 7.7	19.8 ± 1.7	21.0 ± 2.6
192	45.5 ± 4.2	52.4 ± 11.1	23.5 ± 1.8	28.2 ± 6.4
256	77.9 ± 27.2	–	31.7 ± 1.9	38.0 ± 4.0
352	–	–	53.0 ± 8.4	59.9 ± 9.0
432	–	–	74.1 ± 18.7	–

limits for real-time audio processing. Notably, even on lower-end devices, the system can support 192 polyphonic tones with reverb effect on while maintaining reasonable latency, which is sufficient to meet the demands of most amateur music production and arrangement scenarios. The results validate the effectiveness of the AudioWorklet-based multi-threaded audio architecture. Thus, it can provide a stable user experience across different hardware conditions.

5.2 Subjective Evaluation

To evaluate the practicality and user acceptance of the developed web-based DAW in real-world creative scenarios, a subjective experiment was carried out involving specific user cohorts. 32 participants with prior experience using AI music generation applications were enlisted, including 16 professional music producers and 16 music enthusiasts. The evaluation covered three aspects: functional requirement, sound quality evaluation and workflow satisfaction.

Functional Requirement. The necessity of MIDI editing capabilities in contemporary AI music generation applications was examined. Figure 5 illustrates that 24 participants (75%) expressed a strong desire for existing applications such as Suno [1] to integrate MIDI editing functionalities, 7 participants (22%) expressed moderate interest, while only 1 participant (3%) was opposed. This data indicates a significant demand among both professional creators and music enthusiasts for editable music capabilities in AI-generated music workflow, further validating the necessity of developing an editable web-based DAW as pursued in this paper.

Sound Quality Evaluation. To evaluate the audio rendering quality, different versions of the same musical piece were prepared:

- Direct MIDI output (using Microsoft GS Wavetable)
- Real-time rendered version using our web-based DAW
- Professionally produced commercial-grade version

32 participants performed blind listening tests using a 10-point scoring system for two musical pieces: one fusion instrumental music and one pop song intro. As shown in

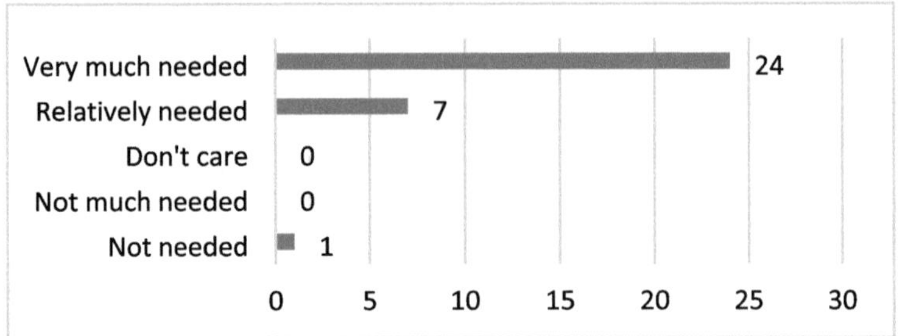

Fig. 5. User expectations for MIDI editing functions in AI music generation platforms.

Fig. 6, the DAW-rendered version received higher scores than basic MIDI synthesized version, while the gap with the professional version was smaller. Although professional producers gave stricter scores than music enthusiasts, however, the scoring trends of both groups were consistent. This indicates that our web-based DAW can effectively address the issue of poor MIDI sound quality and successfully bridge the gap between basic MIDI and professional quality, substantially enhancing the auditory experience and immediate usability of AI-generated music.

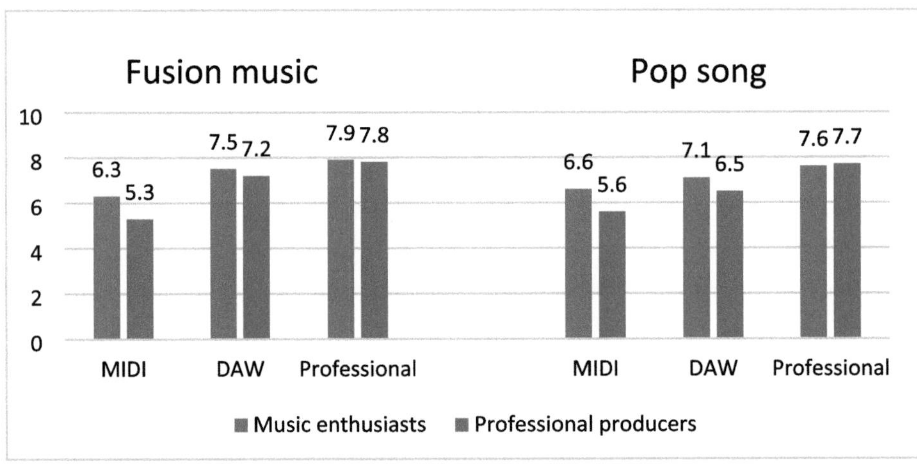

Fig. 6. Subjective blind listening scores of different music versions. Average scores (10-point scale) from 16 professional producers and 16 music enthusiasts for two songs (fusion instrumental and pop intro) across three versions, showing the DAW-rendered version outperforms the MIDI version and approaches the professional version.

Workflow Satisfaction. We used an AI pop music composition system [20] as the front-end, and directly input the generated symbolic file (MIDI) into the DAW for editing and playback. After experiencing the complete workflow of AI music editing-rendering-playback within our web-based DAW, we asked 32 participants whether they would like to use this DAW, and the results are shown in Fig. 7. Among them, 21 participants expressed that they "very much want to use it"; 10 participants said they "want to use it"; 1 participant indicated that he "doesn't care"; and no one said they "don't want to use it". The proportion of users with a positive intention to use it reached nearly 97% (31 out of 32), which not only reflects that the system has successfully met users' core needs in AI-generated music flow, but also lays a good foundation for its potential promotion and application in the future.

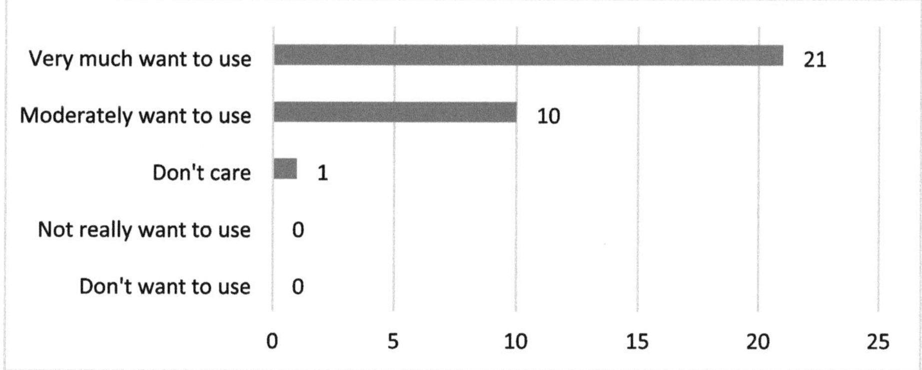

Fig. 7. User intention to use the developed DAW. Distribution of responses from 32 participants, with 21 expressing strong willingness ("very much want to use it"), 10 moderate willingness, 1 indifference, and no negative intention.

6 Conclusion and Discussion

In this paper, a web-based DAW for AI-generated music workflow is designed and implemented. This DAW adopts a layered modular architecture, integrating presentation layer, logic layer, and data layer to resolve the trade-off between editability and sound quality in AI music generation. Via the web page implemented with JavaScript, note-level editing of generated symbolic music is realized. Leveraging a multi-threaded audio processing architecture based on Web Audio API and AudioWorklet, the system achieves low-latency real-time rendering in the browser environment, supporting up to 432 polyphonic tones. Moreover, the output sound quality is significantly superior to traditional MIDI synthesis and approaches professional level. Through in-depth integration with existing AI music generation models via standardized APIs, it supports scenario-specific interactions including regeneration of bars, sections and tracks, enabling a closed-loop workflow from generation to refinement.

Although the system has achieved the expected results, it still has several limitations. First, there is still a gap with top commercial sound sources in terms of the delicacy and dynamic performance of complex orchestral timbres. Second, since performance on mobile devices is constrained by hardware capabilities, polyphony processing and effect handling on low-end phones require further optimization. Additionally, the system doesn't yet support any plugin standards, which in turn limits the expansion capability for professional users.

Based on current research results and limitations, future work will be carried out in several directions. One key direction is to develop a WebAssembly-accelerated audio processing module and an adaptive rendering strategy, which will dynamically adjust parameters according to device performance, thereby improving the mobile experience. Another direction involves referring to the current open plugin standards to explore compatibility with existing plugins, and developing cross-browser audio plugins to enhance extensibility.

Acknowledgements. This work was supported by the Special Program of National Natural Science Foundation of China (Grant No. T2341003), the Major Program of National Social Science Fund of China (Grant No. 21ZD19), and the Central Conservatory of Music General Research Project (Grant No. 25YB14).

The authors gratefully acknowledge the funding support from these organizations, which made this research possible. Any opinions, findings, and conclusions expressed in this material are those of the authors and do not necessarily reflect the views of the funding agencies.

References

1. Suno Homepage. https://suno.com. Accessed 15 Aug 2025
2. Udio Homepage. https://www.udio.com. Accessed 15 Aug 2025
3. Mureka Homepage. https://www.mureka.ai. Accessed 15 Aug 2025
4. Yuan, R., et al.: Yue: scaling open foundation models for long-form music generation. arXiv preprint arXiv:2503.08638 (2025)
5. Liu, Z., et al.: Songgen: a single stage auto-regressive transformer for text-to-song generation. arXiv preprint arXiv:2502.13128 (2025)
6. Wang, Y., et al.: NotaGen: advancing musicality in symbolic music generation with large language model training paradigms. arXiv preprint arXiv:2502.18008 (2025)
7. Tian, S., Zhang, C., Yuan, W., Tan, W., Zhu, W.: XMusic: towards a generalized and controllable symbolic music generation framework. IEEE Trans. Multimedia (2025)
8. Ding, S., et al.: SongComposer: a large language model for lyric and melody generation in song composition. arXiv preprint arXiv:2402.17645 (2025)
9. AIVA Homepage. https://www.aiva.ai. Accessed 15 Aug 2025
10. NetEase Tianyin Homepage. https://tianyin.music.163.com. Accessed 15 Aug 2025
11. Lind, F., MacPherson, A.: Soundtrap: a collaborative music studio with Web Audio. In Proceedings of the Web Audio Conference. Queen Mary University of London, London (2017)
12. Bandlab Homepage. https://www.bandlab.com. Accessed 15 Aug 2025
13. AmpedStudio Homepage. https://ampedstudio.com. Accessed 15 Aug 2025
14. Soundation Homepage. https://soundation.com. Accessed 15 Aug 2025
15. Gridsound Homepage. https://gridsound.com. Accessed 15 Aug 2025
16. OpenDAW Homepage. https://opendaw.org. Accessed 15 Aug 2025
17. Buffa, M., Vidal-Mazuy, A.: WAM-studio, a Digital Audio Workstation (DAW) for the web. In: Companion Proceedings of the ACM Web Conference 2023, pp. 543–548 (2023)
18. Ji, S., Yang, X., Luo, J.: A survey on deep learning for symbolic music generation: representations, algorithms, evaluations, and challenges. ACM Comput. Surv. **56**(1), Article 7, 39 (2023)

19. MIDI Specifications. https://midi.org/specs. Accessed 15 Aug 2025
20. Lu, D., Zhou, Q., Li, X.: Towards the implementation of an automatic composition system for popular songs. In: Summit on Music Intelligence, pp. 83–94. Springer, Singapore (2023) (2023)
21. Choi, H.: AudioWorklet: the future of web audio. In: Proceedings of the International Computer Music Conference, Daegu, South Korea, pp 110–116 (2018)
22. Buffa, M., Ren, S., Campbell, O., Kleimola, J., Larkin, O., Burns, T.: Web audio modules 2.0: an open web audio plugin standard. In WWW '22: The ACM Web Conference 2022, pp. 364–369. ACM, Virtual Event (2022)

A Robot Conducting Performance System Based on Motion Data Transfer

Yan Gao[1], Xiaoqing Wang[1], Di Lu[1](✉), Weiliao Deng[2], Xinyu Guo[2], and Baoyin Cheng[2]

[1] Central Conservatory of Music, Beijing, China
{gyan,wxiaoqing,ld}@ccom.edu.cn
[2] Hangzhou Yushu Technology Co., Ltd., Hangzhou, China

Abstract. This paper presents a semantic, platform-agnostic motion–data transfer framework for enabling expressive robotic conducting in real performance environments. Building on high-precision multimodal motion capture, we construct a four-dimensional **I**ntermediate **R**epresentation (IR) that integrates spatial trajectories, timestamps, musical-event labels, and expressive intensity. This IR serves as the bridge between human conducting semantics and robot-executable motion. A three-stage pipeline—motion capture, semantics-aware data processing and retargeting, and stage-level temporal synchronization—is implemented on the Unitree H1 humanoid. Through rame-skipping delay compensation and joint-limit–aware amplitude correction, the system achieves millisecond-scale visual alignment and preserves key musical intentions despite kinematic differences. The framework has been validated through multiple public concerts and television productions, and further extended to robotic percussion, demonstrating both robustness and cross-modal generality.

Keywords: Robotic conducting · semantic motion representation · motion retargeting · multimodal motion capture · timecode synchronization · robot performance

1 Introduction

In recent years, robots have expanded from industrial and service scenarios into the performing arts, giving rise to the new field of robotic performers. A central challenge lies in stably and reliably transferring human performance motions with their full artistic semantics and expressiveness onto robotic platforms under real-world mechanical and dynamic constraints, while achieving precise synchronization with multimodal stage elements.

Early research demonstrated the feasibility of using human motion to control music, laying the groundwork for robotic conducting [1]. Subsequent systems, such as MIT's Conductor's Jacket, adopted wearable sensing to capture the kinetics and expressive cues of the conductor [2]. In practice, robots like ASIMO (2008) and ABB YuMi (2017)

Y. Gao and X. Wang—These authors contributed equally to this work.

X. Li et al. (Eds.): CCAC 2025, CCIS 2886, pp. 132–148, 2026.
https://doi.org/10.1007/978-981-95-8256-3_8

have acted as conductors on stage, though largely relying on pre-scripted trajectories [3, 4]. More recently, android and collaborative platforms have pushed robotic conducting closer to mainstream artistic practice: the Alter series (2016–2024) explored lifelike android motion and opera-style productions [5–8], EveR-6 (2023) co-conducted with a human maestro in a national orchestra setting [9], and the "Xiao-Yang Robot Band" (2025) performed with a professional Chinese orchestra, signaling broader public adoption of robotic conductors [11].

Despite these advances, key bottlenecks remain in achieving truly expressive, reliable, and deployable robotic performers:

- Semantic-constraint mismatch: Human movement semantics—beat emphasis, dynamics, phrasing—are often lost when mapped to robots with limited kinematic and dynamic ranges.
- Platform dependence: The absence of portable, reusable representations and toolchains impedes adaptation across diverse robot morphologies.
- Cross-modal synchronization: Precise, beat-level alignment of motion, audio, and lighting remains an open engineering challenge, especially under show conditions.

In response, this paper makes the following contributions through the Zhiyin robotic conducting system:

1) We propose a structured, production-oriented motion-transfer pipeline comprising motion capture → semantic cleaning and encoding → temporal synchronization, emphasizing non-real-time preset authoring and strict timecode alignment for robust stage performance.
2) We introduce a platform-agnostic motion **I**ntermediate **R**epresentation (IR) that explicitly encodes musical semantics—beat, dynamics, and phrasing—enabling decoupling of artistic intent from platform-specific execution.
3) We validate the system through repeated public deployments (concerts, TV shows), achieving millisecond-scale synchronization and second-level recovery from disruptions, and report quantitative and subjective evaluations involving both experts and public audiences.
4) We demonstrate the transferability of the proposed IR and pipeline by extending the system to robotic percussion, highlighting its generality beyond conducting.

The remainder of this paper is structured as follows: Sect. 2 reviews related work in robotic performance and motion retargeting. Section 3 details the system architecture and core algorithms. Section 4 presents experimental results from both controlled tests and public deployments. Section 5 concludes and discusses future directions.

2 Related Work

Our work sits at the intersection of robotic motion control for artistic expression and human–robot interaction (HRI) in musical contexts. While related research spans several directions, most existing systems focus either on gesture capture or single-platform demonstrations, and seldom address semantic preservation, cross-platform reuse, and stage-level deployment in a unified framework. In this section, we review prior work in three major directions: gesture-based music interfaces, robotic conducting, and motion retargeting techniques.

2.1 Gesture-Based Music Control and Early HCI

Early systems explored mapping human gestures to musical control. Morita et al. (1991) proposed a computer music system that responded to conducting gestures, laying an important conceptual foundation for using human motion as a musical interface [1]. Marrin-Nakra's *Conductor's Jacket* (2000) used wearable sensors to capture body kinetics and expressive cues of the conductor, and related them to musical parameters [2].

These works established the basic paradigm of "gesture-to-music mapping", but their focus was on interactive interfaces rather than robotic embodiment. They did not consider robot morphology, joint constraints, or the problem of deploying motions on stage-ready robotic platforms.

2.2 Robotic Conducting

Robotic conducting systems are closest to our work. Several milestones can be identified:

- **ASIMO (2008)** conducted the Detroit Symphony Orchestra using preprogrammed trajectories [3].
- **ABB YuMi (2017)** conducted Verdi with Andrea Bocelli at Teatro Verdi, relying on carefully authored motions [4].
- **Alter series (2016–2024)**: Alter 1 demonstrated lifelike, neural-network-driven motion [5]; Alter 2 Alter 2 conducted and sang in the android opera *Scary Beauty* [6]; Alter 3 and Alter 4 further explored android-centered opera and stage presence [7, 8].
- **EveR-6 (2023)** conducted the National Orchestra of Korea in Seoul, co-leading with a human maestro [9].
- **MAiRA Pro S (2024)**, a three-armed robot, conducted the Dresden Sinfoniker, showcasing polymetric gesture handling [10].
- **Xiao-Yang Robot Band (2025)** performed at the NCPA Beijing with the Beijing Chinese Orchestra, signaling growing mainstream interest in robot musicians [11].

These systems convincingly demonstrate the public appeal and feasibility of robot conductors. However, they generally share three limitations compared with our approach:

1) They are typically built around platform-specific motion authoring and lack a platform-agnostic intermediate representation for conducting semantics.
2) Most rely on pre-scripted or demonstration-taught trajectories. Even when motion capture is used, the captured data are not systematically encoded into reusable semantic units (e.g., explicit beat, phrasing, or dynamic labels).
3) Their deployment toolchains for timecode alignment, latency compensation, and cross-modal synchronization are seldom documented in a reusable, engineering-oriented manner.

In contrast, our Zhiyin system proposes a semantic **I**ntermediate **R**epresentation (IR) specifically tailored to conducting, decouples artistic intent from robot-specific execution, and focuses on a production-oriented pipeline that can be redeployed across multiple venues and musical tasks.

2.3 Motion Retargeting Techniques

Motion retargeting methods aim to transfer human motion to characters or robots with different kinematics. Model-based approaches jointly estimate morphology parameters and optimize trajectories to satisfy kinematic and dynamic constraints (e.g., Ayusawa & Yoshida, 2017) [12]. Learning-based methods, such as Neural Kinematic Networks [13] and Skeleton-Aware Networks [14], enable cross-skeleton transfer with high geometric fidelity and minimal paired data.

However, these techniques are usually evaluated on generic motions (walking, dancing, everyday actions) and optimize for geometric similarity and physical feasibility. They do not explicitly preserve music-specific semantics such as beat emphasis, dynamic shaping, or phrasing structure, nor do they tackle stage-level timecode alignment with audio and lighting systems. Our work can be seen as extending motion retargeting into the music-semantic domain, with a dedicated IR that carries beat, dynamic, and phrasing information into the optimization and execution stages.

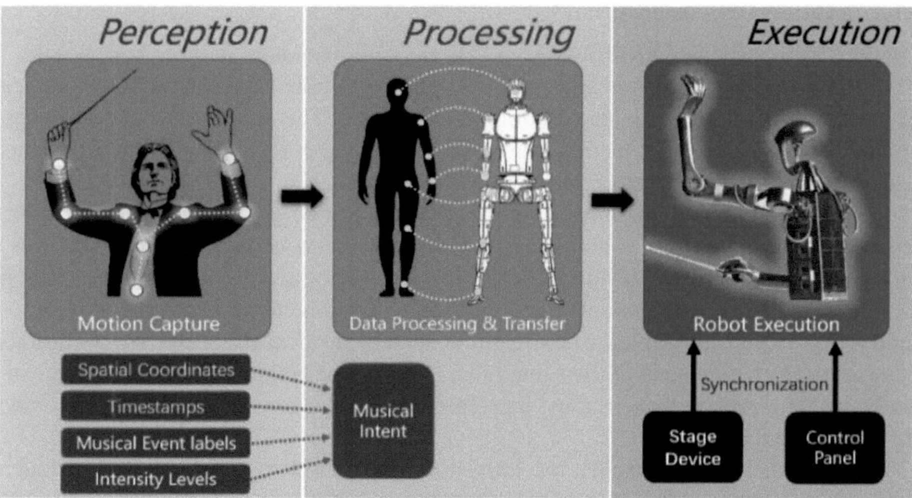

Fig. 1. Overall system architecture. The proposed framework comprises three core modules: Motion Capture, Data Processing & Transfer, and Robot Execution. Arrows indicate the direction of data flow, from human motion acquisition to adapted command generation and final robotic performance.

3 Overall Architecture

The system adopts a modular architecture to establish a complete perception–processing–execution closed loop. As illustrated in Fig. 1, it consists of three core components: a motion capture module, a data processing and transfer module, and a robot execution module. The capture module streams raw motion data to the data processing and transfer module, which subsequently generates adapted motion commands for the execution module, thereby forming a complete pipeline from human conducting motion acquisition to robotic conducting performance. This structure minimizes inter-module coupling to facilitate independent upgrades and maintenance, while supporting flexible feature expansion to ensure both scalability and operational stability.

3.1 Motion Capture Module

The motion capture module serves as the core perceptual unit, whose performance fundamentally determines the accuracy of downstream processing and the quality of robotic execution. To address both the artistic expressivity and the directive, time-critical nature of conducting, we constructed a high-precision multimodal capture system specifically designed to transmit musical intent, thereby overcoming the limitations of conventional motion-capture approaches.

3.1.1 Motion Data Acquisition

Conducting motion capture differs from generic motion capture in three key aspects.

First, conducting gestures are tightly coupled with musical semantics such as beat emphasis, melodic phrasing, and emotional expression. This requires synchronous spatiotemporal labeling of conducting movements with their corresponding musical events, rather than treating motion as context-free kinematic data.

Second, conducting contains a high proportion of fine-grained motions, including fingertip micro-tremors and subtle wrist rotations. Preserving these nuances demands a capture system capable of millimeter-level spatial accuracy and high temporal resolution.

Third, unlike dance segments that often follow fixed meter or prearranged routines, conducting exhibits dynamic variability influenced by musical affect and live conditions. Even across performances of the same piece, tempo and kinematic amplitude can vary markedly. The capture system must therefore handle non-stationary, highly expressive temporal patterns.

To meet these requirements, we implement the following three tailored technical solutions.

Gesture–Music Synchronization. We integrate an audio-trigger module into the capture system that uses musical beat peaks as temporal anchors. Gesture trajectories are aligned to these anchors to obtain frame-level correspondence between motion data and audio.

High-Resolution Optical Capture. A high-resolution optical camera array is deployed around the performance space. Micro retro-reflective markers are attached to critical hand joints, including fingertips, phalanges, and the wrist, to enhance spatial precision.

Additionally, a microsensor mounted at the baton tip provides independent and high-frequency orientation tracking.

Two-Phase Capturing Protocol. To robustly characterize both typical and expressive variations, we employ a two-phase "baseline + enhancement" capture protocol. In the baseline phase, three full takes of the piece are recorded, and dynamic time warping (DTW) is applied to extract common kinematic trajectory features. In the enhancement phase, emotionally salient sections are recorded in 10 + additional repetitions. These repeated segments are used to estimate plausible variation ranges in movement amplitude and tempo, which later guide motion adaptation on the robot side.

3.1.2 Semantic Intermediate Representation (IR)

As summarized in Table 1, the resulting multimodal motion dataset incorporates four types of information: spatial coordinates, timestamps, musical event labels, and intensity level, to support downstream data processing and motion transfer. Building on this dataset, we define a semantic, platform-agnostic **I**ntermediate **R**epresentation (IR) that bridges human conducting and robotic execution.

Unlike traditional motion formats that store only trajectories, the proposed IR explicitly combines kinematic features with music-aware semantics, so that both the "shape" of the movement and the "intent" behind it are preserved. Concretely, the IR is organized around four core components:

Table 1. Composition of the four-dimensional motion data for semantic IR construction

Dimension	Description	Components/Classification
Spatial Coordinates	Precise spatial data points captured from the movement	– 3D position (X, Y, Z), – Orientation
Timestamps	The exact time points corresponding to each data sample	– High-resolution time codes – Beat/bar indices (optional)
Musical Event Labels	Semantic tags describing specific musical events and instructions	– Special Techniques – Phrase and section entries – Meter changes – Tempo-related events
Intensity Levels	Normalized quantitative metrics representing the expressive dynamics of the baton movement	– Discrete dynamic levels – Dynamic trends – Normalized amplitude

- **Spatial coordinates.** This component stores the robot-agnostic target motion, including 3D position and orientation of the conductor's hand or baton. It is derived from the optical capture system and serves as the geometric reference for later retargeting to robot joints.

- **Timestamp.** Each motion sample is associated with a high-resolution absolute timestamp, ensuring precise alignment with the audio track and other stage timecodes. This enables beat-level and bar-level synchronization between motion, sound, and lighting.
- **Musical event labels.** Musical event labels describe the type and role of the gesture in the score. They include:
- Special conducting techniques (e.g., point, stroke, shake, circular motion);
- Phrase and section entries (e.g., phrase start, section start);
- Meter changes (e.g., change of time signature);
- Tempo-related events (e.g., accelerando, ritardando).

These labels are manually verified by expert music teachers to ensure musical correctness.

- **Expressive intensity.** Expressive intensity encodes how "strong" or "soft" the conductor intends the passage to be and how it evolves over time. It combines:
- Discrete dynamic levels following standard notation (*ppp, pp, p, mp, mf, f, ff, fff*);
- Dynamic trends such as crescendo and decrescendo;
- Normalized scalar features (e.g., amplitude) derived from the motion envelope and velocity.

For lightweight cross-platform use, the IR is stored in a JSON-based structure that fuses temporal, kinematic, and semantic information into a single data object, for example:

```
{
  "timestamp": 123.456,
  "target_pose": {
    "position": [0.12, 1.45, 0.87],
    "orientation": [0.0, 0.7, 0.1, 0.7]
  },
  "musical_event": {
    "event_type": "phrase_start",
    "special_technique": "stroke",
    "meter_change": null,
    "tempo_change": null
  },
  "expressive_intensity": {
    "dynamic_level": "mf",
    "dynamic_change": "crescendo",
    "amplitude": 0.72
  }
}
```

This representation transforms traditionally subjective aspects of "artistic expression" into computable, transferable, and reusable data units. By preserving both geometric motion and conducting semantics, the IR provides the foundation for subsequent motion retargeting, amplitude correction under joint limits, and high-fidelity robotic conducting on stage.

All musical event labels and intensity labels are annotated and verified by expert musicians, forming the four-dimensional dataset used in the next section.

3.2 Data Processing and Transfer Module

The data processing and transfer module bridges the semantic IR constructed in Sect. 3.1 with robot-ready joint trajectories. Starting from IR sequences that combine motion, timestamps, musical events, and expressive intensity, the module first aggregates heterogeneous features into intent-aware motion units using an intent-dimension anchoring strategy, and then converts these units into executable joint trajectories. This process consists of two main stages: kinematic retargeting, and semantics-aware amplitude correction under joint limits.

3.2.1 Kinematic Retargeting to Robot Joint Space

We adopt a kinematic retargeting approach to map human conducting gestures onto the Unitree H1 humanoid robot. The H1 platform features a total of 19 joints, including 8 joints in the upper limbs, 1 joint in the waist, and 10 joints in the lower limbs as shown in Fig. 2. Since conducting primarily involves upper-body gestures and waist motion, our mapping focuses on the upper limbs and waist, while the lower limbs are used mainly for postural stabilization.

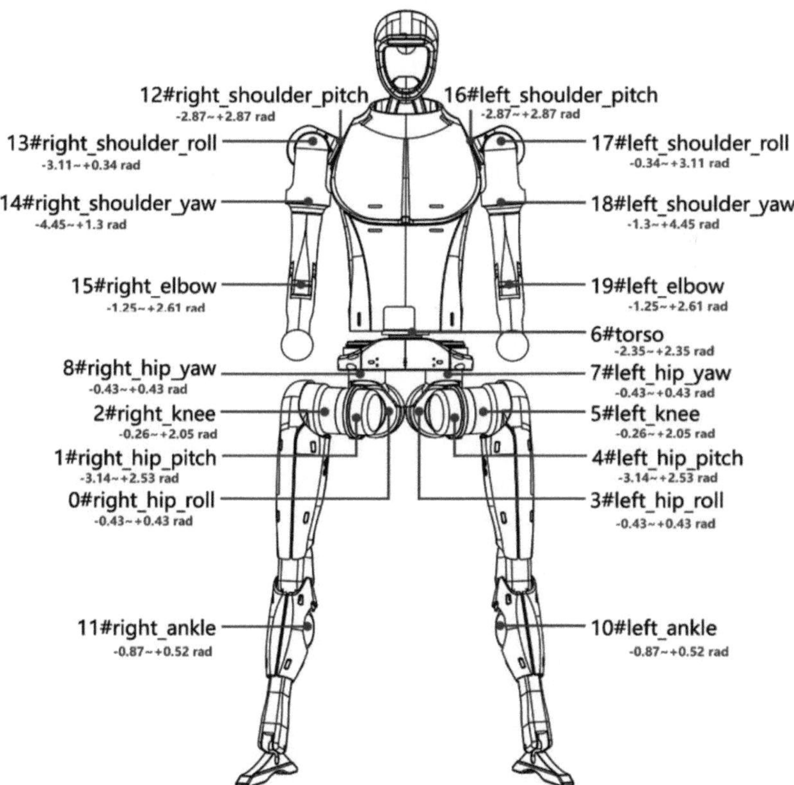

Fig. 2. Joint and Limit Diagram of Unitree H1 Robot.

We first define a human–robot kinematic correspondence, associating human shoulder, elbow, and wrist motions with the robot's shoulder and elbow joints. For each IR entry or motion unit, the motion component provides a target pose for the conducting hand or baton tip. This pose is treated as a task-space objective, and inverse kinematics (IK) or task-space control is used to compute feasible joint configurations.

The IR timestamps determine when each key pose or segment should be realized. Using these timestamps, we generate time-parameterized joint trajectories so that the temporal structure of the original conducting performance—downbeats, phrase entries, and climactic gestures—is preserved. The trajectories are then smoothed to satisfy joint-range, velocity, acceleration, and jerk limits, ensuring that they are physically safe and visually coherent.

The resulting joint commands are validated in **unitree_mujoco**, Simulation allows us to check for joint limit violations, self-collisions, and balance issues before deploying to the physical robot. In cases where the original human motion involves substantial waist rotation that could jeopardize stability, the system can lock or restrict the robot's waist joint and compensate by adjusting shoulder and elbow motions, thereby maintaining the perceived conducting gesture while preserving lower-body stability.

3.2.2 Semantics-Aware Amplitude Correction Under Joint Limits

Due to differences in morphology and joint ranges between the human conductor and the robot, direct kinematic retargeting often results in reduced gesture amplitudes. If left unaddressed, this reduction can weaken critical musical cues, such as strong beats, section entries, or crescendo. To mitigate this, we use the semantic information encoded in the IR to guide a semantics-aware amplitude correction procedure.

Based on the IR musical event and expressive intensity fields, each motion unit is assigned a dominant intent category using the motion–music association defined during data preparation. Typical categories include:

- **Intensity-emphasizing** gestures: e.g., accented downbeats, climactic cues;
- **Amplitude-evolving** gestures: e.g., crescendo and decrescendo;
- **Position-indicating** gestures: e.g., pointing to a specific section or instrument group.

For each motion unit, the retargeted joint trajectory is analyzed with respect to the robot's joint limits and workspace. When the full human amplitude cannot be achieved, we compute appropriate scaling factors and identify which degrees of freedom are most constrained. Correction is then applied in a semantics-dependent manner:

- For **intensity-emphasizing** gestures, we compensate for reduced spatial amplitude by increasing joint velocity and acceleration within safe bounds. This enhances the sharpness and impact of the motion, helping to preserve the perceived strength of the gesture despite limited range of motion.
- For **amplitude-evolving** segments, we scale the trajectory envelope proportionally within the robot's reachable space so that the trend encoded in the expressive intensity—growing or fading—remains perceptually intact, even if the maximum amplitude is smaller than that of the human conductor.
- For **position-indicating** gestures, spatial accuracy is prioritized. Even if the absolute amplitude must be reduced, the end-effector direction and approximate target location

are preserved as closely as possible, ensuring that orchestral players and audiences can still recognize the cue.

After semantics-aware correction, the final joint trajectories are discretized into a stream of joint command packets that follow the Unitree H1 communication protocol. Each packet contains target joint angles, velocities, and timing information, and can optionally retain references to the underlying IR intent labels. These trajectories, having passed both simulation-based validation and semantic correction, are then handed over to the execution module for timecode-synchronized playback on stage.

3.3 Robot Execution Module

The execution module is responsible for turning the retargeted trajectories produced in Sect. 3.2 into safe, timecode-synchronized motion on the physical robot. It encompasses hardware adaptation, motion control parametrization, time-aligned playback with stage systems, and safety-oriented exception handling.

3.3.1 Hardware Adaptation

To ensure that the robot can robustly execute conducting gestures on stage, we first adapt the hardware configuration to the requirements of baton-based conducting.

On the end-effector side, we experimented with both a dexterous multi-fingered hand and a lightweight 3D-printed hand for holding the baton. The dexterous hand allows for fine-grained finger motions (e.g., subtle taps or grips), but its additional mass and inertia noticeably affect the robot's center of mass and response speed, increasing the risk of instability when executing large-amplitude gestures. In contrast, the 3D-printed hand is significantly lighter and easier to balance, but sacrifices very fine finger-level expressivity. Considering the demands of stage reliability, we ultimately selected a lightweight 3D-printed hand that offers a favorable trade-off between visual clarity of the baton and dynamic stability.

3.3.2 Optimization of Motion Control

We implement a parameterized control framework using stiffness and damping as the primary adjustable parameters. By adjusting joint stiffness and damping, we can modulate the perceived "rigidity" and "softness" of the gestures:

- Increasing stiffness (with appropriate damping) produces sharper, more decisive motions, suitable for strong beats and rhythmic cues.
- Lowering stiffness yields more fluid, legato-like gestures, suitable for sustained phrases and lyrical sections.

The waist joint is provided with an independent control channel. During passages where stability is paramount, the waist can be effectively "locked" by setting high stiffness and damping, reducing undesired torso sway. For more expressive passages that benefit from upper-body involvement, the waist stiffness can be relaxed, enabling subtle torso movements while still respecting balance constraints.

To support these functionalities, we developed the web-based "Zhiyin Control Panel" which incorporates a Flask backend with a Bootstrap 5 and jQuery frontend for responsive real-time control. Key features include parameter tuning, mapping configuration, audio-synchronized execution, and comprehensive system logging. The screenshot is shown in Fig. 3.

3.3.3 Timecode Synchronization and Latency Compensation

For stage performances, it is crucial that the robot's gestures be tightly aligned with audio playback, lighting, and other stage systems. To this end, we implement a timecode-synchronized playback mechanism with explicit delay compensation.

First, a common time reference is established between the stage control desk and the robot. The stage system sends standardized timecodes (e.g., via network messages), which the robot uses to align its internal clock. At run time, we adopt a frame-skipping strategy based on the predicted delay. Concretely, when a motion file is scheduled to start at stage time t_0, and the predicted delay for the current setup is Δt, the robot does not begin from the first frame of the motion file. Instead, it jumps directly to the frame whose timestamp is closest to $t_0 + \Delta t$ and starts execution from there, effectively truncating or skipping the initial frames that would otherwise be perceived as late by the audience.

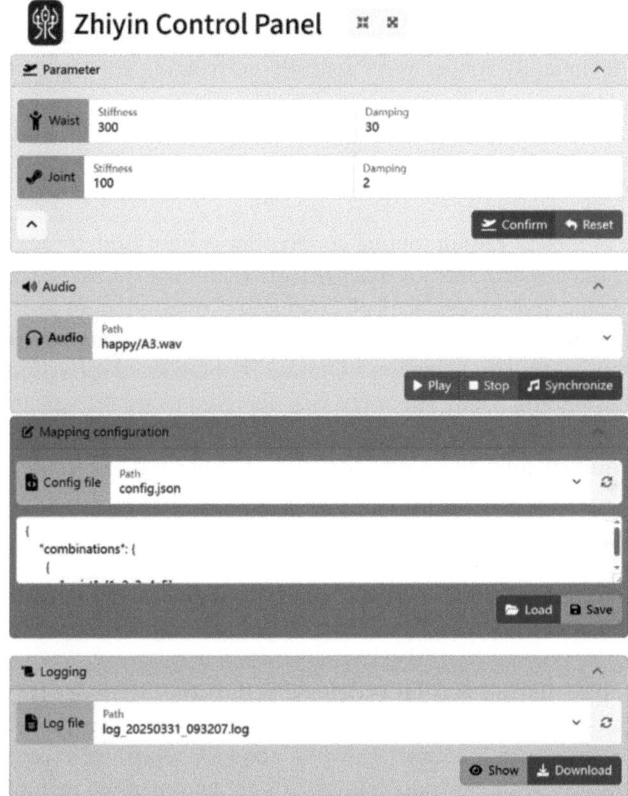

Fig. 3. A screenshot of the web-based Zhiyin Control Panel, illustrating the real-time control interface for motion parameter adjustment (stiffness, damping), mapping configuration, audio-synchronized execution, and system logging.

3.3.4 Exception Handling and Performance Assurance

Given the constraints of live performance, safety and robustness are essential. We design a layered protection and fault-tolerance mechanism to handle typical failure modes:

- **Overload and balance protection.** When overload or abnormal torques are detected in the upper body, the system immediately pauses upper-limb motions while allowing lower-limb joints to adjust for balance. A dynamic center-of-mass rebalancing routine is activated to prevent tipping or falls.
- **Data loss and overheating compensation.** If motion commands are dropped, delayed, or invalidated due to overheating or communication issues, an interpolation-based recovery algorithm fills in missing segments by fitting trajectories between adjacent valid motion samples. This maintains temporal continuity and visual coherence for the audience.

Finally, live rehearsals play a crucial role in refining performance quality. Key motion units—such as openings, climactic sections, and endings—are iteratively fine-tuned in collaboration with conductors and musicians. Adjustments made during rehearsal can be fed back into the IR annotations and control parameters (e.g., slightly advancing or delaying certain cues, increasing the contrast of climactic gestures), resulting in a motion set that is both technically robust and musically convincing for repeated deployments across different venues.

4 Experiments

We evaluate the proposed Zhiyin robotic conducting system from three complementary perspectives: (1) quantitative latency and synchronization performance under stage-like conditions, (2) subjective assessment of conducting quality by experts and audience members, and (3) public deployments in real concert and media environments.

All experiments were conducted on a Unitree H1 humanoid robot equipped with the 3D-printed baton-holding hand. The robot was operated using the semantic IR pipeline and motion-transfer framework introduced in Sects. 3.1–3.2, and executed trajectories generated from human conducting data for a set of orchestral excerpts.

4.1 Latency and Synchronization Evaluation

We first evaluate the end-to-end communication delay between the stage control desk and the robot, and the effectiveness of the frame-skipping compensation strategy described in Sect. 3.3.3.

End-to-end communication delay is defined as the time difference between the emission of a timecode packet at the stage control desk and its reception and execution scheduling at the robot. In a concert-hall-like network setup, we repeatedly triggered the same conducting cue for 50 trials. The results are summarized in Table 2. In the raw condition (without compensation), the measured one-way delay ranged from 510 ms to 620 ms across trials. After enabling the predicted-offset and frame-skipping compensation, the residual misalignment between the intended cue time and the actual execution time at the robot was reduced to less than 15 ms in all 50 trials, which is within the threshold of visual detectability for both expert and non-expert observers.

Table 2. End-to-end delay before and after frame-skipping compensation (50 trials)

Condition	Number of trials	End-to-end delay
Raw (no compensation)	60	500–550 ms (one-way communication delay)
After compensation	60	<15 ms residual cue misalignment

4.2 Subjective Evaluation of Conducting Quality

To assess the perceived quality of the robotic conducting, we carried out a subjective evaluation with 20 participants, using three conditions:

- **HUMAN** – the original human conductor;

- **ROBOT-BASELINE** – Unitree H1 with geometric retargeting only;
- **ROBOT-FULL** – Unitree H1 using the full semantic IR pipeline, including semantics-aware amplitude correction.

For each condition, short video clips of the same musical excerpts were shown from an audience-like viewpoint. After each clip, participants rated the performance on a 5-point Mean Opinion Score (MOS) scale (1 = very poor, 5 = excellent) along five dimensions: (1) Beat clarity, (2) Dynamic expression, (3) Phrasing/structure indication, (4) Motion smoothness and naturalness, and (5) Overall acceptance as a conductor.

Before analyzing the MOS scores, we assessed the reliability of participant ratings. The 15-item scale showed acceptable internal consistency (Cronbach's $\alpha = 0.749$). Corrected item–total correlations indicated coherent contributions across items, and leave-one-out analysis showed no participant whose removal meaningfully increased α. The ratings were therefore considered reliable for subsequent analysis.

Table 3. MOS scores (1–5) for human and robotic conducting conditions.

Dimension	HUMAN	ROBOT-BASELINE	ROBOT-FULL
Beat clarity	4.85	3.05	3.90
Dynamic expression	4.95	2.00	3.70
Phrasing/structure indication	4.90	2.30	3.90
Motion smoothness and naturalness	4.90	2.95	3.80
Overall acceptance	4.95	2.55	3.85

Table 3 reports the MOS scores across participants. The HUMAN condition is close to ceiling on all dimensions (4.85, 4.95, 4.90, 4.90, 4.95), reflecting the expected high quality of professional conducting. The ROBOT-BASELINE condition receives clearly lower scores (3.05, 2.00, 2.30, 2.95, 2.55), with the largest deficits in dynamic expression and phrasing/structure. In contrast, the ROBOT-FULL condition shows substantial improvements over ROBOT-BASELINE across all five dimensions, with mean scores of 3.90, 3.70, 3.90, 3.80, and 3.85 respectively.

These results indicate that the proposed semantic IR and semantics-aware amplitude correction significantly enhance perceived beat clarity, musical expression, and overall acceptance of the robot as a conductor, bringing its ratings closer to the human reference compared with the geometric-only baseline.

4.3 Public Deployments and Case Studies

To evaluate the robustness and practical usability of the Zhiyin system beyond laboratory settings, we deployed the robot conductor in a series of public events between September 2024 and May 2025. These deployments span formal concerts, technology expos, commercial showcases, and a televised variety show, covering both traditional orchestral conducting and extended scenarios such as close-range interaction and percussion performance.

Across all events listed in Table 4, the system operated without critical hardware failures. The same IR-based motion files and control framework were reused across venues, with only minor adjustments to stiffness/damping parameters and timing offsets. A set of snapshots from major public performances are shown in Fig. 4. These public deployments provide converging evidence that the proposed system is not only technically feasible but also robust and musically acceptable in real-world performance environments.

Table 4. Public performance events and system status.

Date	Event	Status
2024-09-10	Central Conservatory of Music's (CCOM) 2024–2025 Opening Ceremony	First public appearance; no execution failures
2024-10-02	2024 International Audio-Visual Works Expo—"Art + Technology" Zone	Continuous operation over 5 days
2024-11-27	Sino-French International Music Festival · Future Concert	Conducting plus vocal trio
2024-12-31	2025 Ningbo New Year Concerts	Two consecutive days of performance
2025-01-30	AI in Haidian for the New Year—2025 Haidian Spring Technology Temple Fair	Close-range performance with audience in near field
2025-01-29	CCTV-3 2025 Spring Festival Comedy Night	New repertoire; conducting both music and audience
2025-03-29	Human–AI Co-Creation 2025 Positive-Energy Creation Conference	First ethnic costumed performance
2025-05-10	Western Percussion Master's Graduation Concert	First percussion performance using the same IR framework

(a)

(b)

Fig. 4. Public performances of the Zhiyin robotic conductor. (a) CCOM 2024–2025 Opening Ceremony; (b) 2025 Ningbo New Year Concert.

In addition to orchestral conducting, we reused the same IR-based pipeline to author and deploy percussion gestures for the Western Percussion Master's Graduation Concert (2025-05-10). As shown in Fig. 5, the same representation and retargeting framework were used to author and execute drum gestures for both experimental setups and a public graduation concert, confirming the generality of the motion pipeline beyond baton gestures.

(a)

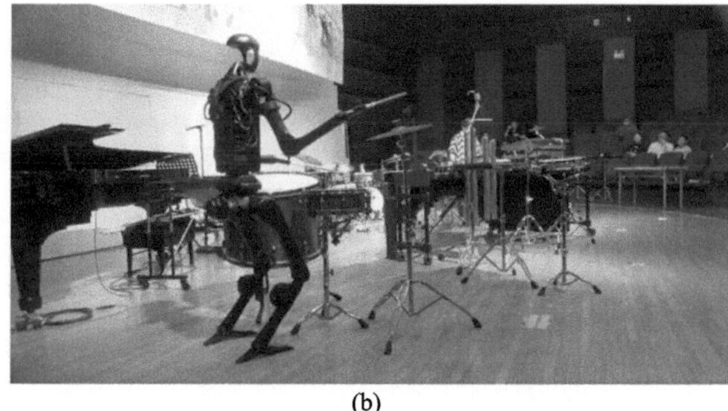

(b)

Fig. 5. Extension of the IR-based pipeline to percussion performance. (a) Robotic percussion performance experiment; (b) Western Percussion Master's Graduation Concert—When S/He Begins to Dream.

5 Discussion

This work shows that a semantic, platform-agnostic **I**ntermediate **R**epresentation (IR) can act as an effective bridge between human conducting and robotic execution. By explicitly encoding motion, time, musical events, and expressive intensity, the system preserves not only the geometric shape of gestures but also their musical function. The subjective results indicate that this semantic layer is perceptually meaningful: the full pipeline with semantics-aware amplitude correction is consistently preferred over a purely geometric baseline, especially in terms of dynamic expression and overall acceptance as a conductor.

A second contribution is the focus on stage-ready engineering rather than purely laboratory demonstrations. The end-to-end delay measurements and frame-skipping compensation provide a simple but robust way to align the robot with external timecode, which proved sufficient across multiple public performances and a TV recording. From the perspective of stage technicians, the robot can be integrated into existing show-control workflows much like lights or video, which lowers the barrier to deployment.

Finally, the successful reuse of the same IR pipeline for percussion performance suggests that the proposed representation is not limited to baton conducting. Without changing the core framework, we were able to author drum gestures and deploy them on the same platform, indicating potential for broader classes of IR-driven musical robots.

At the same time, the current system has clear limitations: it operates in an essentially open-loop manner (no real-time listening or adaptation to live musicians), relies on manual expert annotation of musical events, and has been validated on a single humanoid platform. Future work will focus on integrating real-time audio feedback (listening while conducting), semi-automatic annotation tools, and cross-platform studies on different robot morphologies to further test the generality of the proposed IR and motion-transfer framework.

Acknowledgement. This work was supported by the Special Program of National Natural Science Foundation of China (Grant No. T2341003) and the Major Program of National Social Science Fund of China (Grant No. 21ZD19). The authors are also deeply grateful to all those who contributed to this work.

References

1. Morita, H., Hashimoto, S., Ohteru, S.: A computer music system that follows a human conductor. Computer **24**(7), 44–53 (1991)
2. Marrin Nakra, T.: Inside the Conductor's Jacket: Analysis, Interpretation and Musical Synthesis of Expressive Gesture, Ph.D. dissertation, Massachusetts Institute of Technology, Cambridge (2000)
3. Los Angeles Times. Honda's ASIMO conducts Detroit Symphony Orchestra. Newspaper article (2008)
4. Reuters. YuMi the robot conducts Verdi with Italian orchestra. Reuters, Pisa, Italy (2017)
5. Doi, I., Ikegami, T., Masumori, A., Kojima, H., Ogawa, K., Ishiguro, H.: A new design principle for an autonomous robot. In: Proceedings of the 14th European Conference on Artificial Life (ECAL 2017). MIT Press (2017)
6. ATAK. "Android Opera Scary Beauty. Project description, 2017–2019. Available from the ATAK official website
7. Al Arabiya English. Robot conducts human orchestra in Sharjah. Al Arabiya News (2020)
8. Théâtre du Châtelet and ATAK. Android Opera MIRROR. programme notes, Théâtre du Châtelet, Paris (2023)
9. Reuters. Robot takes podium as orchestra conductor in Seoul. Reuters (2023)
10. Oltermann, P.: Three-armed robot conductor makes debut in Dresden. The Guardian (2024)
11. CCTV.com/Astribot. Xiao-Yang Robot Band performs with Beijing Chinese Orchestra. CCTV.com and related social media posts (2025)
12. Ayusawa, K., Yoshida, E.: Motion retargeting for humanoid robots based on simultaneous morphing parameter identification and motion optimization. IEEE Trans. Rob. **33**(6), 1343–1357 (2017)
13. Villegas, R., Yang, J., Ceylan, D., Lee, H.: Neural kinematic networks for unsupervised motion retargeting. In: Proceedings of the IEEE/CVF Conference on Computer Vision and Pattern Recognition (CVPR), pp. 8639–8648 (2018)
14. Aberman, K., Li, P., Lischinski, D., Sorkine-Hornung, O., Cohen-Or, D., Chen, B.: Skeleton-aware networks for deep motion retargeting. ACM Trans. Graph. (ToG) **39**(4), 62 (2020)

Author Index

X. Li et al. (Eds.): CCAC 2025, CCIS 2886, p. 149, 2026.
https://doi.org/10.1007/978-981-95-8256-3

MIX
Papier aus verantwortungsvollen Quellen
Paper from responsible sources
FSC® C105338

If you have any concerns about our products,
you can contact us on
ProductSafety@springernature.com

In case Publisher is established outside the EU,
the EU authorized representative is:
Springer Nature Customer Service Center GmbH
Europaplatz 3, 69115 Heidelberg, Germany

Printed by Libri Plureos GmbH
in Hamburg, Germany